W9-CFB-729

2 BILLION

UNDER 20

2 BILLI◯N

UNDER 20

How **Millennials** Are
Breaking Down Age Barriers and
Changing the World

STACEY FERREIRA & JARED KLEINERT

FOREWORD BY BLAKE MASTERS

ST. MARTIN'S PRESS ✳ NEW YORK

2 BILLION UNDER 20. Copyright © 2015 by Stacey Ferreira and Jared Kleinert. Foreword copyright © 2015 by Blake Masters. All rights reserved. Printed in the United States of America. For information, address St. Martin's Press, 175 Fifth Avenue, New York, N.Y. 10010.

www.stmartins.com

Designed by Anna Gorovoy

Library of Congress Cataloging-in-Publication Data

2 billion under 20 : how millennials are breaking down age barriers and changing the world / edited by Jared Kleinert and Stacey Ferreira ; foreword by Blake Masters.
     p. cm.
   ISBN 978-1-250-06761-6 (hardcover)
   ISBN 978-1-4668-7608-8 (e-book)
   1. Success in business.   2. Entrepreneurship.   3. Leadership.
4. Generation Y.   I. Kleinert, Jared.   II. Ferreira, Stacey.   III. Title: Two billion under twenty.
   HF5386.A13 2015
   305.235—dc23

2015005981

St. Martin's Press books may be purchased for educational, business, or promotional use. For information on bulk purchases, please contact the Macmillan Corporate and Premium Sales Department at 1-800-221-7945, extension 5442, or write to specialmarkets@macmillan.com.

First Edition: July 2015

10 9 8 7 6 5 4 3 2 1

To the 2 Billion Under 20:
You all have a story to create and share.

CONTENTS

FOREWORD

BY BLAKE MASTERS

xvii

INTRODUCTION

1

START

Collete Davis

LIFE IN THE FAST LANE

7

Bamidele Onibalusi

GETTING STARTED MAKING
MONEY ONLINE

12

Daniel Brusilovsky
HOW FOUNDING "TEENS IN TECH" WHEN I WAS FIFTEEN
CHANGED MY LIFE FOREVER
16

Andrew Aude
APPLE, HOUSE PARTIES, AND LEAVING WISCONSIN
20

Tyler Arnold
THE MOST UNUSUAL WORD FOR AN ENTREPRENEUR
24

Emmanuel Nyame
HOW IT ALL STARTED . . . AND HOW YOU CAN START, TOO
28

Edward Lando
MY 500-HOUR SUMMER
(BECAUSE SOMETIMES ALL YOU NEED IS
ONE SUMMER FREE OF OBLIGATIONS)
31

Kirill Chekanov
MAKING YOUR PASSION YOUR LIFESTYLE
34

Adib Ayay
CURBING POVERTY
37

Zoe Wolszon
FINDING YOUR CAMP HALF-BLOOD
40

Charlotte Bravin Lee
THE IMPORTANCE OF THE TEEN VOICE
47

Jaxson Khan
MAKING STUDENTS PARTNERS IN EDUCATION
51

Safeer Mohiuddin
SELLING $100,000 WORTH OF IPHONES
55

Joe Previte
FROM A COLD E-MAIL TO AN
INTERNSHIP IN SAN FRANCISCO
58

Alexandra A. Saba
ON VULNERABILITY AND FINDING ONE'S WAY
THIS IS FOR THE DREAMERS, THE ARTISTS
62

RISK

Dau Jok
STRIVE TO THRIVE
67

Buntu Redempter
HOW GENOCIDE IN BURUNDI BRED
A GLOBAL INNOVATOR
72

Darby Schumacher
I AM MISS METROPOLITAN,
AND I AM GOOD ENOUGH
75

Jasmine Gao
ON LOSING AND DROPPING OUT
83

Madison Maxey
SKATING ON CALIFORNIAN HILLS
A REFLECTION ON WIPING OUT
87

Noah Centineo
WHAT HOLLYWOOD, IN-N-OUT BURGER, AND PARKOUR TAUGHT ME ABOUT TAKING RISKS
90

Anwit Adhikari
PERPETUAL ENERGY
94

Michelle Lynn
WHAT DOES IT TAKE TO MAKE IT IN HOLLYWOOD?
99

Vijay Manohar
BRIDGING THE DIGITAL DIVIDE
102

Zoe Mesnik-Greene
WHAT'S A SMILE WORTH TO YOU?
105

Alpha Barrie
TURNING GANGSTERS INTO ANTI-DRUG ADVOCATES
110

Brandon Wang
ON FLYING
113

Daniel Ahmadizadeh
CONNECTING FLIGHTS, STORIES, AND EXPERIENCES . . . THIS IS WHO WE ARE
117

Kevin Breel
WHAT DO YOU DO?
120

JOURNEY

Samuel Mikulak
MY ROAD TO THE OLYMPICS IN LONDON 2012
127

Kristen Powers
I LOST MY MOM,
BUT GAINED A PURPOSE
132

Alex Jeffery
FIND YOUR GIFT, GIVE YOUR GIFT!
136

Ryan Orbuch
THE DAY WE BEAT OUT ANGRY BIRDS
ON THE APP STORE
140

Caine Monroy
MY ARCADE
FROM CARDBOARD BOXES TO
A WORLDWIDE PHENOMENON
143

Payal Lal
THAT'S IT!
146

Patrick Lung
WE ARE ALL BETTER TOGETHER
153

Ben Lang
BAD BREAKUPS
157

Brittany McMillan
SAVING THOUSANDS OF LIVES
(AND INSPIRING MILLIONS)
THROUGH SPIRIT DAY
160

Erik N. Martin
ANOREXIA NERVOSA AND ABRAHAM LINCOLN
166

Ash Bhat
WHY TRY IF YOU'RE GOING TO FAIL?
170

Ariel Hsing
RALLYING MY WAY TO THE OLYMPICS
174

Stephen Ou
MY JOURNEY BEFORE PROGRAMMING
178

Corey Freeman
I'M A BLACK, LESBIAN, FEMALE, COLLEGE DROPOUT,
OCD, INTERNET ENTREPRENEUR
183

LEARN

Conrad Farnsworth
FARNSWORTH FACES HIS FATE OF FUSION
191

Mohnish Soundararajan
WHAT KHAKIS AND COOKIE FLAVORS TAUGHT ME ABOUT LIFE
194

Javier Sandoval
WHAT I LEARNED FROM THE
SEVENTY-SOMETHING-YEAR-OLD BACHELOR
198

Michael Costigan
HOW I'M TURNING MY AUDIENCE INTO A PLATFORM
200

Peter Solway
WHAT COMPETING FOR A TENNIS GRAND SLAM
TAUGHT ME ABOUT CHARACTER
206

Fletcher Richman
"THE STARTUP OF YOU" AS A STUDENT
209

Brett Neese
I COULD HAVE RUN AWAY . . . BUT I DIDN'T
216

Nick Liow
THE STEREOTYPE OF A SOCIALLY AWKWARD PROGRAMMER
220

Victoria Chok
CHOICES
223

Tessa Zimmerman
THE THREE LESSONS FOR SUCCESS
228

Romain Vakilitabar
LESSONS LEARNED FROM SURVIVING
IN THE SAHARAN DESERT
232

Zak Kukoff
FIVE MINUTES
237

Arshdeep Sidhu
RUNNING WITH OPPORTUNITIES
240

Aaron Kleinert
FINDING BALANCE AS A HIGHLY RECRUITED
STUDENT ATHLETE
245

Christopher Pruijsen
BIRTH AND REBIRTH AS A BURNER . . .
IT TOOK A WHILE TO GET HOME
247

Eric Arellano
ONE DROP IN A SLOW OCEAN
250

SUCCESS

Jack Andraka
JUST IMAGINE WHAT YOU COULD DO
257

Simon Burns
WHAT IS THE DEFINITION OF SUCCESS?
262

Cam Perron
STEPPING INTO THE BIG LEAGUES
266

Tallia Storm
DISCOVERYOURSTORM
270

Taylor Amarel
WITH PRIDE AND HUMILITY
275

Micaela Chapa
HOW I LOST 165 POUNDS AND
SAVED MY OWN LIFE
279

Pulkit Jaiswal
BEING FIRED FROM YOUR OWN COMPANY
283

Paige McKenzie
ADORKABLE
287

Mariah Spears
WHEN YOU BECOME STAGNANT, YOU DIE
290

Tyné Angela Freeman
THE KEYS TO SUCCESS IN MUSIC AND LIFE
293

Lou Wegner
HOW HUNDREDS OF KIDS HAVE SAVED
THOUSANDS OF ANIMALS
299

Olivia Bouler
SAVING THE GULF
ONE DRAWING AT A TIME
303

Vanessa Restrepo Schild
A SEVENTEEN-YEAR-OLD SCIENTIST
305

Leora Friedman
WRITING THE LYRICS TO A LITTLE GIRL'S DREAM
309

Karan Kashyap
MIKEY'S RUN
A MISSION TO AID BOSTON MARATHON
BOMBING AMPUTEES
313

Siouxsie Downs
PARTING, HEARTFELT ADVICE TO FUTURE DOERS
316

ACKNOWLEDGMENTS
323

FOREWORD

History shows that innovators can't expect to be popular—at least not at first, and often not ever. That's the price of doing new things in a world in which so much of what people do is to repeat what has been done before. A certain class of innovator—young people—must be especially prepared to steel themselves against the scoffing and skepticism they're sure to suffer as they try to do anything new. The world has given up expecting new things from kids—why else would we lock them up in schools and prescribe to each one the same homogenous (and homogenizing) curriculum for years on end?

But sometimes the tracked path doesn't take. Now more than ever, young people are realizing that the future is theirs to create, not something that will simply happen to them. In *2 Billion Under 20* you'll meet seventy-five remarkable individuals who have learned that it's never too early to do something bold. These trailblazers have plenty in common—each is self-taught in one way or another, and not one had yet celebrated a twenty-first birthday. But even more remarkable is just how diverse they are: from programmers, designers, and writers to race car drivers, Olympians, and EMTs, their achievements dazzle—like flying machines in a world used to bicycles and buggies.

If you type "Millennials are" into Google's search bar, the autocomplete feature suggests "doomed." But the crowd's got this one wrong. This book shows what ambitious young people can get done, if only we believe in them. Actually, scratch that: They don't need our faith. Perhaps all that's required is that we get out of their way.

—BLAKE MASTERS,
COAUTHOR OF *ZERO TO ONE*

INTRODUCTION

"Millennials are screwed."

At least that's what Google thinks. When we started *2 Billion Under 20*, if you typed the words, "Millennials are," into the world's most popular search engine, "screwed" was the first suggestion that popped up. Rounding out the top four options were "lazy," "entitled," and "the new hippies."

But we refuse to believe that those words define our generation.

At eighteen years old, Stacey cofounded MySocialCloud with her brother, Scott, and friend Shiv Prakash in an apartment they had rented for the summer in South Central Los Angeles. After hard work, dedication, and a whole lot of learning, they raised just over $1 million from Sir Richard Branson (founder of Virgin), Jerry Murdock (cofounder of Insight Venture Partners), and Alex Welch (cofounder of Photobucket). Just two years later, they made their first exit when they sold MySocialCloud to Reputation.com.

Meanwhile, on the East Coast in South Florida, Jared had been tinkering with startup ideas since he was fifteen. After starting (and failing) to launch both NowIGetIt.com, an edtech platform, and Synergist, a crowdsourcing site specifically for social entrepreneurs, he found his groove working remotely for two venture-backed Silicon Valley startups in 15Five and Learnist before consulting as a marketing specialist for some of the world's top authors and entrepreneurs, including individuals like Keith Ferrazzi, number one *New York Times* best-selling author of *Never Eat Alone*, and Brian Smith, founder of UGG Australia.

The two of us met by accident in November 2012 at the Thiel Foundation Summit in New York City. Jared's flight back to Florida was delayed, giving him time to watch the event's final keynote speech that sparked the idea for the book, and we soon realized in the months following that our combined experiences in entrepreneurial endeavors, network building, and overcoming various obstacles along our paths, coupled with our thirst to share the untold stories of our community, would allow us to be the necessary guides needed to share this book and its insights with you today.

Right now, there are more than two billion people in the world at or under the age of twenty. These Millennials represent almost one-third of the entire global population and, more importantly, their actions determine the world's future, despite what Google's most skeptical searchers would hope for.

What these skeptics don't know is the type of young people we have met, befriended, and worked alongside over the past four years while working on our own endeavors. We are an ambitious melting pot of go-getters; members of a generation who are breaking down barriers in all walks of life and in all corners of the globe, working together to act on our passions and accomplish truly remarkable feats for anyone at any age.

Our contributors in this book are doing amazing things. Jack Andraka has found an 85 percent more effective way of detecting pancreatic, lung, and ovarian cancers. Daniel Brusilovsky started Teens in Tech to bring teens interested in technology to Silicon Valley each summer to immerse themselves in the atmosphere. After running Teens in Tech for five years, he created, pitched, and landed his own job to work as a technical guru for the Golden State Warriors. Brittany McMillan rallies tens of millions of people through the Internet each year to support the LGBT movement that continues to play a massive role in securing marriage equality for all. Kevin Breel travels the world speaking to teens about his battle with depression through a comedy skit that shows that things get better. Conrad Farnsworth became the first person in Wyoming to build and operate a nuclear fusion reactor, at just seventeen years old! And there are many more.

We have watched them begin their journeys and grow into successful teenage entrepreneurs, award-winning scientists, internationally recognized singers, Olympic and collegiate athletes, mission-driven nonprofit founders, renowned public speakers, multifaceted actors, and remarkable individuals who inspire us every day and show that the Millennial generation isn't "screwed" after all.

We are the ones who are going to change the world, and, in fact, we already have.

This book is sectioned into easily digestible chapters that you can read little by little before you go to bed every night. Each chapter is comprised of, on average, fifteen anecdotes that can be read in less than ten minutes each sitting. The anecdotes shared by the selected contributors leave readers with vast knowledge on various ways they can find their passions (START), take the required first steps in accomplishing their own personal goals (RISK), handle adversities that will come their way (JOURNEY), gain experience and expertise from everything they do (LEARN), and ultimately (SUCCEED).

Our contributors are on the cutting edge of their various industries and lines of endeavor. Their stories will offer valuable inspiration and practical takeaways, whether you are a young person looking to get ahead in life or an older reader who wishes to innovate in your chosen craft or better understand the Millennial generation.

No matter who you are, this book, and the development, efforts, and success of the Millennial generation, will impact your life in some capacity, so let's get started.

We have brought together seventy-five ambitious, successful, and forward-thinking young people from all walks of life in order to deliver this message to you and introduce you to the 2 Billion Under 20 movement.

Why?

Because if the two billion people in the world under twenty years old spent every day pursuing their passions and working together to solve the world's most pressing problems, just imagine what the world could be.

It is our hope that you'll read these stories and connect with each of the seventy-five contributors who have generously shared their most intimate thoughts and stories with us. We hope that you'll be inspired to join our 2 Billion Under 20 community and make your own contributions to our future books, growing online community, and society at large, and we invite you to do so online at 2BillionUnder20.com and in the real world whenever we have meet-ups or make a visit to your city. Know that, behind the seventy-five people who are sharing their stories with you today, there stand thousands of other extremely talented, giving, and supportive Millennials, all of whom work with us every day to tackle some of the world's biggest problems, assist one another in our endeavors, and bond over the stories that make each of us unique.

We can't wait for you to join us, too.

—STACEY FERREIRA AND
JARED KLEINERT

START

The starting point of all achievement is desire.

—NAPOLEON HILL

Collete Davis

LIFE IN THE FAST LANE

Collete Davis is founder/CEO and racing driver at Collete Davis Racing, LLC. Starting college at fifteen, and, after receiving a scholarship from the National Science Foundation to attend Embry-Riddle Aeronautical University for Mechanical Engineering at sixteen, she quickly became a national STEM ambassador for young girls and women. She won her first championship in racing at fifteen and made her pro debut in motorsports alongside the IndyCar Series at eighteen. She's set a track record in Florida, represented Team USA on an international racing platform for F1 development, and was one of the first drivers in the world to test Ford's new Formula EcoBoost200 race car at the Silverstone Circuit in the UK. She was also part of the inaugural class at Draper University's entrepreneurial program.

As a military brat, my life has seen constant moving and changing, but one thing has always been there for me: racing. From taking apart lawn mower engines as early as age eleven, to winning a championship title my first year of kart racing, I was blessed to discover my life's passion early—and have since been designing my entire life around becoming one of the best drivers in the world.

Lots of kids get into racing go-karts shortly after they learn to walk, often because the sport runs in the family and the financial support is there to back them. My story is quite different—I started at age fourteen and my passion for racing was completely organic; no one in my family had been in the sport, had connections, or even watched racing for that matter. At first, this was my biggest challenge. As an outsider looking in, I had to work my way into the industry by brute force, make connections from nothing, establish my presence, and learn a whole lot about the business of the sport to pilot myself through the early stages of my career. I let being the "underdog" fuel my drive, and I hustled every day.

I knew what I wanted to do in life and did everything I could to excel in school so I could graduate early and pursue my dreams. I had already skipped sixth grade, so at fifteen I was a junior at Fountain-Fort Carson High School in Colorado. I was taking classes not only at my school but also at a local college campus (where I became president of my automotive class) as well as online. For my school allowing me to do this, I am endlessly grateful—if not for my school counselor, Cathy Matthynssens, who helped me convince the dean to allow me to take such a ridiculous workload, I don't know where I'd be today. By the end of my junior year I had enough credits to graduate two years early, as well as sixteen college credits.

People often ask what motivated me to work so hard that early, and the best answer I have is that I was, and am, hungry. I've always been hungry. Hungry to succeed.

Racing captivated me. From the first moment I sat in a go-kart I knew I wanted to be a professional driver and compete against the best in the world. Growing up, I was ultracompetitive and played just about every sport from basketball to cheerleading . . . but racing was something different altogether—it spoke to my core. Racing is about pushing yourself, improving on every minute detail. It's engineering. It's about becoming a master of real-time physics and learning, and working, and growing with a team to collectively become the best within the pack. And all that aside, it's the single biggest adrenaline rush on earth. I have yet to fire up a race-car engine without wearing a devious grin.

When you find something that ignites that fire within you . . . you *must* chase it.

After graduating high school, I received a scholarship from the

National Science Foundation to attend Embry-Riddle Aeronautical University for Mechanical Engineering at sixteen. That scholarship represents another constant force in my life—the help of others. Were it not for a number of positive influences in my life, I know I would not be where I am today, and the funny thing about those who help you along the way is that they have usually been assisted as well along their own journey. Thus, I learned the importance of giving back, and vowed to use my unique experiences as a racing driver to promote STEM education for today's youth (especially young women), in hopes of captivating and inspiring other youngsters early on. I even became Embry-Riddle's youngest national STEM ambassador in history and, through that role, was able to inspire hundreds of middle school girls to potentially pursue STEM-related careers. I was also able to create a hands-on education program for the university, bringing students to the racetrack to help apply our STEM studies in the real world. During my time as their ambassador, I spoke to hundreds of middle school girls across Florida and was shocked to find that all they needed was someone to tell them that they can. They can be smart. They can be interested in math and science. They can be successful in motorsports, in engineering, in coding. I literally had girls come up to me after many of my talks saying how they just didn't know they *could* do that, too, alongside the guys. They didn't know it was "normal." As ridiculous as that may seem, that is the cliché that still exists in America during those crucial moments in a kid's life where they are shaped as individuals. They just need someone to show them that girls *can,* and more importantly, girls *are.* After some of my talks, I even had girls e-mail me asking me questions about cars, or telling me that they went home and starting working on cars with their parents and continued excelling in math and science. After realizing how big of an impact I could have, I knew I needed to do whatever I could to continue to inspire others and make a change.

My dedication in promoting STEM, enriching the education experience, and being a pioneer for the university led to me to land my first corporate sponsor . . . Embry-Riddle! With their partnership, I went on to win every race that year, set a track record, speak at multiple events across Florida, and continue my engineering studies as a full-time student.

Fast-forward to today (and at the ripe old age of nineteen), I find myself a woman in a male-dominated sport. I have progressed through racing in Formula 500, Formula 2000, Formula Atlantic, Grand-Am Rx-8, Panam GP Series, and Pro Challenge Mustang. I have a track record of success, winning races in many different types of cars, making my pro debut in the USF2000 National Championship Series (a development series for IndyCar) in 2012 where I got two top-ten finishes (placing sixth and ninth) in a field of thirty-six drivers, and was the highest-running female in the history of the series at the Grand Prix of St. Petersburg. I was later selected as one of two drivers to represent Team USA on an international F1 development platform, and had the opportunity to be one of the first drivers in the world to test Ford's new open-wheel race car at the famous Silverstone Circuit in the UK. Racing success generally comes with lots of practice in the specific car type (which equates to needing a lot of financial backing just to practice) and having the support of a teammate—of which I had neither.

There will always be bumps in the road as you start chasing your dreams. My "bumps" were that my sport of choice is a *very* expensive one, and not only did I not come from a wealthy background (which is often the case), but I also didn't know anyone when I started. All that aside, I kept pushing. I accepted the fact that many things were against me, but I kept pushing. Tenacity, dedication, and persistence are what I've held on to over the years, and it's what's needed to chase success.

I was forced to become very entrepreneurial early on if I wanted to pursue my passion of racing for the rest of my life. I've also had to adapt and evolve as a person. Becoming a professional racing driver involves most aspects of starting a business and crafting a brand. I've had to learn a variety of skills, from coding websites and editing videos to managing social media channels, creating pitch decks, raising money, planning events and executing promotions, convincing corporate decision-makers, and building business partnerships.

Because of all these challenges, I realized I needed to do something much bigger to set my career up for long-term success.

In September 2012 I met with Tim Draper, one of the most famous venture capitalists on the planet, about his revolutionary vision for a new kind of university. A few months later, I received a scholarship (again, the help of others at work) and was accepted into the inaugural class of the Draper University of Heroes entrepreneur program, where I absorbed everything that was thrown at me, and I mean everything—complex business planning and development, advice from hugely successful entrepreneurs, wilderness survival, first experience driving an electric car, and even my first big pitch to a panel of some of the most prominent Silicon Valley VCs. It was here where I learned how to transform my racing career and brand into a high-growth business opportunity.

Having essentially bootstrapped everything to date, I'm racing toward that critical tipping point when I can finally stop fighting for entry fees and track time and proudly start racing for one of the top teams in the world—and I'm close.

If you couldn't tell by now, I'm on a mission to thoroughly disrupt the motorsports industry, make history, and inspire millions of young girls along the way to chase after what they want in life. This is just the beginning.

Bamidele Onibalusi

GETTING STARTED
MAKING MONEY ONLINE

Bamidele Onibalusi *is a nineteen-year-old Nigerian entrepreneur who got his first computer when he was sixteen. He soon discovered blogging and has been devoted to it ever since. He's also the founder and CEO of popular writing blog,* Writers in Charge, *which is read by tens of thousands of people monthly and employs at least seven people at any given point in time. He has been featured in* Forbes, *in* Millionaire *magazine in Italy, and in several local newspapers. He is recommended by Under-30CEO, Blogtrepreneur, and Retireat21 as an entrepreneur to watch.*

Growing up in Nigeria has been tough. Making a living here has been even tougher. But early on, I decided that nothing would get in the way of my success.

I lost my father when I was seven years old. After he passed, it became my mother's sole responsibility and mission to take care of me and my six brothers and sisters. Being the second oldest of seven children, I soon realized that not having a father significantly impacted the lifestyle my siblings and I were able to live. With no father figure and no second income, we needed to stay home and pitch in around the house and take care of each other while our mother was at work. And as we did, my siblings and I watched the other children go running off together after class, playing sports and making inside jokes that we were never a part of.

I saw how hard my mom worked for a weekly paycheck that would only cover the basic necessities of what my siblings and I needed to survive: food, clean water, a home. Yet, across the town, I saw the rich schoolkids' parents making their money work for them, not putting in much physical effort to live a lavish lifestyle, and therefore being able to spend time with their families. Being in my formative years, I gushed with envy and went to bed at night dreaming about a time that I wouldn't have to see my mom do manual labor—and I wouldn't have to, either.

In 2009, I started hearing about this thing called "the Internet" and its "endless possibilities." The only problem was that to be able to access this mystical world called "the Internet," I had to learn how to use a computer. At that point in my life, I'd never seen a computer up close. Computers sat behind a glass window at my school and looked too complex to me . . . lots of buttons, a blank pad that I later learned was a touchpad mouse, and software that mimicked paper. But when other kids started talking about how people were making $7,000 a year (which, in my country's currency, is the equivalent of being a millionaire in the United States) through the power of the computer, I knew that it could be my ticket to a better lifestyle. So I knew I needed to learn.

I started at school, taking peeks at the computers and hitting some keys to see what effect that had on the screen. But after a while, I knew that if I was going to dedicate the time necessary to learn enough to make money, I needed a computer at home.

Considering our financial situation, convincing my mom to make the investment of buying a computer wasn't easy. I talked to everyone I knew who knew anything about computers. Some of them told me not to bother learning, saying that it was too complex. Others said that once I paid for a computer, I'd start working with the software that would "mess up the screen," but others encouraged me to invest my time and money in learning. When I found out that my pastor was computer literate, I started working with him to create a plan to pitch the idea to my mom. I outlined the upfront costs ($300 for a PC) and explained that the benefit was beyond imaginable. Because of this little box with buttons and a screen, we might never have to worry about money again.

Though computers were a household necessity in other countries, computers in Nigeria were extremely rare. So when the day finally came that my mom made the investment and bought a computer, I was ecstatic. I spent all night practicing typing with two hands and learning the meanings of all the strange icons I'd never seen before (i.e. ESC and screen brightness icons).

Over the course of the next couple of weeks, I kept learning new things about the computer and the software that came with it. My church community began to notice how well I was beginning to type and how well I could enter numbers and words into programs on the computer to keep track of things. Shortly after they caught on, I was offered a data entry job by a church member.

In my spare time, I searched the Internet to get ideas for how to make money through the Internet. I had learned enough to know that if I set up a website to sell products, I could make money off the products I sold. I just needed a domain name, a product to sell, and a way to accept the money.

After working enough hours through my data entry job, I made enough money to register my first domain name and host my first website for a few months. I spent an entire day building and putting up a very simple webpage to sell one type of product and used PayPal to accept the money. From there, I realized that even though I had a website, no one was visiting it. And after four months without making a single sale, I knew I needed to rethink my approach.

After researching ways to make money online, I came across an article by Steve Pavlina, a self-help speaker, entrepreneur, and author, titled, "How to Make Money from Your Blog." Steve was a very persuasive writer who seemed to have tangible results to show for his blogging, so I thought I'd give his strategy a go. Steve's strategy for blogging success was to give value without expecting anything in return in order to build an audience over time. This audience would then be used to reach my financial goals—by selling them things like the product I had initially been trying to sell.

I decided to give this a try and began writing about small business, entrepreneurship, and social media. Every day for a few months, I kept writing and kept creating other blogs where I would write about my main blog. After a year of blogging, I received my first e-mail from someone who asked me to write content for his websites. The opportunity of the Internet hadn't exactly manifested itself in the way I was expecting, but writing became an avenue to making more money for my family, so I slowly started to embrace my career as a freelance writer and blogger and began looking for more clients.

Today, I'm continuing to write on a monthly basis (with four others working for me), making a good enough salary that my mom doesn't have to work so hard to support my family, and getting ready to attend college (that I'll be able to pay off in full) to get a better education. I'm still searching for the next opportunity that my computer can bring, but in the meantime, I reflect and am glad that I took that risk to invest and get started.

Daniel Brusilovsky

HOW FOUNDING "TEENS IN TECH" WHEN I WAS FIFTEEN CHANGED MY LIFE FOREVER

Daniel Brusilovsky leads digital initiatives for the Golden State Warriors, working on emerging technology, innovation, analytics, special initiatives, and more. Prior to joining the Warriors, Daniel was the head of business development and growth at Ribbon, the simplest way to send and receive money from anyone. Daniel also founded Teens in Tech Labs, a community, conference, and incubator for young entrepreneurs. He has spent time as a summer associate at Highland Capital Partners, a twenty-five-year-old $3-billion-plus venture capital firm that focuses on investments in seeding early and growth-stage companies. Prior to joining Highland Capital Partners, Daniel was on the founding team of Qik (acquired by Skype) and also worked at TechCrunch.

My story starts with curiosity, the same force that eventually inspired me to help hundreds of young entrepreneurs around the world get their "start."

I was fortunate to have been born in San Francisco, California. I've always been at the epicenter of next-generation technology. Both of my parents work in the tech industry, so I grew up with technology around the house, in my parents' office, and as the central topic of dinner table conversations. From a very early age, my dad and I would take apart spare computers at home as he explained to me how each part contributed to the whole and why the computer wouldn't work without each specific component. Technology became an integral part of my life and, as I grew up, I wanted to further explore the field.

In middle school, I got a job as an IT associate at a company called Remend. While Remend didn't end up being a Facebook IPO story (the company eventually went bankrupt, and its assets were sold off), it was one of the best learning experiences of my life. I learned a lot of the core technical skills (like learning how to code) that I still use to this day. Looking back, I'm thankful that my manager at Remend gave me projects that helped me grow personally—even if they didn't always directly correlate to the company's bottom line.

It was at that time—between 2006 and 2007—that I began listening to Leo Laporte, a technology broadcaster, author, and entrepreneur, on the radio as recommended by my dad. During this time, and with Leo as inspiration, I began blogging, podcasting, and vlogging on my own.

In late 2007, all my interests converged at a single space, a startup called Qik. At the time, Qik developed an app only available on Nokia phones that allowed users to stream live to the web with only a millisecond delay. I was blown away when I first saw a demo from Bhaskar Roy, cofounder of Qik, at a local Starbucks. A few weeks later, I was offered an internship with the team, and ended up spending three years with Qik before their acquisition by Skype in 2011.

While I was at Qik, some of my biggest responsibilities early on were evangelism and marketing. I frequented tons of conferences, events, and meet-ups showing people the awesome technology behind Qik. After attending all these events, I started noticing a trend—I was always the youngest person in the room. As I continued to attend these conferences void of young people, I continued to ask myself "Why?"

With that question in mind, I started Teens in Tech Labs in February 2008 to meet other young, entrepreneurial-minded people in Silicon Valley. I knew deep down that I couldn't possibly be the only young person who felt alone among techies twice our age. With my knowledge of the industry and with the broadcasting experience

I had recently developed, I wanted to start bringing these people together. Four years later, by the end of 2012, Teens in Tech Labs had produced six Teens in Tech Conferences (five in Silicon Valley, one in Los Angeles), organized the first incubator program exclusively for young entrepreneurs (which helped start over ten companies over two years), and launched other initiatives that helped create a community of thousands of young entrepreneurs. In the five years that I was CEO of Teens in Tech Labs, companies like Microsoft, Google, Intel, General Motors, JBL, and others supported our initiatives by sponsoring our conferences. All of this stemmed from the simple notion of wanting to meet other people my age who were interested in tech and entrepreneurship.

Because of the Teens in Tech Conference and Incubator, numerous people have gotten involved in the tech industry. Mark Daniel, cofounder of GoalHawk (one of the companies in our 2012 Incubator program) moved from Nashville to San Francisco after he was accepted into the Thiel Fellowship "20 Under 20" program. Mark is just one example of people who gained experiences in entrepreneurship firsthand through Teens in Tech and turned the opportunity into a career worth pursuing, and various other young entrepreneurs (including my fellow 2 Billion Under 20 contributors Brandon Wang and Ben Lang) also trace parts of their roots back to Teens in Tech for the lessons in fundraising, networking, and community building that we provided to them.

What's happened since Teens in Tech? Well, a lot. My experience running Teens in Tech allowed me opportunities to work at a variety of interesting places like TechCrunch from 2009 to 2010. In 2010, I joined the creative interactive agency JESS3 and worked on data visualization projects for some of the biggest brands in the world. In 2012, I joined Highland Capital Partners as a summer associate, working with an amazing venture capital firm that's been around for twenty-five years and has $3.5 billion under management. In late 2012, I joined a payments startup called Ribbon, as the head of business development and growth (the founder/CEO of Ribbon, Hany Rashwan, and I met through Teens in Tech in 2008), and most recently, I joined the Golden State Warriors basketball organization as their digital initiatives lead.

In 2008, I would have never guessed that the desire to meet young, like-minded people would lead me to where I am today. The community we built around this notion of "Teens in Tech" was the seed that started numerous companies and changed hundreds of people's lives. It's a community that I'm incredibly proud of to this day.

Every day, I wake up humbled and thankful for everything that has happened since my first job at Remend in 2007. My life would be so much different if I hadn't taken a chance in following my dreams at a young age. The course of my life would be so much different if I had feared being the youngest person in the room, but I didn't. I let it fuel me to change the world around me, and with that mindset, I'll never know who I'll meet in the future or what experiences I'll have, but I know they'll be meaningful and life-changing.

Andrew Aude

APPLE, HOUSE PARTIES, AND LEAVING WISCONSIN

Andrew Aude has been into computers from a young age, and once the iPhone came out he had an intense drive to program the iPhone to do just about anything. He taught himself C, Objective C, and the iPhone API out of a book and later released his first iOS app iWhiteboard, which has more than 155,000 downloads, when he was just a college sopho-more. When he was a senior, Apple awarded him a WWDC student schol-arship ticket that drove him to move from Wisconsin to Palo Alto just two weeks after the conference to begin an iOS development role at Refresh, Inc. Currently, he's studying computer science at Stanford Uni-versity and works as a section leader (undergrad TA) for introductory computer science classes. He has previously worked for Venmo and is currently working at Apple.

It's safe to say I've been fascinated with technology and the entire tech industry since I was little. In elementary school, I was addicted to TechTV, the twenty-four-hour TV channel dedicated to everything tech. Because of this show, I wanted every gadget on the market (way before my allowance matched the price of those "toys"). In high school, I became hooked on the iPhone, so I taught myself app development.

At the end of high school, I planned a trip to WWDC, Apple's annual flagship conference for developers. Being a "broke teenager" with a student ticket, I looked for the cheapest lodging possible near the Moscone Convention Center in San Francisco. I booked a room at Startup House, a hostel for entrepreneurs, at a measly $50 per night.

The room was basic, to say the least. It didn't even have a window. However, shortly after getting settled in, I realized that this place was actually quite special. Despite the hostel's aesthetic shortcomings and crowded quarters, for the first time in my life I was surrounded by a ton of passionate and friendly people who appreciated technology as much as I do. Each night, I stayed up late conversing with people in the lounge. One of them, Chris, was a community manager for a startup (and at the time, I had no idea what a "community manager" even meant!). He explained how easy it is to network in the Bay Area and how to get "plugged in." From how I understood it, all one had to do was just talk to people, share a bit about yourself, find out what they're into, and exchange contact info. That's about it, which as it turns out, is the same way to network in pretty much any industry, tech-related or not.

The next person I met was Paul Henry, a seventeen-year-old working as a full-stack computer engineer for a company called Wanelo. He had just graduated from high school as a homeschooled student and had recently moved to the Bay Area from rural Texas. Now, he was making oodles of money compared to what I could ever earn working in Wisconsin. Paul and I shared stories of being the lone kid in the middle of the country interested in technology, and he set an incredible example of how a person can capitalize on their interests and make a comfortable living out of them.

Paul and Chris are just two of the fifty-plus people I met that week. I went to WWDC after-parties each night and met tons of incredible people. I met CEOs, developers, designers, recruiters, and even Apple's vice president of iOS. Connecting to people was so easy now that I knew where to find the ones I could relate to!

As you can imagine, I didn't want to leave. It seemed like I had made more friends in one week than I had made in all of high school. The worst part of the whole experience was knowing that, after WWDC was over, I would probably never see these people again after going back home to Wisconsin. I was not okay with that. The thought of quickly losing my first real sense of belonging to a community that finally understood me overtook any reservations I had about leaving home before this trip, so on the last day of the conference, I started a full-on job hunt in the Bay Area. The founder of Startup House sent my resume to his list of connections. I even walked into nearby start-ups and applied for jobs on the spot. Something had lit a fire under me, and I was not going home empty-handed.

As much as I wanted to stay, I had to fly home to clean up some important loose ends. That didn't end my job search though. I decided on the two-hour drive from the airport to my house that I was 100 percent committed to moving out to the San Francisco Bay Area. I told my parents this right when I got home, and I insisted that the decision was final. Over the next few days, I interviewed with a few companies via phone and I gave my two weeks' notice at my old job, signed with a startup in Palo Alto, California, booked a one-way ticket, and found housing online. Two weeks later, I was working in the Bay Area as a front-end engineer.

Within a week of living in Palo Alto, I received a Facebook invite to a housewarming party in San Francisco. The host was Paul Henry, the seventeen-year-old engineer I thought I would likely never meet again. I, of course, attended the party and again met many of the people there. They quickly became my best friends that summer. Because of that housewarming party, I eventually met hundreds of other people I would not know otherwise, and many of them are close to me to this day. I've gone to hackathons with them, partied with them, vacationed with them, and skydived with them. With these friends, I chatted with founders of companies like Venmo, Twilio, and Stack Overflow. A group of us even attended the TechCrunch Disrupt Hackathon. I ended up on the winning team, and got to see Mark Zuckerberg in person. I guess I was lucky.

None of these awesome experiences I've had in the San Francisco Bay Area would have happened if I hadn't gone to Paul's party and talked with the people there. On that note, had I not stayed at Startup House and talked with Paul Henry in the lounge, I wouldn't have known about Paul's party in the first place.

Looking back at my first night at Startup House, Chris was right: networking isn't hard. It literally involves going to a party, talking to people, and maybe exchanging contact info. Find an event, conference, or party that suits your interest, and just go for the sake of meeting people like you. I guarantee you'll meet someone awesome that will have a major impact on your life that you'll have missed out on otherwise.

Making the effort to talk to people you don't know pays itself back a hundred times over. It's never a waste of time to sit and talk to someone you don't think you'll see again, because there's a fair chance you will.

Especially if you make the effort.

Tyler Arnold

THE MOST UNUSUAL WORD
FOR AN ENTREPRENEUR

Tyler Arnold *is the founder of SimplySocial, which helps organizations properly utilize social media tools and content. Previously he cofounded two other companies, Purlize and Tyler Systems, both of which held contracts with large companies like Microsoft, HBO, and McKinsey. Tyler has been featured in* Forbes, VentureBeat, The Huffington Post, *and* TEDxAnchorage, *and he was the 2011 SBA Young Entrepreneur of the Year in his hometown of Anchorage, Alaska.*

"No!" I said. "I don't want to do it."

"No? What an unusual word for an entrepreneur!"

Andy Holleman was my computer teacher in middle school, and he was largely responsible for my interests in technology and business. He was one of the few adults who met my level of passion and fueled my curiosity by patiently answering all of my questions and enticing more from me. At the time, I was making some extra money buying and selling computers online, finding ways to channel my passions into business (even at age twelve). Brokering computer deals online gave me a chance to get my hands on the latest technology and play with the latest toys.

Andy and I always kept in touch even after I graduated to high school. One summer, shortly before my sixteenth birthday, he gave me the book *The World Is Flat* by Thomas L. Friedman and told me to read the whole thing.

"Why would I spend my summer reading something that's four hundred and fifty pages? No. It's too much. I don't want to do it."

We continued our conversation as we walked around the local supermarket. I was brought along for Andy's Sunday afternoon shopping.

He began his rebuttal, "Someone on the other side of the world is going to eat your lunch. Read the book and realize how globalization is taking over. It's going to change everything."

"Yeah, sure. Whatever, I'll be fine," I responded. I felt confidently safe and cut off from the rest of the world. Reluctantly (out of respect for my former teacher), a few weeks later, I opened the book and started to read. I was one chapter in when I realized a piece of paper had fallen out of the book. As I unraveled the note, I soon saw that it was a letter from Andy. This unusual, sentimental move caught my attention.

In the letter, Andy outlined what he described as an "exciting time," as our modern world is continually growing and evolving. "Read the book and recognize what a great time this is to be alive," he wrote.

Finally, I understood what all the fuss was about. The book had outlined a future that included the rise of a global middle class. It portrayed entrepreneurs that connect the developed and developing worlds as the new early economic prophets of the twenty-first century global economy. I immediately realized that, for Andy, my reading of this book was important. I then decided to continue onward, now referring to the book as my gospel instead of an unwanted summer reading assignment.

After the first 25 pages, I went from being an isolationist (it happens, growing up in Alaska) to being open to the idea of a global world. By page 50, I even began to think it was a good idea. "A global middle class sounds like a terrific thing," I thought. By page 100, however, I began to see opportunity. There was this whole generation of individuals profiting off of an increasingly global world, creating wealth that spanned borders. I desperately didn't want to be left out.

When I put the book down at page 125, I was inspired to start my own business. I knew a bit about web development, and started searching for overseas outsourcing teams. The book revealed opportunities on a global scale; I realized I could create relationships online with pro-gramming teams in Romania and Pakistan and deliver their services at a reduced cost, through a business I could offer to advertising agencies located around the United States and Western Europe.

Since my sixteenth birthday was just days away, I wrote up (what in hindsight could be called) a little business plan and asked my parents for $400 worth of seed money to start my first business. I knew my parents would want to know what I planned to do with the money, so I tried to do everything I could to sell them on the idea by showing them the same version of the future I saw. I explained how that $400 would take me there. That $400 would get me a down pay-ment on a website design so I could start advertising my business and make enough money to pay the web designer back. Since web designers at advertising agencies were our target customers, I posted links to our website in online discussion groups for designers, asking for feedback on our website design. It was a great way to get feedback, but it was also an easy excuse to put our website in front of our target market in a very noninvasive way. Shortly after launching, we did a few $100 projects for advertising agencies in the United States, Neth-erlands, and Germany. Wise investment, parents!

I was running the business out of an e-mail inbox on my BlackBerry phone at the time. When the school year started, I quickly lost inter-est in my schoolwork and focused almost all my energy on the busi-ness. After eight months of aggressive advertising online, asking for referrals from everyone I knew, and pouring almost all of our reve-nue back into more banner ads online, we started to do some large projects for clients like Microsoft, eBay, and HBO. They just started filling out the order form on our website without any sort of sales pro-cess. They either heard about us from their friends at other agencies, or had worked with us directly on a previous project and changed jobs. We built a solid reputation around our website and promised our customers to uphold it. I ended up getting a C (my first and only) in precalculus soon thereafter, as school slipped to a second priority. I craved an environment where I was tested, challenged, and growing. I couldn't relate to precalculus, but working with people in Romania, Pakistan, Europe, and the United States was inspiring.

The business ended up generating enough revenue to attract investors. I sent a cold e-mail to a major business figure in Anchorage,

Alaska, named Allan Johnston. There's a great phrase, "If you ask for money, you'll get advice, and if you ask for advice, you'll get money." Allan and I connected immediately when we met, and whether it was blind luck or some powerful instinct, I started asking for advice. I told Allan of my dreams to grow the business and what I would need to make it happen. Thirty days later I presented him with a business plan that he passed around to a group of friends and fellow accredited investors. I ended up offering those investors a positive return, and fortunately they decided to take a chance on me, allowing me to continue growing the business and travel the world after graduating high school. I spent most of my time in Europe where we had a few customers and where I had participated in a German American exchange program (GAPP) a few years earlier. It was my active learning MBA. The experience also ended up introducing me to the cofounders of my most recent startup, SimplySocial. One is Dutch (he clicked on our banner ad) and the other is Romanian (he won an outsourced job of ours previously on oDesk). We ended up spending a lot of time together during all of my business travels, and later started a business together.

Today, SimplySocial employs eighteen people and is growing. Since I had worked with investors before, even at a young age, I had a track record that allowed me to pull from existing relationships to pool a small amount of capital together to get the business off the ground. We kept things "lean and mean" until we could grow and expand overhead through customer revenue.

In hindsight, every START story feels like things were "meant to be." It feels like your destiny was set all along. But that's not true. What every START story is missing is the endless questioning and self-doubt that's felt throughout the entire process, at every step of the way. Sometimes you think you are wasting your sixteenth birthday gift, or putting school second for all the wrong reasons, or traveling to a different city for a client you'll never win. Not everything goes smoothly, but, as one of my mentors, Douglas Grobbe, says, "That's how the cookie crumbles."

Indeed, I guess if you've been around long enough to see these things, you realize that luck, spontaneity, and good timing count for a lot (and every successful career contains elements of all the above).

The only thing you really have to do, is just start!

Emmanuel Nyame

HOW IT ALL STARTED . . .
AND HOW YOU CAN START, TOO

Emmanuel Nyame, a Kairos Global Fellow, doubles as a multiple award-winning business strategist with an distinct focus on strategy development, commercial intelligence, and entrepreneurship development. He organizes the U.S. Department of State's StartUp Cup Accelerator program in Ghana, and is a partner to a New York–based venture capitalist firm, iYa Ventures, assisting growth potential startups with funds and support services. Emmanuel is a prolific speaker and writer, having been guest speaker for high-profile events such as the Ghana SME Summit, and has a dedicated column in Ghana's most-read business newspaper, Business & Financial Times, *where he talks extensively about starting a business in today's developing world. Emmanuel is also a contributor to* The Huffington Post, *authoring thought-provoking articles on Africa's development and sustainability.*

Looking back makes me reflect greatly on my early beginnings, when nobody really cared whether I succeeded or not. Life seemed to be about obtaining good grades in school and becoming responsive to what the future would bring. My challenge at that time was discovering who I really was so as to get out of the pack, especially when there was pressure from all angles to conform.

I had quite an interesting upbringing, thanks to my parents and church. And strangely enough, I had no idea what I wanted to become—until I started becoming the hero at home. Almost everything that was faulty at home became a priority of mine to either repair or improve. I remember when our tap screw malfunctioned one time, and within seconds I solved it. This was just the beginning. I translated this mentality of solving problems to my academic work, but honestly did not produce the kind of results that everyone would acclaim.

A very poor score in my mock examination at the junior high school level, just before taking my final entrance exams for senior high school sent me over the edge. My friends made fun of me, and my most frequent thought became, "Why don't you give up?" Like everyone, giving up was the easiest thing to do. How on earth could I score five marks out of one hundred in my mathematics exams? I wept, yet moved on. My mathematics teacher at that time encouraged me to look for my mistakes, correct them, and give the test a second try in the final exams. I followed his advice, and it worked! I passed my finals with distinction and gratefully accepted admission into senior high school.

What had been an abysmal performance in school turned out to be one of my best experiences ever! I represented my school in quite a number of competitions both internal and external and came out with flying colors. Notable among them was the National Quiz on Finance, which hosted fifty secondary schools across Ghana to battle it out on financial literacy. I won first place for my school! I also started a financial model to assist students in their educational progress. We helped fund their textbooks and other school needs. This venture earned me and my friends two awards within a year of operation.

What I want to do is show you how you can begin to see the world on your own terms from a perspective that will add more zest to your life. Helen Keller once said, "Life is either a daring adventure, or nothing."

Every great thing that you see around emanated from a small idea. Your idea must be something you are passionate about. Passion is what keeps you moving when things don't go as well as expected. For instance, I have passion for helping build businesses, and that's the reason I'm a strategy consultant for corporate organizations. Not only do I feel at ease executing my job, but even in bad times I feel very okay.

Change the status quo. This is a fact in business. Don't repeat what is already on the market. Distinguish yourself. Be unique! Have a unique selling proposition! This refers to a component of your business that makes it stand out. Most investors really concentrate on this aspect of your business. If you're not competitive enough, you're out of the competition!

Be very realistic in your goals and be sure to have a resounding vision for your company. This works especially when your company is expanding. Your visions and goals provide ultimate direction.

Keep working till you achieve. My advice to some of the corporations that I consult for is this. Some products require a lot of design and infrastructure in order to attract buyers. It is therefore the responsibility of the chief executive to prevent the human behavior of relaxing among employees until the job is done and an exemplary product has been made. If you truly want success in business, this attitude needs to stop. Work day and night, make contacts, and push your company into the limelight!

My final word of advice is that you do not allow the system to determine your future. One of my favorite spoken word artists, Suli Breaks, sums it up this way: "We all have different abilities, thought processes, experiences, and genes. So why is a class full of individuals tested by the same means?" You're meant to be a superhero at home, school, or in business! Find your passion and your way and may you experience so much joy every day! Act *now*!

Edward Lando

MY 500-HOUR SUMMER

(BECAUSE SOMETIMES ALL YOU NEED IS ONE SUMMER FREE OF OBLIGATIONS)

*Born in Paris, **Edward Lando** is an undergraduate at the Wharton School of Business at the University of Pennsylvania, where he focuses on entrepreneurship, computer science, and international studies. He previously founded Famocracy, a site that allows people to become famous for their talents, and currently is an aspiring novelist and entrepreneur. Edward is a regular contributor to* The Huffington Post *and won the Bartleby Snopes "Story of the Month" award in their online literary magazine.*

Not all those who wander are lost. I quit an internship after three days and decided to spend every day of my summer reading and writing novels. As I'm writing this, I'm one month into my decision, eighty pages into the draft of my first novel, and eight books down.

I feel privileged that I'm able to do this, and I am. I'm living for free in my cousin's basement in San Francisco, so at least I don't incur the cost of rent. However, this isn't just "free time," although there may be no boss to report to or schedule to rule my day, if only for a summer. This time is more of a philosophical proving grounds: Can I make a living on my own accord doing what I love and following my major life goals? To me, finding out the answer to this question was certainly worth risking a summer without a safety net.

Something strange happened to me a year ago. It might have come from getting older, but it probably came from reading Vonnegut and Tolstoy. And Salinger. Those guys will mess with your brain if you read them at the right time of your life. You feel something happening inside your head. You think of everything differently. It's scary and interesting and you know you won't ever go back.

You start questioning all the rules of life. You start realizing they're total BS and that everything is absurd. And so you decide that maybe you'll spend the rest of your absurd life being free. Or at least one summer to try it out, worst case being a return to an internship like the one I turned down, or redirecting focus to my grades so I can get the most out of my education and utilize those in a traditional job search. One 500-hour summer was worth sacrificing to escape "absurdity," right? For me, this freedom involves trying to reach mastery at something. Many people are good at a lot of things, but few are really good at one thing. And being really good at one thing makes life very pleasurable and creates an illusion of higher meaning that's convincing enough to convince you that you are very happy (which isn't so bad, is it?).

I feel privileged to have had this insight before I was forty, or fifty. That's pretty much what people call a "midlife crisis," but it's not as useful then because you have much less time to do something about it. I think about mortality tens of times each day. It used to make me desperate, but less and less so now. Now it just makes me impatient to get back to work. I'm more and more breathless in everything I do, and feel a sense of wonder when confronted with just about anything in the world. The other day I had no fixed schedule just like every other day of my summer, and I started my day by walking from the Financial District to the Embarcadero, all the way along the water past the Golden Gate Bridge. That walk got me high on everything. Every minute I jotted down several scenes and thoughts on my phone, because everything was fascinating.

I believe in the 10,000 hour Malcolm Gladwell analysis. In his book, *Outliers,* which is potentially one of the most famous business books of recent memory, Gladwell states that it takes roughly 10,000 hours of practice to achieve mastery of a given skill. He studied the lives of extremely successful people to find out how they achieved greatness. From professional violinists to the founders of Microsoft and even the Beatles, time and time again, Gladwell found that those who had this significant amount of practice time in their history outperformed those who were less experienced. It's because of this principle that I risked an internship, and the money, security, "prestige," and opportunities that could result from it. I knew writing was the singular skill I wanted to master, and the best way to improve my skills and develop to a point where I could become happy, self-sustaining financially, and able to contribute to society was . . . you guessed it, to continue writing!

I've probably spent a couple thousand hours writing before this summer. This summer can get me 500 more. Ninety days away from college, times 24 hours times ¼ because you don't realistically write well for more than 6 hours a day . . . in my case at least. That's 500 hours. Doesn't look like much, but it really is a lot. They are the tipping point for us to commit to our goals even if we wander a bit along the way. Remember, 10,000 hours are required to reach mastery.

I encourage anyone who doesn't know where to start in accomplishing his/her goals to simply commit 500 hours of effort along some determined path. If that doesn't take you where you want to be, then start 500 hours of something else. Just starting something, anything, will help you in seeing if it's something you want to continue investing your time and energy in.

Kirill Chekanov

MAKING YOUR PASSION
YOUR LIFESTYLE

Russian native **Kirill Chekanov** *started his first business at fourteen and at seventeen, started Hippflow—a brand new format of sharing data with mentors, investors, and other interested parties. Hippflow started as a network of business incubators and accelerators and was evaluated at more than $1 million a few months after its launch. Soon after, investors helped to grow the company more quickly and provide a better service to the customers. Now Kirill is developing Hippflow as a web platform and Google Glass application and doing his part to aid the startup community all around the world by mentoring various startups in business development and strategy. He has been featured in TechCrunch and PandoDaily among other media outlets.*

When I was growing up in Russia, I saw business as a very romantic career. I saw businessmen that I looked up to having fun, laughing, and shaking hands: "doing business." In my mind the job required talking, it required being friendly, and it required just having fun. The reality, I learned, was much different.

In high school, I began working on a project to connect local university students with brands that wanted to advertise to students. After the first week of trying to sell this value to brands, I realized how hard I was going to need to work to build relationships in order to get their business. In the beginning, I didn't get much traction. E-mails I sent would never be returned or people that I asked to meet with straight up said "no." For the meetings I was able to land, I saw the way people looked at me (a high schooler) when I walked in the room. I noticed that "doing business" meant starting at square one: proving that I should be in the room.

I started attending a few events in my community that revolved around startups and startup founders. I found that there were a ton of people like me experiencing the same problems. Many of them were trying to pitch investors (mostly individuals—because VC firms in Russia are known for taking too much equity in a company) to put money into their company to build and distribute their product. As I began forming friendships with these people, I realized that the things that set the successful people apart were their networks. The people getting their business ideas funded had a connection or warm introduction (through a mutual friend) to investors who would put in money, which left the rest of the people without connections with nothing.

After a year or so of learning about this problem, I decided to switch my project altogether. Rather than connecting young people with brands, I wanted to connect startup founders with targeted potential investors (i.e., investors that had experience or expertise in the industry that startups are being built in). Once my team and I had an initial product built (we called the product Hippflow), we began testing it in a few incubators in Russia and collected as much feedback as we could about the onboarding process (to make sure people stayed with us throughout the whole signup process without giving up), product ease of use, and the value of the product. This allowed us not only to learn more about Hippflow, but also build deep relationships with startup founders and investors, our two customers.

With those connections and the work we had done in building our initial product, we were able to prove that we deserved to be in the room with investors. Once we were in the room, we had to let our product and the work we had done so far do the talking. We showed off the core of our product as well as little experiments with building sub-products, like a Google Glass app that compiles data (both media data and data input by the founders) about investors' portfolio companies to track their achievements and needs. These connections and our hard work allowed us to raise a seed round of money ourselves, which has allowed us to continue following this passion.

As a college student now, I look back on the days that I romanticized my "idea of business." It's true that "doing business" does require talking and laughing and shaking hands—but it takes work to get there. And putting in that work upfront, to build a solid network, will help ensure that doing business will be fun.

Adib Ayay

CURBING POVERTY

Adib Ayay *is a nineteen-year-old social entrepreneur and peacemaker. He founded Fair Farming to empower smallholder farmers in developing countries. His work has strengthened the financial stability of hundreds of households in rural Morocco. He got his start as an active member of SIFE Morocco (Students in Free Enterprise) and the Moroccan Center for Innovation and Social Entrepreneurship during his time studying at the African Leadership Academy. He has since been invited to the Global Youth Summit in London and the Three Dot Dash Peach Summit in New York, where he was named "Global Changemaker" by the British Council and a "Global Teen Leader" by the We Are Family Foundation. He is now studying at the University of Chicago and working to expand Fair Farming to growing markets like Nigeria and Bangladesh.*

Hoping to escape the brouhaha of the city and recharge my inner energy, I retreated for a few weeks to an isolated inn nestled somewhere deep in the Atlas Mountains of Morocco. Each morning, the locals offered me a basket of delicious red apples as a gift to accompany my stay. Delighted by their warm hospitality, I insisted on meeting the man behind this gesture to thank him in person. Soon afterward, I was taken to see Miloud, the owner of the surrounding farm where the delicious fruit came from. Judging from the size of the land, I expected to walk through the doors of an ostentatious residence.

When I walked through the doors, however, I was shocked by the deplorable state of Miloud's mud house and miserable living conditions. With the same fervor the fruit on his land flourished and ripened, his walls deteriorated and cracked. What we'd consider common conditions could only be perceived as luxuries of the highest order for him and his family.

How could one live like this? Gratitude for the generous gift I had received just hours ago quickly turned into guilt; how could one be constrained to such distressing lifestyle standards, and how could I sit by idly eating Miloud's harvest, carefree, without the urge to help? His kindness deserved my wholehearted reciprocity.

Puzzled by Miloud's situation, I mobilized a small group of students within a local student organization, SIFE Morocco (Students in Free Enterprise), and we conducted a field survey to decrypt how the owner of paradisaical prairies receives such minimal benefits. The results highlighted how the market prices were five times higher than those charged by the village farmers. As explained simply by the laws of supply and demand, Miloud's produce was in much higher demand than dictated by what he was charging, and because Miloud, who had never left his small town, hadn't realized most of the market realities, he became easy prey for unscrupulous middlemen who atrociously exploited his blissful ignorance, buying his produce at extremely low prices so they could sell them at market value and make most of the money for themselves.

I returned to the village determined to incite Miloud to increase his selling prices. The notion of change terrified the man because he feared losing his clientele under the impression that all his neighbors would continue to charge low prices. After a long and heated discussion about his current living situation, and after reasoning that his children deserved better if he had the opportunity to provide more for them, Miloud finally agreed to gather the remaining farmers of the region with the goal of finding a solution to end the clear exploitation they faced.

The feeling of fear and inexplicable dread regarding change and resisting the ruthless middlemen recurred in the farmers' interventions, but they were all equally (if not more) concerned about the future of their families, and hoped to offer them a better life. After listening intently to their insecurities, I suggested they put their harvests in the same basket, decide together on the selling price, and never let anyone exploit them again. With the help of business students from SIFE, we developed an action plan for the farmers' cooperative initiative and stayed in touch with them during their first two years of operation under this new collective trade agreement.

Today, their collective (the Rhamna Cooperative) has developed several added-value products and has received support from the National Initiative for Human Development. As a result, in less than two years, each of the farmers has reported a staggering 70 percent income increase, including Miloud.

Miloud's success story inspired me to start Fair Farming (FFarming for short), an initiative that promotes fair trade and helps smallholder farmers derive maximum benefit from their products. Since its inauguration, FFarming has partnered with 7 agricultural cooperatives and has impacted more than 300 farmers from all over the country. FFarming has received awards from the Global Changemakers program (given by the British Council), and was adopted by the We Are Family Foundation under its Three Dot Dash initiative. At the moment, we are initiating expansion of FFarming to Nigeria, Brazil, Colombia, and Bangladesh.

Miloud's continuous phone calls updating me on the progress of the Rhamna Cooperative always bring flashbacks of the delicious red apples he gifted to me just a few years ago, and remind me that our little actions can and will change the world around us for the better.

Zoe Wolszon

FINDING YOUR CAMP HALF-BLOOD

Zoe Wolszon is a recent graduate of the University of North Carolina at Chapel Hill, where she studied biomedical engineering, worked as an emergency medical technician (EMT), traveled as much as she possibly could, and eschewed any form of regular sleep schedule. She is currently living and working in Daegu, South Korea, as a Fulbright Korea English teaching assistant (ETA), and plans to return stateside after the fellowship to join the Boston Consulting Group's San Francisco office as an associate consultant. Zoe is also a health entrepreneur who is fascinated by the intersection of medical devices, clinical medicine, global public health, and sustainability.

I started working as an intern at BookPeople, the largest independent bookstore in Texas, when I was twelve years old. I already knew the kids section like the back of my hand after countless hours spent curling up in a corner with a good book. I loved being able to help people find what they were looking for while putting my OCD toward a good cause by alphabetizing and straightening the shelves. I quickly befriended the amazing staff, and got involved with our teen book club, becoming especially good friends with Topher Bradfield. Topher is not only a guru on children's books, but he's also quite the storyteller (in every sense of the word); all the neighborhood kids loved listening to him read, and would often gather at the store once a week to hear a selection from one of his favorite new releases. It was an innocent question at one of these readings that tipped the first domino in a chain that, although I didn't know it at the time, would change the course of my life. He was reading us Rick Riordan's *The Sea of Monsters* that night, and paused at one point to pose a question to the group: "Would you all like to go to Camp Half-Blood?"

For those of you that haven't read the series, I should take a moment to explain. *The Sea of Monsters* is the second novel in a series entitled Percy Jackson and the Olympians, which chronicles the adventures of a young Percy Jackson. Percy finds out the hard way that the Greek mythology he learned in school isn't a thing of the past; nor is it, in fact, mythology. Nope, the Greek gods are alive and well in the twenty-first century, sitting atop their thrones on Mount Olympus (located on the six-hundredth floor of the Empire State Building in New York City) and causing trouble per usual. In the series, Percy discovers that he is a demigod (half-human, half-god), and must immediately travel to the only place where he will be safe: Camp Half-Blood. As a training camp for demigods, Camp Half-Blood offers activities that go far beyond the norm: sword fighting, archery, intense games of capture the flag (all weapons and armor allowed), lava-wall climbing, chariot racing, and more. Throughout the series, Percy travels around the world encountering all sorts of mythological beasts, but Camp Half-Blood is never too far from the action. So when Topher posed to us that simple question, there was no hesitation. The phrases "Yes!," "Of course!," and "Duh" filled the room from our eager, innocent, excited faces, and Topher just smiled; you could see the wheels turning in his brain.

A few short months later, we held our very first session of a real-life Camp Half-Blood in Zilker Park, located in Austin, Texas. The campers varied in age from about seven to fourteen, and were sorted into cabins according to a questionnaire meant to draw out personalities and align them with those of the Olympian gods. The questions ranged from favorite activities to lovely oddities such as, "What would you tell a five-hundred-ton pig sent to squash the earth?" and "What color is thunder?" Over the course of a week, we learned to fight in a Greek phalanx, throw spears through Hula-Hoops hanging in trees while riding in the back of a pedicab (our "chariots"). We sword-fought, participated in history lessons, and chose Greek names for ourselves, all in the name of competition with other cabins for pieces of a mythical Apple of Discord, whose scattered presence was causing problems among humans around the world. At the end of the week, the campers came together and realized that the only way we could succeed in our quest to restore order to the world was to work together and make the apple complete once again. As cheesy (and crazy) as it seems, the camp was an enormous success. The growth in confidence, friendship, and appetite for literature was visible in nearly every single participant.

Although a triumph, the week ended with sad news. Topher's wife, Ceci, had just finished school, and they were going to have to return to California in order to find jobs with benefits and more than a basic retail salary in order to support themselves. I was devastated to learn that we were going to lose this visionary and the opportunity to continue making magic like we did that summer.

I couldn't let that happen. So I began a letter-writing campaign and a petition to make BookPeople understand the immense value of someone like Topher, and to ask them to find a way to keep him in Austin. I talked to all of the parents whose kids had attended Camp Half-Blood that summer, and contacted some of the librarians who had witnessed Topher's story discussions. Word spread, and BookPeople was quickly flooded with letters, e-mails, and phone calls from kids, parents, and librarians from around the city. As of that August, Topher had a new job title, children's outreach coordinator, a position created solely for him and his unique talents. And the best part? A significant portion of his job description included the continuation and expansion of the literary camp program. I knew that we had won, but the significance of that victory far exceeded anything I imagined at the time.

A little over a year later, I began having some musculoskeletal problems that forced me to take a hiatus from my hobbies of tennis, kung fu, and violin. When my doctors predicted I would shortly need surgery on my wrists, I was forced to quit all physical activity, a move that only proceeded to make things worse for the rest of my body. I was restless, frustrated, and desperate for a way to fill my time, so I was overjoyed when Topher asked me to join the BookPeople staff in order to help him grow the camp program. I started out as a secretary, taking messages, responding to e-mails, and talking to parents about what we did. When it came time for registration (in November, mind you, more than half a year before the camp started) and Topher had meetings elsewhere, I took responsibility for running the process at the store. I had no idea what I was in for, and neither did BookPeople. People swamped the store, phone calls frequented us more than ever, the fax machine broke in the middle of important faxes, and cashiers stumbled, wondering how to process this new type of transaction. "Running around like a chicken with my head cut off" doesn't quite do justice to my state of being, but I can say without a doubt that, at the end of that day, I felt immensely proud of what I had accomplished. There's something different about achievements that occur out in the "real world," outside of the bubble of school, surrounded by people with families and careers. It was the first time a significant number of adults ever looked to me for guidance, where I felt that weight of responsibility and the thrill of opportunity and confidence. When I was voted Employee of the Month just a couple weeks later, you could see in my smile and sense in my stride that I felt like I was on top of the world.

My commitment to the camp program only grew, and I began spending hours at the store every day after school working on creating and managing an organizational database sufficient to keep all of the campers' information in order. I got my own desk and computer (at least for some time), began sitting in on budget meetings, and going to off-site meetings with Topher. I gained confidence in my ability to reach out to parents and members of the community as needed, via phone or e-mail, and learned how to use corporate mailing systems such as RatePoint to send out mass mailings with important information. I learned how to calmly, confidently, and effectively talk to a displeased or confused parent or customer, a skill whose importance in business and in life cannot be understated.

I would tell people how much I loved my job and then describe what I did (data entry, data filing, budget meetings, etc.), and would constantly be met with blank stares and confused faces. I knew it didn't make logical sense to love entering information into huge Excel spreadsheets the way that I did, but I also knew that it didn't matter what others thought of these seemingly mundane tasks. Why? Because I was so deeply passionate about what we were doing, and about the power and importance of the camps we ran. I loved the people around me, as well as the feeling that I was actually doing something that mattered, something that went far beyond writing an English paper or taking a history exam.

I inherited this unique situation where I earned the opportunity to grow with my job description, take on more responsibilities as I continued to become comfortable with my duties, and perpetually embody deeper involvement. As one of only two people working on these camps year-round, there were no limits to how much I could grow and learn, no boundaries to contain the expansion of my experience into new realms.

The camps grew exponentially, quickly. The next year was the first in which we had parents camping out in front of the store to get a spot in line for registration. The line has started earlier and wrapped farther around the block every year since (now parents will camp out for almost twenty-four hours just to enroll their children in our camp!). We expanded into other literary properties like the Spiderwick series, the Kiki Strike series, the Ranger's Apprentice series (still running), and even Star Wars, but Camp Half-Blood has always remained the flagship camp. In the summer of 2013, nearly 800 campers attended one of the sessions of camp, and received an experience shaped by an ever-growing pool of people, resources, and ideas. This included detailed professional makeup work, a whole troop of dedicated actors and fighters, a number of custom-made props, and an ever-changing storyline whose skeleton was filled in by snippets of conversation and cool ideas contributed by the kids each day.

My responsibilities at the camps grew as well. From a counselor-in-training and administrative assistant, I eventually became a camp administrator and assistant camp director. I was in charge of all administrative duties including paperwork, organization, and legal matters (including the surprise state inspection of our files, employee records, and more that happened every summer), and was usually the point of contact for parents, kids, staff members, and other stakeholders. I also directed the day-to-day activities of the camps, which involved everything from explaining the rules of the games, writing up schedules, directing the staff, and being the safety officer (hey, someone had to be the mean one). I also checked in on sick or hurt campers, acted as a resource for the growing staff, and helped run staff meetings before and after camp. I certainly kept busy.

But here's what made our camp (and my job) special: None of that was ever straightforward. This was no ordinary summer camp, and the number of moving pieces (in terms of actors, props, encounters, changing story lines, and random occurrences) was . . . let's just say, pretty crazy. I can most likely say with confidence that I am the only assistant camp director to ever encounter texts and calls multiple times a day with messages like "We're putting a spybot in the tree—make sure the kids don't come down to the capture-the-flag field yet," which I of course received as we were walking the camp down the hill to the capture-the-flag field. Suffice to say that I enforced a number of very randomly timed and located water breaks, story times, scouting missions, and . . . more water breaks.

I worked seventy-plus-hour weeks over the summer simply because I wanted to, because seeing the shock, surprise, and excitement in the kids' eyes made it all totally worth it. I witnessed kids with dyslexia form relationships with characters and worlds within books, realizing the immense power of a novel; I watched children who, according to their parents, had never been able to stay at a camp for more than a few hours fight those same parents to stay longer at the end of our nine-hour days so that they could continue sword fighting with their new friends; I heard a parent say that she had seen her daughter cry for the first time in two years on that Thursday night, all because she didn't want camp to end; and so much more.

It wasn't just the kids who absorbed a wonderful camp experience. I watched myself grow in confidence as I developed my interpersonal, organizational, and management skills, and saw the same growth in the staff members around me. I benefited from the wisdom, trust, and support of an unbelievable crew who worked tirelessly to create an unforgettable experience for our campers, and I built relationships with them that I know will endure for years to come.

Even though I have had to give up my role at these camps in order to attend an out-of-state college, I know that those experiences will never leave me, nor will my passion for the camps, their purpose, and the people who make them what they are today. I know now the importance of the people with whom and the environment in which you work, that passion and purpose can turn even the most menial tasks into worthwhile investments that inspire happiness and feelings of worth and accomplishment, that I am capable of so much more than my age or number of diplomas may dictate if I can devote myself to a cause, and that I am not meant to be a person in a lab coat doing academic research. I am meant to be out in the world, interacting and learning from new people every day, in the quest to find or to create the next Camp Half-Blood.

Charlotte Bravin Lee

THE IMPORTANCE OF THE TEEN VOICE

Charlotte Bravin Lee *is an eighteen-year-old writer, artist, and cura-
tor. She is the current adviser and former director of Teen Art Gallery,
whose mission is to provide creative teens with a place to display their
work in New York City. She has completed programs at the Iowa Young
Writers' Studio, The Kenyon Review Writers Workshop, and New England
Young Writers Conference at Middlebury. She has had her poetry and artwork published and won a Scholastic gold medal for painting and gold
keys for art and writing. She currently curates Young Creators, a Tumblr
site for work by young writers and artists. She attends Kenyon College,
where she is a Gund Gallery associate.*

I was the kid that couldn't kick a soccer ball or emote onstage. I couldn't
read musical notes or follow dance steps, but the moment I discovered
what I could do with a piece of paper and a pencil, my parents never
signed me up for a single ballet class again. My family replaced sports,
drama, music, and dance with canvases, notebooks, colored pencils,
and motivation. "Oh, that's nice Charlotte!" became "I really like what
you did with these lines, but I think this paragraph could be worked

on to bring it up to speed with the rest of your writing." They taught me to appreciate their criticisms of my work just as much as their encouragement, and over the years I would draw constantly, filling every inch of every piece of paper I touched, writing poems and short stories in notebooks and making lists of words that appealed to me. For a while, I only shared this part of myself with family and a small group of friends. I didn't think anyone else would want to see my work, and so it stayed hidden among my inner circle and insecurities.

When I reached middle school, however, I realized I had a distinct voice that needed to be shared with others. Certainly I wasn't the only one shy about sharing my talents, and I wanted to give my peers permission to be their own creative selves should they also face the same insecurities I possessed. During one of the first few weeks of sixth grade, I remember sitting in math class letting my teacher's voice trail off as I focused on my own thoughts, something I generally did in math class (I'm sure you can relate!). I scribbled down charlottehatesmath.com and decided I would create a website for everything I considered to be the opposite of math. I would include my own art and writing, but more importantly I'd include a submissions page. I was eager not only to showcase my own creative endeavors, but to also give others a chance to have their work seen.

It wasn't the biggest success, as I was only eleven years old and received only four submissions (one of which was from my younger brother), but the website did have its fifteen minutes of fame during my sixth-grade year. Kids would come up to me and ask if my math teacher knew of my site. I would smile and nod, explaining that, despite its name, it was not about math at all. It was a way for kids to view work from their friends and become inspired. This was the first time I felt as if I had scored a goal.

In the beginning of tenth grade, I read a *New York Times* article about a seventeen-year-old who had started an art gallery for teenagers. It was called Teen Art Gallery, and her goal was to give teen artists a chance to have their work displayed in New York City art galleries. Her ideas fascinated me and I knew that this was something I wanted to take part in. I wouldn't entirely forego my website, but this was a new and exciting path I needed to pursue. Even then, however, the article stared dauntingly at me from my bulletin board for a few weeks before I summoned the courage to contact the girl who started Teen Art Gallery. After a few e-mails back and forth, she finally gave me the simple task of posting flyers on the walls of my school.

I made sure to be diligent about completing any tasks she asked of me. An important lesson I learned in the process is that it is crucial to show that you can be relied upon. Showing your dedication is important because if you can do a job, in a timely fashion, you will be given other, more rewarding assignments to take on. I've also found that it is important to make an effort to reach out to the person in charge and ask if anything more is needed. Don't be afraid of appearing too eager.

When I was invited to my first Teen Art Gallery meeting, I didn't actually have anything particular in mind about how I could improve the mission. I was simply excited that I was going to have the opportunity to join a community of young artists and art lovers. I was two years younger than the rest of the members, so I was a little intimidated at the outset. That feeling quickly went away when they invited me to make suggestions and then asked me to take Teen Art Gallery over when they graduated.

This was now my opportunity to give other teen artists a platform for their voice. I asked myself questions like, "How could we showcase even more teen art during times when a show wasn't scheduled? What magazines would be interested in reproducing teen artwork? Are there any teen organizations with which we could collaborate?"

I quickly realized how much could be done to expand on what already existed. The website needed to display a lot more artwork, so we created a "featured artists" page and asked artists to send me images of their recent works. We also exhibited every piece of artwork we'd ever showcased at various galleries on the site as well. We embarked on small changes like putting the artists' names on announcement cards, which previously had only listed the show title and location. We used Facebook to continually post different images of work and include bits of interesting information about each artist. We even created a YouTube channel to show off films by students as well as videos of our openings.

Before taking over, I was a little nervous about taking on such responsibility. I had never been the type to take on roles of leadership.

I always considered myself too shy to delegate and remind fellow students about impending deadlines. But, as the year went on, I learned that being the director of Teen Art Gallery was not about telling people what to do; it meant giving people opportunities to use their skills and recognize what they are capable of contributing. Teen Art Gallery is all about teens giving to other teens, and that became our leadership structure as well. On the night of a recent show, I caught myself thinking about how proud I was that the artists and their respective families were so supportive of each other, seeking one another out, learning more about each other's work. I can't imagine not being able to be a part of a community like this. Teen Art Gallery gives artists the type of audience that athletes and actors have, a crowd of people celebrating their talent.

Even now, years after first realizing the importance of my own voice and sharing it with my sixth-grade classmates, I often find myself questioning the importance of the teen voice. I believe that, due to the fact that we are on the cusp of adulthood, putting thoughts to paper and creating things for others before reaching adulthood may be better for us both in the moment and in the future. This is a time of freedom, and it is an important one to capture before we make different, difficult choices as we grow up. When we are young, we have a certain kind of freedom in making mistakes and taking chances without being judged too harshly. We have the freedom not to worry about our future careers too stringently, and as teenagers, we may never have another opportunity to create our own paths or think creatively in the same unfettered way we enjoy now. So, if you find your passion at a young age, do something with it!

When I graduate high school, I, too, will pass Teens Art Gallery on to a new group of teens. I have thought long and hard about how this has been the start of an exciting path, and one that I will continue, perhaps online, for the four years when I am in college. I simply cannot imagine not waking up to submissions in my in-box from others eager to share their voice.

Jaxson Khan

MAKING STUDENTS
PARTNERS IN EDUCATION

Named one of Canada's "Top 20 Under 20" young leaders and a global "One Young World Ambassador," **Jaxson Khan** *studies global development at Huron University College in London, Ontario. Jaxson cofounded and is the executive director of the Student Voice Initiative, a national movement to give students a voice in their education. Jaxson is an established social activist, and has spoken before audiences of more than 5,000 youth on positive change-making. Formerly a student trustee of the Peel District School Board, he served as CEO of the Ontario Student Trustees' Association, where he represented two million students across Ontario to the Ministry of Education. He advises AstraZeneca Canada's Young Health Program, reaching more than 50,000 youth and advocating for youth mental health nationwide. He is the president of Impact Entrepreneurship Group, a decade-old organization that facilitates mentorship for young entrepreneurs across Canada, and served as the youngest member of a 15-person human rights delegation to Rwanda, as one of two Canadian representatives, working with multiple NGOs, health development initiatives, and various refugee camps through the UNHCR.*

Students in high schools are, arguably, at the cusp of maturity and at a principal point of influence in their lives. They are a fulcrum between older and younger students, who I believe—and which successful precedents demonstrate—can generate enthusiasm, activism, volunteerism, and strength in a community. So, why do we not engage them?

First, let me tell you my story of being a student and youth leader, and both the challenges and successes I have encountered. I started off in something familiar to anyone who has been through school in North America—student council. Yet, though I had a good experience, I wanted to do more. I thought we could do more than running school dances and bake sales—I wanted to work with my peers to change education itself. And that is why I ran for student trustee when I was sixteen for the Peel District School Board in Mississauga, Ontario. It was the biggest thing I had ever done. I ran against more than a dozen other candidates, competing for the votes of 45,000 high school students in our district. We were the youngest politicians in the country. I was elected to represent more than 150,000 students, impacting educational decisions made by the (adult) school trustees involving $1.5 billion budget.

The lesson I learned in getting votes is that I value representation over politics. Truthfully, in those student elections, I had a hard time seeing where the roots of the demagoguery and hypocrisy in chambers of Congress or in the Canadian House of Commons come from. Sure, you could say that students are more likely to vote for who's popular—but what do adult taxpayers do? I think students, given the right opportunity and venue, can be sincerely engaged in the public sphere, and indeed, have unique insights as key stakeholders in the education system. We have proven it in Ontario, Canada, where the student trustee position has existed for the last fifteen years and led to significant adult-student collaborations to improve education. During my campaign, I had dozens of students message me about policies they wanted to see in their schools, and I realized that we had potential to make positive change. I ended up running to represent even more students, being elected an officer and then selected as CEO of the Ontario Student Trustees' Association. We represented two million students directly to the Ministry of Education, and were able to advocate for policies in mental health, technology, social justice, and even curriculum reform and development. I realized then that students could have power if they were not tokenized or paid lip service, and if a genuine feedback loop existed between students and decision-makers to improve educational policy.

After my experience as a student trustee and as a provincial representative, I started a movement four years ago called Student Voice Initiative (studentvoicei.org) to work to spread the student trustee position to provinces and territories across Canada. I believe that the position is more than a tokenistic entity. Ideally, the student trustee is substantiated by a regional student senate, which comprises itself of student council presidents from every school, and thereby, from the students up, ensures democratic representation at the board and even provincial or state level. This is a student voice framework. I think that a student voice framework is critical to establish, because it improves educational decision-making, and simultaneously instills values for democracy and citizenship in young people.

It has not been easy. I have faced lip service—people hearing me, but not really taking me seriously—at multiple turns. I considered quitting the journey to spread the student trustee across Canada. My team and I are students from across Canada, and we went two and a half years (a long time when you do not have many years in school) before we had our first big break—a nationwide presentation to education decision-makers. But that foothold is exactly what we as students need. To a young person, there is nothing more encouraging than having an adult champion to enable us to share our voice. My journey now is focused on finding adult champions who can work with students as partners in education.

For me, I think high schools are the ideal targets—to start—for student voice movements, because we have successful precedents in Ontario, Canada, supported by Section 55 of the Education Act. Since we have begun our advocacy, this position has spread to four other provinces, principally British Columbia—our advocacy secured a province-wide policy change for forty-five school boards and over half a million students to ensure student representation—as well as Alberta, Quebec, and Saskatchewan. Hence, student voice for me is focused on advocacy for a student voice framework in high schools—even though I am now in university, and far past my high school years. I recognize that this legacy of student voice is one that the whole community can invest in and share in, both young and old. The intergenerational gap is one that we can bridge, if we engage in sincere dialogue in our schools and our communities.

I believe in democracy, in education, and I believe in not only the principle, but also the value of having young people and students involved in decisions. In thinking about the future, perhaps this is with whom the educational decision-making process should begin: the students of today. If students are not heard, they will not be fully engaged, and will not be nearly as successful. The alternative is the status quo, which, in a rapidly changing world, is simply not enough for today, or for tomorrow. Investing in the leaders of tomorrow by listening to them now is the solution, and it starts with our schools and our students. Student voice is the next frontier for education, and we can start listening—now.

Safeer Mohiuddin

SELLING $100,000 WORTH OF IPHONES

Safeer Mohiuddin is a twenty-two-year-old Silicon Valley entrepreneur. He started his first business when he was sixteen years old and ended up selling $100,000 worth of iPhones. He recently graduated from the University of California, Irvine, with a BS in computer science and currently works at Amazon Web Services.

He is also the founder of Cordoba Labs—a boutique iOS/Android consulting firm specialized in building MVPs and its own in-house products. He is also the founder of Underage Investor—a resource for young people to educate themselves about personal finance from credit cards to investing in the stock market that has helped serve more than 20,000 people.

It was that time of the year, post-finals winter break and universal holiday season; the time when everyone is on vacation and spending time with their families. The only thing that could possibly go wrong was getting my report card from the previous semester. As always, this was the time I hated the most. The conversation always started out with "How come you didn't get all A's" and my answer was always the same: "I don't know . . ." However, this time my dad came prepared for battle and incentivized both me and my younger brother with something that was just too good to shrug off. It almost seemed too good to be true. He said, "If you each get all A's next quarter, I'll buy each of you the new iPhone." Both of our jaws dropped and, before we could even think, we shouted, "No way! You have a deal!" With all those ads about the new iPhone, the first of its kind, I knew that I needed to pull off getting all A's. At that moment, I decided that I was going to do whatever it took to get my reward.

However, the next semester quickly passed and history repeated itself, but this time, the worst possible thing happened. My younger brother got all A's and I didn't. I was furious. It was embarrassing, and I knew I would need to find some way to get my hands on my own iPhone as well to redeem myself.

Due to the demand for the iPhone, my brother had to resort to finding one on Craigslist and eBay. While looking at various prices, my dad pointed out a $50–$100 difference between the prices on eBay and Craigslist and even mildly suggested how it could be a good way to make some quick money.

I jumped on the opportunity, given my obsessive hunt to get an iPhone. Two days later, I came to my dad with a spreadsheet detailing the price difference between iPhones on eBay and Craigslist. I showed him that there was at least a $100–$150 difference and that (even after having to pay eBay fees and shipping costs) I could make a solid $75–$100 margin on each iPhone I bought and resold. He agreed that the math certainly made sense and that this seemed to be a good opportunity. But I needed one more thing from him.

My dad is a serial entrepreneur and I definitely wanted to get his advice, but I also needed some way to get capital in order to start this business. At that point, I decided to ask him for $2,000 in order to start. iPhones on Craigslist were selling for around $600 for 16GB and $700 for 32GB, so that amount of startup capital would allow me to at least buy a few iPhones and get a fast start. It was not easy convincing my dad to give me $2,000, but I was insistent that the math proved this investment was feasible. Finally, I convinced him to invest by promising to return the base cost of the iPhone as soon as the sale was complete. That helped ease his mind as he was sure to get his money back immediately.

As planned, I bought a few iPhones on Craigslist and, within days, sold them on eBay. The margins were clearly visible, but how would I be able to get more capital? I had returned the money that I had used, keeping the few hundred dollars in profits already. However, I still needed more capital to scale, so I made a deal with my dad. I asked him if I could borrow up to $2,500 a week, but on the condition that the money would be immediately returned once the item was sold. This allowed him flexibility with his money and freedom from inconvenience with the operations of my business. The idea was that if I could do this for a few weeks, I could gather enough money from my profits and finally be able to buy and sell iPhones on my own.

And that's where it all began.

As quickly as possible, I tried to acquire as many iPhones as I could, borrowing from my dad on a daily and sometimes even hourly basis.

Once I was able to collect enough funds to buy a few iPhones for inventory on my own, I decided that it was time to get what I really started all of this for—my own iPhone. I took one from my inventory and claimed it as my own. Finally! And, while finally having an iPhone felt incredible, the feeling I got from succeeding and being a self-starter was the addicting part. Just to play it off, I even called it a business expense because, at the end of the day, it was. It allowed me to find deals quicker and more efficiently no matter where I went. Anytime I had a spare moment, I could be caught surfing Craigslist to find the next few iPhones to buy.

Fast-forward two years and I had sold $100,000 worth of iPhones. It seems silly talking about buying and selling iPhones as an entrepreneur, but that's how it all starts. Entrepreneurship is about hustling. It's about doing whatever it takes to get the job done no matter the circumstances that you are under. It's putting your mind to something and achieving it. The stories that you will read and the people you'll learn about all have one common theme: hustle. It doesn't matter whether they are athletes or artists, entrepreneurs or scientists, advocates or philanthropists; they didn't wait for someone to tell them what to do. They took matters into their own hands and found ways to be successful. They were persistent and never gave up, qualities that help individuals—in any scenario, at any given time, and at any place in the world—push the envelope and truly innovate.

Joe Previte

FROM A COLD E-MAIL TO AN INTERNSHIP IN SAN FRANCISCO

Joe Previte *is passionate about languages, traveling, cultural under-standing, music, writing, and inspiring others. He sent a cold e-mail to the language-learning startup called Verbling and has been working there since January 2012. Since then, he has worked with other startups including Process Street and Aerolab. He has traveled to nine countries and spent a semester in Buenos Aires in fall 2013 to immerse himself in the culture. Now, he speaks Spanish fluently and studies Portuguese. He will finish with a degree in general studies with a focus on global and intercultural understanding from the University of Arizona in May 2016.*

Sitting at my desk with *mi amigos*, I patiently waited for my high school Spanish class to begin so I could get into *español* mode and practice what I love, language-learning. "I just found out about this really cool website where you can practice with native speakers online," *Señor* Klasky said to us *en español*. He pulled up Verbling on his projector and then attempted to connect with someone.

A few minutes went by as we chatted about the weekend, waiting and hoping someone would connect to us from a Spanish-speaking country such as Spain or Argentina. "Well, no one is available right now, so you guys will have to try it at home and then let me know how it is," he said, as he closed the website and opened up his notes for the day's class. Class went on, but I could not stop contemplating the idea of practicing Spanish with someone who lived more than 5,000 miles away. Without thinking twice, I wrote down "Verbling" in my planner and promised myself I would try it when I got home.

Later that night after finishing my calculus homework, I went on the Internet, typed "Verbling" into Google's search bar, and seconds later created an account on the website. I selected English as the language I speak fluently and Spanish as the language I am learning. I found the "connect to native speaker" button and hesitantly clicked it. I felt nervous about my abilities to comprehend and converse with a native speaker from another country. The only prior experience I had at practicing my Spanish was with the baker at Einstein Bagels where I used to work.

Two minutes following my decision to click and connect, I was introduced to a man named Juan from Peru. "*¿Hola?*" I nervously uttered into my microphone. A few seconds went by. Then Juan replied, "*Hola. Soy Juan de Perú. ¿Cómo estás?*" "*Whew!* An easy question. I can do this," I thought to myself as a feeling of relief rushed throughout my body and slowed the speed of my heartbeat. I replied and, immediately following, the conversation flowed like a river as we chatted about our respective lives for thirty minutes before I had to leave for *cena*.

Throughout dinner, I could not get over the fact that I had just spoken Spanish with a native speaker from Peru, and that it went so well! I *loved* the idea of Verbling connecting native speakers with language learners and I wanted to be a part of the team. Not thinking twice, I e-mailed the "jobs" link on their website, detailing my experience in Photoshop and Final Cut Pro and asking for a job opportunity as a high school student. I had no idea what I pictured myself doing for the company, but I decided to test my luck by sending an e-mail. "What's the worst thing that could happen? They never reply? Oh, well!" I confidently told myself with a smile on my face. In the following months, I continued to use Verbling every once in a while to practice my Spanish.

Three months later, I was visiting my grandparents in California when I checked my inbox to see an unexpected e-mail. It was a response to my cold e-mail from Jake, one of the cofounders of Verbling, asking me to Skype with him. I could not believe it! I thought certainly that it was a mistake. One of the cofounders of Verbling wanted to Skype with me, some random senior in high school from Arizona? It did not make sense at first, but then I realized the domain was "@verbling.com" so it had to be legitimate. I replied back, "I'd love to!" with more excitement than a fifth grader visiting Disneyland for the first time.

Less than a week after his e-mail, we Skyped, and he explained to me that he and two friends had dropped out of Stanford to start the company. A surprised look came across my face. I felt like I was in a scene from *The Social Network*. He told me a little more about himself and then offered me a job working as an administrator on the site to test the system and get feedback from users.

I hardly slept the next two weeks. I could not believe I would be working for Verbling. Life seemed too good to be true. I felt giddy that I was getting paid to work with the engineers and speak Spanish and English with people from all over the world. I imagined I had the most awesome job in the world and was extremely grateful for it.

Through my job, I became passionate about language-learning and cultural understanding from meeting different shades of people every day. I knew I was exactly where I wanted to be and that my desire was to help make this company succeed.

I took it upon myself to e-mail Spanish teachers in almost all the public high schools and universities in the state and inform them about this online platform that changes the way we learn languages. I even worked with a high school Spanish teacher named *Señor* Cordova from Brophy College Preparatory who contacted me via my first round of e-mails. We incorporated Verbling into his curriculum and created a blog for him to post weekly homework assignments.

Jake and the rest of the team in Northern California was pleased with my contributions after only a few months, and so they asked me to find friends who would do the same work as me for Verbling. I hired a few friends from high school who spoke Spanish, which grew into the administration team that I led for eleven months. We were a fantastic team of seven high school students who maintained the site's functionality and secured the Verbling community for all the language learners.

Then in November 2012, the company took a big step forward: live online language classes. They suggested that I learn how to teach because they wanted to move me up and have me become an English teacher. I felt so grateful to be given the opportunity to teach. I fell in love with teaching and then told myself, "Whatever I end up doing after I graduate from college, teaching in one way or another *must* be involved."

Before the school year ended, I asked my boss, Jake, if I could come to San Francisco for a month to do an internship. He spoke to the rest of the team and told me they'd be happy to have me helping out at the office.

During the thirty days I spent on the fifth floor of an office building in downtown San Francisco, I gained tremendous insights into the daily cycle of a startup, such as measuring metrics for success, developing new features, communicating with investors, working with the engineering team, and deciding the future path of the company. I learned how to communicate with customers to solve issues, manage the company's Facebook and Twitter pages, propose a new feature project to the team, measure the success of a website product, collaborate with my team, and several other aspects of running a startup company. I gathered more knowledge in that month than I could have ever possibly imagined. I feel grateful that the Verbling team gave me such a wonderful learning opportunity.

As long as you overcome fear of rejection, you never know where you'll end up. Many people think you have to get lucky and create your own startup to be a part of one. But that's not the case. I encourage you to take a leap of faith and send a "cold e-mail" to that company you are dying to work for, or chase that opportunity you've been eyeing for the longest time. Follow your passions. Don't worry. You don't *have* to know where you will end up. Let life be unexpected. Go out and create your story.

Alexandra A. Saba

ON VULNERABILITY AND FINDING ONE'S WAY

THIS IS FOR THE DREAMERS, THE ARTISTS

Alexandra A. Saba is a creative visionary, designer, artist, writer, and social entrepreneur working to integrate these passions to create a more sustainable future. She's a contributing writer and editor at fashion media company FutureClaw, where she has covered events like Art Basel and Mercedes Fashion Week. She has been a freelance writer and designer while working on her goal of opening an artistic makerspace.

At nineteen, I'm truly just starting to believe in the knowledge, power, and good that is present within me and my peers as I dive into the waters of social change and entrepreneurship. My journey is just beginning, though some days it feels like I've been thrashing around in this river my whole life. However, I feel as if I've learned more from my peers, and the communities of which I am a member, in these last two years than I have in my entire life previously.

When I first arrived in San Francisco to attend Draper University (the same alternative education program *2 Billion Under 20* contributors Collete Davis and Anwit Adhikari have been through), I had no idea of what hacker or maker culture was, but quickly found out what this lifestyle was all about through living in a "hackerhouse," or in other terms, a communal living space occupied by members of the tech community. I realized that my interests in creating wacky art projects, living life as a grand science experiment, and filling my head with whatever obscure knowledge I could get a hold of intersected greatly with these cultures. Before I found myself within these confines, I was very timid about expressing myself to others and opening up about my passions. I had experiences in which others found my interests and personality to be weird or odd instead of unique and beautiful. For awhile, I hid the real me in an attempt to shield myself from pain and rejection. Living in hacker communities with loving, supportive people ushered my true self out of the protective shell I had created. I felt safe and accepted in a way I hadn't felt in years.

I believe that the personal growth I've experienced is attributable to the supportive environment, optimistic atmosphere, and coura- geously creative culture of community. Those most influential to me appeared at a critical period of my life, when I was beginning to heal from continual experiences of abuse and trauma growing up. With- out the support, guidance, and love of the communities I found, or rather that found me, I do not believe I would be where I am today. And, when trauma strikes these days, it's the same group of people that helps keep me sane despite life's toughest challenges, like loss of a loved one.

I'm continually humbled by and in awe of the extraordinary intel- ligence, dreams, and achievements of others within these groups. We're all contributors in this swirling madness of light and despair called life. Many of us choose the hardest, yet most rewarding path, of radical self-expression. To me, radical self-expression means being unabash- edly honest, vulnerable, and open with others, and with yourself.

Engaging in radical self-expression requires the courage to be vulnerable and wholehearted: the courage to dance to the beat of your own drum, to be imperfect, and to fail. In fact, the original Latin defi- nition of the word courage is, "to tell the story of who you are with your whole heart." Through this comes the realization of "I am" (what we are individually). In turn, we gain a feeling of coalescence with others, that we're all bonded together by a sense of greater purpose. The "I am" soon becomes, "We are."

Dreamers, artists, makers, creators of a new reality—courageously embrace your vulnerability, in work, in love, in learning, in all that you do. It is not comfortable, nor excruciating, but necessary. It is the very core essence of your being, that which makes you uniquely you.

Take the first leap into vulnerability and start something you have always dreamed of doing! Have the courage to take risks, ones like my friends will soon share with you, and radically expose yourself.

Embrace the ebb and flow of this evolving journey, and learn from the inevitable failures you'll experience.

The real secret to finding one's way lies in being courageous and vulnerable enough to start, risk, journey, learn, and ultimately, succeed.

RISK

The biggest risk is not taking any risk . . .

In a world that is changing really quickly,

the only strategy that is guaranteed

to fail is not taking risks.

—MARK ZUCKERBERG

Dau Jok

STRIVE TO THRIVE

Dau Jok is a Sudan native and refugee of the Sudanese civil war, founder of the Dut Jok Youth Foundation, and a cocaptain of the men's basketball team at the University of Pennsylvania. He founded the foundation after winning the 2011 University of Pennsylvania Kathryn Davis 100 Projects for Peace award to fight violence and poverty in South Sudan through access to sports and academics. He participated in the first Penn Hillel service trip to Agahozo Shalom Youth Village in Rwanda in 2011 and also partook in We Play to Win's Benin City 2013 Youth Development Sports Camp in Nigeria while at Penn. Dau is a philosophy major with a minor in African studies, and managed to master the English language in less than six years to be admitted into an Ivy League institution. He is also the recipient of the tenth annual Coach Wooden Citizenship Cup alongside Drew Brees, legendary quarterback of the New Orleans Saints, and was also selected to the 2014 Allstate/National Association of Basketball Coaches Good Works Team.

I am an outlier.

I am not supposed to be where I am today. I have overcome unfathomable challenges in life. I am not supposed to exceed expectations, nor am I supposed to be drug and alcohol free, having been raised by a single mother in a misogynistic culture. The terrifying sounds of an AK-47 piercing through the chaos of war, against the backdrop of the beautiful Kush Kingdom, along the Nile River, could have taken my life, but they would never define it.

Life was normal in the beginning. I had parents, relatives, community, and the essentials. People showered me with love and shielded me from the reality of suffering and death that was all too familiar to the elders. The Sudanese Civil War, a result of religious intolerance and disputes regarding division of resources between the mostly Christian South and predominantly Muslim North, took with it the humanity of millions of my people. Sudan gained its independence from the British in 1956, but the nation has been plagued by war for most of its history. It was our second civil war, Africa's longest civil war (1983–2005), which dramatically altered Sudan. Life was suppressed in the ashes of the dead.

The Khartoum regime, led by the president of Sudan, Omar al Bashir, used Antonovs, Russian-made airplanes, to indiscriminately bomb southerners, forcing them to seek refuge in underground bomb shelters near schools, soccer fields, houses, and hospitals in town settings. The pain in the faces of my grandparents told stories of lost generations. Faces resting against the palms of their hands, eyes hopeless, bodies suspended in motion; their demeanors embodied the tragedy of war. This was the only truth my family failed to protect me from. They could try to hide their terror of war, but it was always revealed by the numbness in their faces whenever someone wobbled into the house with news of yet another death. I helped my father and his band of helpers and bodyguards farm the gardens. Well, I did nothing but keep them company and occasionally drop seeds as bulls marched through the gardens violently turning the brown dirt, raped by the long dreaded dry season.

My father, Dut Jok, was a frail, six-foot-six figure of hope, compassion, law, love, pride, care, and responsibility. He was the provider and leader of selfless men who had given their lives to the Sudan People's Liberation Army (SPLA) to combat the better-equipped government. He was the glue of a fragile family traumatized by the war, and a man of great character at heart. Under my father, I learned, lived, laughed, and enjoyed life despite the constant threat of guns and death.

Sudan's second civil war took nearly 2.5 million lives, my father's included, before South Sudan seceded as a sovereign nation in 2011. My father's absence caused unfathomable misery in my own life. I was no longer shielded from the desolate realities of war or the effects of greed and selfishness within the family. The compound we called home, that had accommodated numerous visitors on a daily basis, had now become lonely, gloomy, and lifeless. His death stripped away the facade of love. I had lost a friend, mentor, father, and the only person I thought understood and cared for me.

I was unable to fully comprehend what death meant, but I knew something was wrong when hundreds of relatives and tribesmen alike filled the Nile River with tears mourning my father. My father had taught me a few lessons that still serve as a foundation of my character to this day. He taught me to never let family fight alone; to be selfless, honest, and trustworthy, and he shared the importance of respect. And, of course, he taught me to never play with guns.

Every morning at the crack of dawn, select groups of South Sudanese children, me included, would gather under the shade of large trees, a peaceful space in the midst of civil war. We were the lucky ones; while our counterparts dodged bullets from the Khartoum regime, we were afforded the opportunity of an education. Schooling was only available to children whose parents possessed the means and the desire to spend these means on education. Our parents believed that, despite the fact that violence was their only tool in the fight for liberation, their children should only ever fight with pens and intellect. Craving this, we hungrily congregated around a teacher—who, given the limited availability of schooling, had not finished the eighth grade—using the beautiful African sand as a notebook, and sticks as instruments for mathematics and writing. With death and violence clouding our daily lives, we quickly learned to value our education.

My father's death left me in a confused and vulnerable state, but my mother suffered most. My mother was left to play the role of father and mother for my siblings and me with little support from our family. I have a huge family (my grandfather had 37 children, 107 grandchildren, and nearly 40 great-grandchildren upon his passing) but my father's death brought to the surface the greed, hate, and envy that came with a lack of resources. My mother is a savvy, intelligent woman, and I am simply amazed by her determination and wits. She was blessed with wonderful sisters and a mother whom she depended on as we migrated to Uganda and later to the United States in December of 2003. Her youngest sister, Achol, had dropped out of college so she could support my family while we were in Uganda. It is family members like Aunt Achol and my mother to whom I owe my perseverance and ambition.

I am an outlier because I am here against all odds. I was raised by a single mother in a culture that explicitly reinforces gender inequalities. I am an outlier because I was not quick enough, good enough, or smart enough to play Division 1 collegiate basketball or attend an Ivy League institution, but I did gain admission to the University of Pennsylvania. The fact that I mastered the English language in six years well enough to not only be admitted into one of the finest institutions of higher education in the world, but also excel beyond the boundaries of a student athlete is a testament to hard work and resiliency. I am an outlier because I saw my mother struggle to make sure we didn't feel the void of not having a father. She taught us to have faith. Faith that an education would open doors to borders of human capability and imagination. Her lessons have been manifested by small things I have accomplished in life, thus far. I am an outlier because the influence of education in my journey is profound, because I met a mentor, Bruce Koeppl, who expedited my learning curve by years. I was an immature youngster with anger problems because all I knew was violence as the lone solution to every obstacle. Bruce communicated the power of reasoning, a nonviolent approach, a seeking of understanding, and the importance of education. He nourished my self-confidence. His efforts came at an opportune time, as I fell in love with philosophy, a subject that changed the way I perceive the world. I am an outlier because the combination of strong support from my family and Bruce, my basketball family at Penn, the Penn community, and the rigor of the philosophy course load forced me to solidify my self-identity and mature. This combination permitted me to aspire to give back to the world because I have been blessed with more opportunities than most people could dream of.

I am determined to leave the world a better place than I found it. That is only possible if I am radically honest with myself, fully aware of my weaknesses and strengths. While I have been blessed to receive numerous honors for my philanthropic work and leadership, including being selected for (in front of tens of thousands of fans at the 2014 NCAA Men's Final Four Tournament in North Texas) the Allstate/ NABC Good Works Team, in areas I lack competence or skill, I find capable people whom I can trust to do the job, as I have done in founding the Dut Jok Youth Foundation in order to grow Southern Sudanese youth into academic and social leaders. By using education and athletics as vehicles to teach hope, hard work, and resilience, we can create a future group of individuals who can collectively restore post-conflict South Sudan. We are all in the same boat, and this boat will stay afloat and travel far if we realize each other's strengths and cooperate to achieve the common good. I am an agent of change. I am a voice of the voiceless. I am the guide for the blind and I will not rest until the world is better.

I am an outlier, refusing to be defined by life's circumstances or other people's naïve limitations of what I can achieve in life.

I want to know: Are you an outlier, too?

Buntu Redempter

HOW GENOCIDE IN BURUNDI
BRED A GLOBAL INNOVATOR

Buntu Redempter *is a twenty-year-old doer. He was born in Burundi, but just nine months after he was born genocide began in his country, forcing him and his family to flee to Tanzania. There, he lived in a refugee camp for fifteen years, where despite poor living conditions his interest in technology grew tremendously. When he was around eight years old, he started tearing up watches and tried to put them back together, hoping that he would figure out how they work. Now at the age of twenty, Buntu is creating his own success story by founding and owning Doers.bz, Wikindu, and a few other startups.*

Entrepreneurship is a funny word. To this day I debate if I was born with an intrinsic "entrepreneurial ability" or whether it was developed over time and conditioned into me. Thinking about my upbringing, I swing toward the former—but I digress.

I was born in a refugee camp in Kinyinya, Burundi (a small country smack dab in the middle of Africa) where everything was scarce. Demand was always more rampant than supply, and simple necessities like food, water, and light were extremely limited. People scrounged for any little form of entertainment they could get their hands on, and only the lucky few had technologies like watches and radios.

At a young age I realized that my family was one of the lucky few. We had some electronic devices, a few French books (although I hardly understood them, they were still exciting), and even a radio with music. During the day, I found myself reading and trying to figure out how the technology worked. How, when I pushed the ON button, did the device power up and start playing? What was making this happen?

When I grew older and started to understand the world around me a little better, I became increasingly interested in learning the exact nuances of how these devices worked. Shortly thereafter I became focused on one central question: How could I produce my own electricity so that I could stay up at night and have light in my refugee camp to read?

In refugee camps and villages, people dig toilets outside, granting me access to everyone's waste-space. So I started there. I tried everything from harnessing the toilet's heat to produce electricity to using acid and copper to create a longer-lasting battery on a makeshift flashlight that I had built. Try as I might, I only just managed to get fifteen minutes of light with every charge. Not having a lot of books on the topic, it was extremely difficult for me to create continuous electricity just by using my imagination and consulting my confusing French books. But by the time I was fifteen years old, I had marginally succeeded at creating my own electricity to recharge my batteries, and had experimented with a few other projects that allowed me to be seen as an innovator in the village. During those few couple of years, I had tried and learned a lot more about electricity and taking apart/building electronics than most people probably do in their lifetimes. I was scrappy, determined, and proud of what I had built.

Everything changed in 2007, when my family and I came to the United States. Everything that I had spent almost a decade working to create was taken for granted. People walked into a room and flicked on their light switches thinking nothing of it. And at night when the sun went down, I reflected on the significance the switch on the wall had in defining my life's ambition when I was younger. All my dreams and everything I had worked to learn about became irrelevant.

Yet as I became Americanized, my will to create more items to make lives better kept growing little by little. I wanted another chance to create something in this new place. I wanted to build something that hadn't already amazed people and wouldn't be taken for granted. I wanted to build something that could provide a unique value in a way that only I could create it. I discovered the Internet and noticed that, although the United States is extremely advanced, there are still a lot of opportunities to create new things with the Internet network. I immediately began building my own websites and blogs that share inspirational stories and how-to guides for young people.

While these websites have had some level of success, I always feel like it's not enough, and that's because there will always be other projects to build or room for improvement (both here in the United States and in countries like Burundi). But I've made it my mission to take every day in, not take simple things for granted, and to take advantage of the unique possibilities and opportunities I have by being in the United States. Every day is another chance for me to find focus, learn something new through experimentation, and get one step further toward making my mark.

Darby Schumacher

I AM MISS METROPOLITAN, AND I AM GOOD ENOUGH

*At eighteen, **Darby Schumacher** was one of the premier junior scientists in the nation. She has received local, state, and national acclaim for her research paper "A Filter Today Keeps Pollutants Away: A Study of Nanofiber Based Stormwater Filtration." She was the second-place winner in the Environmental Science category at the 2013 National Junior Science and Humanities Symposium in Dayton, Ohio, where she received a Department of Defense medal and an $8,000 college scholarship. She was also awarded a $10,000 from Nordstrom, and is currently the crown holder for the Miss Metropolitan beauty pageant in Chattanooga, Tennessee. This year, she began her journey of higher education at Stanford University.*

Standing in front of my mirror, blood dripping from my forehead and a severed pencil lying on the ground, I knew I had a problem.

I never learned how to internalize failure. I don't know if I just inherited a fear of failure or if my surroundings as a child instilled in me the idea that failure was the most detestable result possible. Regardless, I could not allow myself to fail, ever. This was most evident in my schoolwork, where, even in elementary school, I never turned in an assignment unless it met my standards. The problem was that my standards were perfection. For as long as I can remember, this elusive "100%" hung above me on every test or assignment. I didn't just *want* to be perfect; I *had* to be. My actions were out of necessity. A's filled my report cards, but I found myself focusing more on the grade I received than on what I actually learned.

I would argue that I am a product of the educational system. I think that many students would agree that failure is not welcomed with open arms in schools. It is not perceived as having any value. This isn't doing anyone any favors. In kindergarten, the kids who could write the entire alphabet without mistakes were released for recess first. As someone who mixed up the letters "d" and "b," I never had extra time on the monkey bars. Ingrained in my five-year-old mind was the idea that if I made a mistake, I deserved punishment. When a teacher or authority figure failed to punish me for my mistakes, I felt obligated to punish myself out of guilt for not being perfect. Serving my penance did not fulfill my desire for excellence, so I would work harder and study more as my aversion to failure grew stronger. I became my own "tiger mom." Don't get me wrong—I still had a fun childhood filled with joy and laughter, but in the back of my mind there was always a reminder that I was not good enough.

"Good enough" never gets the credit it deserves. When a paper receives a comment of "good enough," it is not perfect. Although the word "enough" means plenty, "good enough" is not thought of as meeting or exceeding standards. Greatness exceeds standards. Excellence exceeds standards. Perfection exceeds standards. I was never taught that I was good enough. Never did I feel like I was good enough because I had flaws and I made mistakes. My idea of "good enough" was being *more* than I was, when in reality, I truly was good enough, but my own fear of failure never let me believe it. Unless I was perfect, I wasn't happy. It was impossible to meet my unattainable standards, so this cycle of self-loathing and feelings of inferiority continued throughout my childhood. I avoided taking risks because failure was a likely outcome. Taking a risk without the assurance of success requires vulnerability. By definition, if there is assurance of a specific (usually positive) result, the action is not a risk. My fear hindered my ability to be vulnerable and relinquish control.

At the core of a perfectionist is the desire to control. I craved regulating every aspect of my life. I thought that by manipulating each variable in my life, I would achieve total bliss because I would be dictating situations to my satisfaction. I was wrong (as a reformed perfectionist, I am now able to admit that). Putting myself under the intense pressure of perfection did not morph me into a diamond. Rather, I witnessed my life reduce to ashes. Ironically, my quest for absolute control went awry as my two best "frenemies"—the elusive "100%" and perfection—took the reins.

The distinct moment when I realized that I had become a slave to perfection occurred in fourth grade. When most people look back on fourth grade, they remember recess, memorizing multiplication tables, and the anticipation of becoming a fifth grader—the elementary equivalent of becoming the "big man on campus." One specific night in fourth grade continues to haunt me—the night my addiction to exceeding "good enough" became frighteningly evident.

Each week my teacher assigned a spelling list, and on Thursday nights a parent or sibling would proctor the test. Simple words such as "whether," "bicycle," and "believe" filled the lists. I prided myself on my flawless spelling record; I had never misspelled a single word. This spelling test began like any other. I sat, or rather bounced, on an exercise ball in the living room while pestering my brother to quiz me. Believing that the test was below me and "so elementary," I hardly gave it my full attention. My brother graded my paper and handed it back to me with a wide-eyed face of shock. "You spelled act wrong. It's A-C-T, not A-T-C." A careless mistake. A three-letter word. A. C. T. I knew how to spell the word. So you're probably thinking that the moral of the story and what I took away from it was that on any task, no matter how small, it is imperative to dedicate yourself and give a focused effort. While that is a valid lesson, that never crossed my ten-year-old brain. Shock and utter disappointment in myself were the only two emotions I felt. A typical student would be happy with a nineteen out of twenty, or 95% correct. I was atypical, and so was my response.

Unable to internalize and process this foreign feeling of failure, I sulked to my bedroom. I was disgusted with myself. I was better than a 95%. Anything less than perfect was failure in my mind. I walked to my bathroom, staring at myself in the mirror thinking, "You are not worthy." At the time, jungle-themed wallpaper covered my bathroom. I could feel the beady eyes of hundreds of lions and tigers staring me down with a sense of burning disgust, seeming to unanimously agree that I was a disappointment to the world. The pressure overwhelmed me. I could no longer handle the need to be perfect. Release. I needed release. A blood-curdling scream into the abyss of my basement bedroom would not suffice. Desperate times called for desperate measures.

Still gripping my pencil from the test as if I was blaming this inanimate object for my letter mix-up, I experienced a moment of clarity. I knew what I needed to do. Not only did I need release, the voice of self-deprecation told me that I needed to discipline myself. In the next few seconds, I lost total control. I became a monster consumed by an obsession with perfection. I looked into the mirror and in my reflection saw a broken, imperfect, unworthy girl. My arm swung through the air. I felt no pain. As I dropped the pencil to the floor, I focused on my reflection. I now looked as imperfect as I felt. Blood dripped from the top of my forehead. I had a problem.

Something in my world, in my surroundings, and in my thoughts pushed me to the edge. What causes a ten-year-old to stab a pencil into her forehead? Is it an internal or external influence that drives a stake through a child's psyche? Why does a little girl think that self-harm is the answer? Everything in my life told me that I needed to be perfect. I wanted to be better than my older brother, a talented athlete, school leader, and valedictorian in his own right. I wanted to prove to my parents and teachers that I was perfect and therefore worthy of their adoration. What I did not understand was that the world around me loved me for my imperfections, and I did not have to prove my worth or value. Only one person believed that I was not good enough. Me.

Walking up the stairs in disbelief, I knew I had to face my mother because I needed a Band-Aid and some antibiotic cream for the gash on my head. As soon as she laid eyes on me, she knew something was wrong. She took me to her bathroom, cleaned my head, and asked me about what happened. My mother did not know how to handle the situation. As much as she tried to hide the pure fear on her face, her eyes could not lie. She believed that I had become a victim to the villain of perfection, but she did not know how to process my actions or help me with my addiction, so she decided to just let me deal with it myself.

The pressure to be perfect dominated my life for the next three years. Spending hours on all of my schoolwork, I received nearly perfect grades. My obsession carried over into every facet of my life. It consumed me. In sixth grade I tried out for the soccer team at my new middle school. When the coach cut me from the A-team and the B-team, and instead placed me on the C-team full of amateurs (in hindsight, I was not the most athletic child), I burst into tears. I cried to the coach and quit on the spot. I did not want to let myself be imperfect, and I feared that my peers' perception of me would tarnish because I could not run as fast, score as much, or kick as hard as other girls. I have not played soccer since that fateful afternoon. Because athleticism did not prove to be my calling, I bounded toward the world of musical theater. At the age of six, I graced the stage for the first time and loved it (most likely because of the attention center stage provided), so I knew I wanted to invest my time in the theater. As any actor knows, the ruthless entertainment business demands perfection. Entertainers face hundreds of rejections before achieving success. To a perfectionist, this probably seems like a dangerous world to take on. For me, it became my safe haven.

There were times when it felt like the cycle of auditions and callbacks and rejections would break me, but each time I plummeted toward rock bottom, I would soon find success. Obsessively refreshing the webpage of the cast list, I waited in anticipation to see if this time, maybe, I would find my big break. This was local community theater, not Broadway, but nonetheless, if I was cast in a musical, I felt validated.

One director finally asked me to take on a character role, even though he had a myriad of other actresses to choose from. I finally felt worthy. Onstage I could shine without even a fleeting feeling of trepidation. Under the spotlight stood the Cheshire cat, a high school cheerleader, or a ladybug. I could become vulnerable because this was acting and I played a character. The distance between my own story and the story in which I portrayed—the idea of fiction—replaced my hard exoskeleton, the armor I wore as I fought to banish all blemishes in my life. The dark cloud of compulsion to achieve perfection dissipated under the bright theater light. I transformed into the powerful heroine of my own life. I was in control.

As cliché as it sounds, the lights *do* dim and the curtain *does* close. I found peace when I told a story that was not my own. Realizing I could not play dress up for the rest of my life, I returned to reality.

However, my perfectionist nature continued to afflict me. My fear of failure and vulnerability plagued me. Overworked and unhappy, I knew the expectations that I demanded of myself were unhealthy. Someone needed to come into my life and help me discover that I was enough. Hearing people say that I was a great scholar or very smart only increased my cravings for perfection. My situation necessitated a person who would acknowledge my brokenness, show me how to break the chains of my binding obsession, and encourage a realization that I was enough, flaws and all.

I do not personally believe in guardian angels, but I reckon that something in the universe sent an earthly equivalent into my life. Walking into my seventh grade American studies history class, I held high expectations for my teacher, Mr. David Cook. I heard that he was one of the favorite teachers of past students, so I was excited to learn from a passionate teacher. An advocate for peace and human rights, Mr. Cook plastered his walls with posters of civil rights demonstrations, powerful female role models, and famous quotes about loving humanity. He taught me about the strength of Aung San Suu Kyi, the courage of Ruby Bridges, and the bravery of Rosa Parks. These women overcame great adversity in their lives. Their former brokenness strengthened them. It was in their light that Mr. Cook taught me the most important lesson in my life. You wouldn't find it in any American history curriculum or discussion of current events. David Cook forced me to control my fear. He required me to fail.

Until this point, I thought that all teachers provided their students with the material, explained the material, and then assessed their students' ability to understand and retain that material. Mr. Cook shattered those expectations. On the day of our first test, I felt prepared. I had made a lengthy study guide and memorized all the dates and names regarding famous explorers. The class settled down as he began to hand out the tests. I was ready to correctly answer every question and earn a "100%." I was not ready to fail.

Mr. Cook stood at the front of the classroom ready to give us instructions. "I want you to fail." *What? Excuse me, but aren't we supposed to master this material and get an A?* "You all must be okay with failing." *No. No. No. I am not okay with failing.* "Take your tests and get the answers wrong. I will put a big, fat, red 'F' on your paper and you can show it off to the world." *I must be perfect. I cannot flaunt an imperfection.*

Completely confused, I began the test. I knew every single right answer. Out of habit, I circled the correct answers. When I finished the assessment, I walked to his desk and told him that I knew the right answers and did not want to have a bad grade by getting an F. "I will not accept the test until every answer to every question is incorrect." Walking back to my desk, I felt something click. He told me that he did not want me to be perfect. He demanded total imperfection. Erasing my answers, I began to embrace the absurd. Each time I circled a wrong answer, the volume of my inner voice of self-deprecation quieted. Mr. Cook celebrated failure and I felt free. I looked up and saw the faces of my classmates. They smiled out of pure joy while taking that test because they, too, no longer needed to live up to the pressure of high expectations. Proudly walking toward Mr. Cook, I turned in my test with a bright smile. He, too, smiled back as he marked the page with a bold, red F. I doubt he realized his impact at the time, but that was the first time I allowed myself to fail. Not only did I fail, but I also received validation that failure was something to celebrate. A moment of triumph. The perfectionist surrendered control and empowered Darby to finally be in charge.

You do not have to be perfect. People always said that to me, but no one made me believe that it was true until Mr. Cook. I *was* good enough, and being enough was better than reaching for perfection. Embracing "good enough" provided me with the freedom to take risks and truly enjoy them. The idea of "good enough" is not an excuse to be lazy, but rather a philosophy that your best effort, within reason, is your own version of perfection. Being "good enough" is being fearless. Taking risks. Failing. Failing *forward*. Repeated failure makes success that much sweeter.

I believe that perfectionism is like alcoholism and other addictions. For the rest of my life, I will be a recovering perfectionist. With the passage of time, the days when I revert back to obsessing with reaching the unattainable have become less and less frequent. I still am conquering my fear of failure, but each risk I take provokes celebration because I am progressing. I do things that make me uncomfortable and I am happier because of those actions. Perfectionism will always be a part of my past, but I am working toward minimizing its role in my future. At the top of my forehead, on my hairline, my scar remains as a reminder of when perfectionism consumed me. The scar tissue is tougher than the surrounding skin. I am stronger because of my brokenness. My name is Darby Schumacher, and I am good enough.

Jasmine Gao

ON LOSING AND DROPPING OUT

At fifteen, **Jasmine Gao** *got her first taste of startup culture working for myCollegeSTAT. She loved it so much that she applied to and spent four months at Google NYC participating in their Technovation Challenge, where she helped build a fashion app called Trending. Later, she found herself at another startup, Plum Alley, before being accepted into the Enstitute apprenticeship program. Through Enstitute, she dropped out of college to work at Bitly as a data strategist under chief scientist Hilary Mason. Currently, she leads the product and analytics teams at Made, a food company serving lovingly crafted meals by independent chefs. Through these experiences, she has been featured in* Forbes, The New York Times, CNBC, *and more. You can reach her by saying hi@jasminegao.com.*

I think we can all agree that losing sucks. Whether it be losing in a video game, athletic match, professional competition, or creating the next Facebook, no one can make sexy the feeling you get in your stomach when you try really hard at something and don't come out on top.

For me, that feeling came after placing second in the Technovation

Challenge, a prototyping and business plan competition at Google's office in New York City. Second place meant there would be no flight to San Francisco, no $25,000 development grant, and no professional release of the Android app my team and I spent four months developing.

I essentially failed. But from an entrepreneurial perspective, I had succeeded. Why? Because I had failed. Confusing, I know. Let me explain.

Nowadays, failure is the new black. You are encouraged to fail early, fail fast, and fail often because of the notion that what you learn during challenging times improves your chances of succeeding in the future. While I disagree with the whole idea of striving to fail, I do think it is important to know how to fail or, rather, make the most out of negative outcomes in business and life in general.

In my case, I learned the powerful lesson that a window of opportunity only closes when you let it. I could have easily gone home empty-handed after finding out the results of the Technovation Challenge, but the sore loser in me approached the judges afterward to repitch both the app and myself. I simply asked each one of them for their contact information and made it known that, even though the competition was over, I was still interested in pursuing my team's app further and continuing work in the field of technology. What resulted from those conversations were two interviews and ultimately my next internship at a startup called JumpThru. Looking back, it was a lot of the same stubbornness (or, as some kinder folks like to call it, perseverance) that helped me get from that internship to where I am now in my life at the time of writing this: a college dropout working at Bitly, the leading URL shortener and data analytics company.

Long story short, I left school after being accepted into Enstitute, a two-year fellowship that places eighteen to twenty-four-year-olds in apprenticeships under entrepreneurs and top-level executives. Through Enstitute, I now apprentice under Hilary Mason, who serves as chief scientist at Bitly.

Dropping out was the easy part. In fact, it only took a few clicks of a mouse to completely erase my existence on my college's upcoming roster for the fall 2012 semester. Telling my parents, on the other hand, was hard. I remember having to do a few deep-breathing exercises before I could even begin to explain that I was leaving school to work at some Internet company that shortened links. What resulted was a reaction from my parents that very closely resembled Elisabeth Kübler-Ross's model for the five stages of grief (the five stages being denial, anger, bargaining, depression, and acceptance), but laced with arguments—in person, over the phone, and even via e-mail. However, my mind had been made up and soon enough they realized I was legally an adult and, as a part of Enstitute's agreement to cover the living expenses of its first class of fellows, no longer financially dependent.

All in all, the world didn't end when I stopped listening to my parents. Eventually they came around and no longer wanted to send me to a reform school in the outskirts of mainland China. But since then, many people have asked me some variation of the questions "Why did you make such a risky decision?," "How will you survive without a college degree?," and "Are you crazy?" Well, to me, I had two options: either spend another three years of my life studying abstract concepts and textbook case studies while accruing thousands of dollars in debt, or go straight into the workforce and start solving real-world problems with meaningful outcomes.

Believe it or not, it didn't take much self-convincing to choose the second option. Three years was simply too much time to waste pursuing an unrewarding and, more importantly, passionless endeavor. So from an opportunity-cost perspective, it would have been much riskier for me to stay in school than to drop out.

Yes, I know, those education public service announcements you saw after every cartoon when you were growing up said otherwise. However, it is important to note that society is naturally risk averse. When you evaluate risk based on the perspective of someone or something that has no tolerance for it, you will ultimately be left with what is safe rather than what is best.

Had Tim Westergren given up after his three-hundredth rejection from venture capitalists instead of maxing out eleven credit cards to keep his music discovery company afloat, we would have no Pandora. Had Sara Blakely not quit her job selling fax machines to invest her life savings in panty hose, there would be no billion-dollar company, Spanx. Had Elon Musk let his inexperience in the aerospace industry stop him from exploring space transportation, SpaceX wouldn't be the first privately held company resupplying NASA's International Space Station.

Staying on the safe side and taking "no" for an answer is simply not characteristic of our generation, as we have grown up surrounded by rapid innovation and disruption that would not have been possible had we done just that. And so, I encourage you to seek and embrace the opportunities hidden behind risk and failure, because without them, who knows what we will all be missing.

Madison Maxey

SKATING ON CALIFORNIAN HILLS

A REFLECTION ON WIPING OUT

Madison Maxey *is passionate about fashion, technology, and the inter-section where the two collide. She learned to sew when she was eight and has been working in the fashion industry since age fifteen, with compa-nies like Tommy Hilfiger,* Nylon *magazine, and Peter Som. After living abroad in France for a year at age sixteen, and running a popular fashion blog that received invitations to Paris Haute Couture and Mercedes-Benz Berlin fashion weeks, she won a CFDA/Teen Vogue Scholarship for college and interned in California and New York. After taking a leave of absence from Parsons to start her own clothing company, Madison Maxey Blazers, she has worked for tech companies like Enstitute and General Assembly and she became a Thiel Fellow in 2013. Featured in* New York *magazine,* The Wall Street Journal, Her Campus, *and many other press outlets, Maddy has been named a "Female Founder to Watch" by Women 2.0.*

I love the empowered feeling one gets when learning something new. It's the thrill of your mind making a new connection, allowing your body to achieve something you were unaware you could do beforehand. I find it intoxicating. I believe strongly that the best way to spend a day is learning something outside of your comfort zone. It's this mentality that has driven me to learn about hardware, programming, and yes, even skateboarding.

In general, I assume that I am only unable to do something because I haven't tried it yet; however, this mindset was questioned the other day while practicing the last-learned skill.

Unlike New York, where I grew up, Northern California is notoriously hilly, which can make skateboarding, at least for me, an awkward, incline-dictated combination of skating and walking.

With a free hour or so of time (a hot commodity in this community), I decided that learning to conquer hills while on wheels would be the perfect way to spend those moments. Things were off to a good start, but then came the inevitable.

I hit a bump at high speed, felt a bit wobbly, my feet came out from under me, and my breath was cut short.

I found myself flat on the pavement, skateboard rolling downhill.

Luckily, a woman with her young daughter at the bottom of the hill picked up the board before it rolled into oblivion, but not without leaving me with these words:

"Maybe you shouldn't be riding this thing."

As obvious as that comment may have been, it was never a thought I had considered. Why shouldn't I ride it? Not to come off as an ultra feminist, but she never would have made that comment to a guy. Was she telling me I shouldn't do things I'm not good at?

Speaking of which, risk aversion dictates the majority of our lives.

"I'll wear the plain shirt instead of the colorful one because it's less socially risky," he says. "Maybe I won't try salsa dancing because there's a risk I'll be bad or awkward at it," she thinks. Although risk aversion is essential for physical safety, it seems as though the majority of our decisions are based on societal fear and security; concepts taught to us from our youth. That woman, the one who thought she was being wise by advising me to trade Mary Janes for wheels, also muttered to her daughter, "That was scary, wasn't it?" after seeing me fall.

Translation: Falling is embarrassing and scary. Don't try, so you won't fall and then other people won't have to be scared for you.

As embarrassing as it was for me, sprawled out on the pavement in front of absolute strangers, I so wish she would have used me as an example for her daughter and said something like, "Look! She fell, but got up again. Perseverance is key!" Or, "Look! You can do anything you want, and even if you fall, don't give up." However, in those few words, she expressed to her daughter that "scary" is bad and that "scary" means that you shouldn't do it.

Yes, it was just a blip in time on a skateboard, but it's societal norms like these that make me question what we're teaching children.

My immediate response to hitting the pavement (after the obligatory "WTF?!?") was that I should skate more so that I can improve. Skating more often means gaining a skill, which means less risk of falling.

It seems as though society's normal reaction is "I fell once, so I should stop trying because then I won't fall again." It seems as though the risk of failure is so paralyzing that attempting success isn't even an option.

As doers, we live in a world where risk is common, but this bubble isn't everywhere. In reflection of this moment, I realized how much our mindset is unique. How failure or pain can be a signal to push forward instead of to come to a full stop.

So, for those of you out there who've fallen flat, lying facedown on the pavement, it's your decision to make. Are you going to give up, or get up and keep pushing forward until you've mastered everything that has made you fall?

Take your time, no rush to decide, but in the meantime, I'll be skating the ups-and-downs of life as a doer and dreamer.

Noah Centineo

WHAT HOLLYWOOD, IN-N-OUT BURGER, AND PARKOUR TAUGHT ME ABOUT TAKING RISKS

Noah Centineo is a seventeen-year-old actor who has appeared on hit Disney Channel shows such as Austin & Ally *and* Shake It Up. *He has also been in nationally broadcast commercials for companies like Monopoly, Old Navy, and Coca-Cola. He was also featured in a couple of movies, most notably* The Gold Retrievers, *which he starred in back in 2009. Noah was also an investor in his father's movie,* Legends of Oz: Dorothy's Return.

Risk is all around us. In fact, without risk, life would be a lot less interesting.

When I was sixteen, I illegally trespassed onto government property with a friend en route to swinging, jumping, and hanging on the famous Hollywood sign. After about twenty minutes of this insanity, switching off between posing for pictures and looking out onto the Los Angeles skyline, a police helicopter hovered over us and ordered us off the mountain.

Could we have been arrested? Maybe. Was the risk worth it to cross something off our bucket list? Absolutely! The experience added another blotch of color to my life or (as I like to call it) my canvas.

A few months before that, I remember picking up my buddies from out of town at the airport. Wanting to give them the classic L.A. dining experience upon their arrival, I took them to an In-N-Out Burger and demanded they each order a "Double-Double" (complete with the special sauce of course), a milkshake, and fries—the quintessential fast-food combination. Our cashier was a cute Persian girl about three or four years my senior, but I flirted with her anyway and passed her my number on a napkin before heading outside to enjoy our fast-food feast.

Did I ever get a text or call from her? No. (Instagram follow? Maybe, I don't remember.) What was the worst thing that could happen though? She'd yell at me in front of a restaurant full of people I'd never see again? I didn't know what would happen when I shared my number with the cute cashier, but I did know that absolutely nothing would happen if I didn't take a chance.

There are two outcomes of taking a risk, and these outcomes sculpt who you become as a human being. They shape us and make us who we are. It's the difference between stagnancy and progress.

I'm talking about failure and success.

You cannot succeed without eventually undergoing some form of failure, or (as I like to call it) a learning experience. You cannot "learn" without taking risks. It's those risks that help you discern what works from what doesn't, and I believe that a life without failure is a boring, blank canvas. Every experience we go through, whether it be negative or positive, adds color to our canvases, and we grow through these moments. Risk-taking is a skill that takes confidence, intelligence, and a whole lot of balls, but I'd rather create a masterpiece with my life than stare at an untouched palette.

I don't know how many of you know about parkour, a sport where people attempt to get from point A to point B as quick as possible by running, jumping, swinging, climbing, etc., over and through any obstacles in their path, but the first thing you're taught to do in parkour is learn how to fall. In fact, my first lesson was strictly jumping off a ten-foot platform and landing properly onto a pad, and I had to master that before attempting to scale walls, jump from rooftops, or hang from stop signs.

This approach to learning parkour is highly relatable to risk-taking. In risk-taking and even life in general, we need to learn how to fall.

"Failure" is not actually failure; it is merely an experience to learn from. As Captain Jack Sparrow would say, "The problem is not the problem. The problem is your attitude about the problem." From now on, look at failure as a stepping-stone and testing grounds for your ambitions instead of an end to the pursuit of your passions. Captain's orders.

Personally, I started acting when I was eight years old, and although I had minor successes over the course of my young life in school plays, never-looked-at modeling opportunities, and a low-budget movie no one has heard of called *The Gold Retrievers* (I did get my first on-screen kiss in that movie, so maybe it was actually a success!), I wasn't getting very far with my career. However, instead of giving up, when I was fifteen years old I made the decision to give my full, undivided attention to acting, convincing my parents to let me drop out of my high school in Florida and move across the country to Los Angeles.

It was as if all my previous risk-taking endeavors had prepped me for that jump off the proverbial cliff. Truth is, if I was really serious about chasing my goals and dreams, I needed to be at the epicenter of all the action. It wasn't easy leaving behind my friends, family, and lifestyle I had grown accustomed to and felt comfortable with, but it needed to be done if I wanted to succeed. I had to take this risk, and whether it panned out or not, my canvas would certainly become more colorful.

I am eighteen now and have taken many steps forward in my career. I have been fortunate enough to appear in Disney channel shows like *Austin & Ally* and *Step It Up,* shoot nationally broadcasted commercials with brands like Coca-Cola, Old Navy, and Monopoly, and (at the time of writing) am set to appear in both the Disney Channel Original Movie *How to Build a Better Boy* and *Girlfriend in a Coma,* a planned NBC sitcom currently in pilot stage starring myself, Miranda Cosgrove, and others!

Without taking risks, I would never have been able to learn how to be successful. While I may have had moments of improvement, without knowing what failure looks like I wouldn't be able to discern what I'm doing that's positive from what I'm doing that isn't helping me get ahead. The sad truth is that most of the people who read this book will agree with me, but decide not to take risks, or will be motivated to change their lives for about two weeks before returning to their normal state of complacency and comfort-seeking.

That's not going to be you, however. I want to challenge you to stay motivated and keep pushing yourself to take risks and learn from those risks every single day. You can do it!

Don't be afraid to change your life.

Anwit Adhikari

PERPETUAL ENERGY

Anwit Adhikari *is a former Seasteading Institute intern from Nepal working on a device to generate perpetual energy through his company Anveya. He is an alumnus of Draper University, the entrepreneurial academy started by billionaire Tim Draper to help foster more entrepreneurship in Millennials.*

I grew up in the beautiful hills of Nepal, where I spent my early years as a lonely and curious child. I couldn't understand what to make of a shoelace, but I always knew what I wanted to make out of my life. I wanted perpetual energy: creative, free energy for everyone. Interesting thing to want as a child, but maybe I was inspired by Nepal's daily power cuts. Nevertheless, the idea of having a world with abundant, pure energy has always fascinated me. Even back then, I genuinely believed it could happen, and I believed that those imperfect ideas based on my childish imagination could change the world. I believed I could be the one to make it happen.

And so, at the age of nine, I retreated into my school's library and started reading. I read about everything I could, from the design of car engines to the science behind powered flight, and used that knowledge to design my first perpetual energy machine. After researching the idea for two years, I finally felt I had enough "expertise" to make a prototype. So I did, and it failed miserably.

I was crushed. I trashed the prototype and never looked back to it again.

I was eleven at that time, and there was no one to teach me what failure was, or how one should treat it. Therefore, at the age of eleven, I swiftly gave up on my dreams of changing the world.

I still had a lot of spirit in me, but my dream of building a perpetual energy device was all but over. Soon, I tried writing my version of the seventh installment of the Harry Potter series (before *Harry Potter and the Deathly Hallows* was published) but I left it after the first few pages. Then, when I was fifteen, I tried making a documentary to raise money for the epidemic-stricken regions in Nepal, but the plan didn't go past the paper-and-pencil stage. I even burst into my teacher's room one day, declaring that I wanted to feed 500 beggars in the city, but was quickly shot down and never ventured to explore potential solutions to that problem again. Without a main purpose in my life, I didn't know what to do with the energy I had. I was lost, clueless, and deeply unsatisfied.

A couple of years later, I turned seventeen and chose to rebuild my life by immersing myself in a new project: designing and building a wind turbine. The plan was ambitious. I'd build a personal wind turbine that could fit on every rooftop and provide enough energy to free consumers from corporate control. I believed it could be the next step in solving the issue of energy, and I worked feverishly to finish it. But again, I hit walls of iron. Deadlines passed, expectations were bashed, and my designs stayed on paper. Every effort to raise money went down the drain. My attempt to publish a scientific journal to raise money didn't work, my talks with two major banks went nowhere, and the National Academy of Science and Technology didn't believe in me. My team members were so fed up that they left. The deadline for the wind turbine slowly extended from two months to four, then to half a year, and then finally to three years. I was alone, and out of the hundreds of people I knew, fewer than five actually believed in me.

I didn't realize how big a mess I had made out of my life until the time came to apply for college. I was so busy with my project I had completely forgotten about the application process, and subsequently my applications were possibly the worst they could humanly be. I was rejected by every American college I had applied to—twenty in total. It was humiliating.

By the summer of 2011, my friends were giving hearty farewells to friends and family and flying off to the United States for their education. I, on the other hand, was left with a single-person company, an incomplete project, rock-bottom self-confidence, zero college prospects, and no clue where my life was heading.

Out of the many themes in J. K. Rowling's commencement address at Harvard in 2008, there is one that I always connect with: how failure affects you. Knowing you've failed can be a hard truth to realize, but it eventually gets rid of the unnecessary clutter in your life, leaving you naked with the only things that really matter. If you love something or some pursuit enough, you'll have the courage to start over again.

I eventually found my niche at a small college in Thailand. It was here in the secluded peace Thailand offers, away from the naysayers and terrible failures back in Nepal, that I chose to start anew. I worked, read, and researched whenever I could, on a flight between Nepal and Thailand, in class, or in a hotel trying to escape the devastating Thai floods of 2011. Eventually I stopped attending classes altogether, choosing to spend my time in dorm rooms and coffee shops, with whiteboards and loose papers, working away on this project that meant more to me than anything else in the world. It became an obsession and, slowly, the wind turbine grew. It grew from crazy, naïve ideas into designs for nanotech skins and beautiful wings. There were massive stacks of paper and megabytes upon megabytes of research files dedicated solely to the project. Soon enough, Anveya, the company I'd founded three years ago, had two more designers, and even though the wind turbine was still on paper, I could realistically see it coming to fruition one day.

But the solitude Thailand offered had another effect on me. In those hours of careful reflection, I finally understood how my past, present, and future connected together. I looked at my wind turbine, and saw how it was a less ambitious version of the prototype idea I had dis-

carded when I was a kid. I realized that I wasn't designing a wind turbine because I loved it, but because I was scared my vision of perpetual
energy could never come true. I was scared by the magnitude of my
own dreams, and was settling for something less.

What was there to be scared about? If I could die one day knowing that I had made my dream come true, wouldn't that matter more
than any fear, insecurity, or excuse? Of course it would, so I decided
to put my wind turbine designs through a major evolution, focusing
instead on creating the perpetual energy device I'd always wanted to
make. The world needed energy, and Anveya was going to deliver it
to the world.

Once I finally knew what I wanted to do with my life, the next step
was all too obvious. I decided to leave college and pursue my dreams
in the United States. Anveya was a Nepali company, but I needed the
financial and technical resources that only America could provide.
Anveya's first product would have to be made on American soil.

The only way I was going to get into the States was through working for someone else part-time while I developed my own research. I
could get a visa through work. After searching intensely for companies and organizations where I could apply my skills, I came across the
Seasteading Institute. Simply put, the Seasteading Institute is a nonprofit that wants to build floating ocean cities. It sees ocean cities as
potential platforms for making innovative, government-free systems
that would benefit humanity as a whole. It interested me, but it was
nothing compared to what I found next. I saw the title of one of their
blog posts that literally changed my life forever.

Undergraduate Interns Wanted

I immediately contacted them, asking if I could be an intern in their
organization. For their part, they couldn't understand why a Nepali
student studying in Thailand would travel halfway across the world
to come to the United States to participate in a two-month voluntary
internship. It took me one month of back-and-forth e-mails to convince them that I was a good fit. They were initially hesitant, but slowly
things took a turn for the better, and on February 2013, they gave me
the green light.

I was finally coming to America.

On a chilly February night, I packed my bags, kissed my dorm room good-bye, and headed out. I took a taxi, and as it cut through the night, outside the college grounds, an unforgettable tingle ran down my spine. It was pure elation. A light, crisp, wonderful feeling of pure freedom. I was finally starting to live my life. I was finally free.

Less than a month later, visa in hand, I finally arrived in the United States and started working again on the concept of perpetual energy. Anveya, the company I started to try and create this breakthrough, has a five-member design team now, and we are slowly developing the plans for what we hope will be a major revolution in energy. In two months, I've met more amazing people and made more connections than I did in my entire lifetime previously. My crazy, crazy risk is paying off wonderfully, and I'm finally working on my childhood dream without the thought of surrender ringing in the back of my mind.

If I could go back ten years in time, I would let my younger self know that our resolve is much bigger than any obstacle we come across in life. Usually, people have a remarkable ability to brave even the worst of situations, and that makes our fear of failure just a primitive thought that we have to train ourselves to ignore. I wish I knew this when I was young. But now that I do know this, I hope I can use it to fulfill my life's dream.

It's only a matter of time.

Michelle Lynn

WHAT DOES IT TAKE
TO MAKE IT IN HOLLYWOOD?

Michelle Lynn is the twenty-year-old president/CEO of video produc-
tion company VIP Studios. By age seventeen, this award-winning FIRST
robotics electrical team leader earned thirty college credits, made the
National Dean's List (Who's Who Among American College Students),
and interned at NASA Kennedy Space Center. She had also been her high
school's valedictorian at age sixteen. Now, as a video production entrepre-
neur with ten years of experience in electronics technology and robotics,
nineteen years of experience as stage talent, and six years of experience
practicing every job behind the camera, as well as six years of experience
as an on-camera interviewer and researcher, analysis and implementa-
tion are her forte. She has a wealth of technical and formal college edu-
cation as well as hands-on experience, having previously filmed for
various businesses and the NFL.

A lot of people ask me about what it's like working in the entertainment business. They usually want me to share advice from personal
experiences and/or advice from some famous person I've met along
my path. Well, here's probably the best, most straightforward, and

honest advice I can give to anyone "thinking" about getting into entertainment . . .

Are you ready?

If you have to *think* about getting into entertainment, this isn't the career path for you! If this isn't something you eat, drink, breathe, sleep, and dream about every moment, this isn't the business for you! This is a business that's left a trail of drug addicts and dead bodies. This is a business where you have to be a self-starting entrepreneur dictating your own future or risk being taken advantage of by someone who may lead you astray.

This business isn't cheap. I mean that financially, mentally, physically, emotionally, and energetically. If there is *anything,* and I mean *anything* else you can do that will *even possibly* allow you to live a reasonably stable/happy/satisfied life, that's *exactly* what you need to do! Don't feel ashamed if you turn back now. Taking care of yourself is first and foremost.

But if you have an abundantly flowing well of passion for this business . . . If you do indeed eat, drink, breathe, dream, and contemplate this stuff. . . . If you feel like you have to create meaningful work or you're going to explode . . . then, by God, don't explode!

Give birth to those beautiful creations!

Manifest the visions you're compelled to realize!

Populate the earth with the children of your dreams!

Those who are most successful in this business don't do it because they *want to*; they do it because they *have to*!

And while I breathe for the entertainment industry, don't be fooled if you aren't in this business. "This business" is whatever *you* can't stand *not* doing in life. Once you find that passion, for anything, hold on to it for dear life and don't let go!

John Singleton, whom I've had the pleasure of meeting a couple of times now, was nominated for two Academy Awards at the tender age of only twenty-three, for writing *and* directing his very first feature film, *Boyz n the Hood.* He's certainly one of *the* most passionate people I've ever met, so much so that I believed him when he said he felt like he was going to literally *explode* if he didn't hurry up and give birth to that film. Spike Lee said the same thing about his film *She's Gotta Have It.* That was actually the second feature film he attempted to make; the first fell through because he did not have all the focus behind him to make it happen. When he built up so much passion for film number two that he was nearly combustible, failure simply wasn't an option. His fiery passion alone ignited his eventual success.

I'm not saying this to be discouraging. What I'm saying is that you need to go big or go home. Because more likely than not, if you're going to be successful, it's going to take blood, sweat, and tears. I'm talking about the real *work* it takes to reach the top! And it takes even more to stay there. Steve Harvey said becoming successful is like powering through a hundred push-ups for the first time and longevity is the will to hold that same position even after you've given it your all!

I can relate because, to be perfectly honest, about halfway through my senior year of high school I said, "I've got to become valedictorian or I'm going to explode!" And guess what? I was the first black valedictorian of my high school since before I was born. I don't like to toot my own horn, so I don't brag about it often, but my valedictory address comprised the proudest moment of my life . . . thus far.

Most people want to get into entertainment because of the glitz and glamour. *Hollywood* is meant to appear magical, and of course it can be tantalizing. Did you know that the *wood* of the holly tree has long been considered by various groups to have magical properties? Do you think that's a coincidence?

But becoming an "overnight" success actually takes years. And each year is filled with a lot of work.

Yes, I know there are people who admire my life from afar. They imagine my days are filled with carefree adventure as I travel to places they've only dreamed of, meet people they admire, and do things they find to be amazing and awe-inspiring (these are not arrogant statements of fantasy, but shocking admissions from my own good friends). Well, news flash, my life isn't nearly that carefree. Yes, I truly enjoy my work, but I struggle every day. And whenever I'm about to have a breakthrough to a new level, I encounter greater opponents and new levels of opposition. I don't need to play video games because I'm living an action-adventure-suspense-thriller that is certainly not rated "E" for Everyone!

But every time I meet a seemingly insurmountable obstacle, I come back to the realization that I simply cannot live life if I don't continue chasing my dreams. Once you feel the same way, you'll know you're in business.

Vijay Manohar

BRIDGING THE DIGITAL DIVIDE

Vijay Manohar *spent his junior and senior years in high school at the Texas Academy of Mathematics and Science, a selective early college entrance program at the University of North Texas. It was here that he got a first taste of entrepreneurship. The Murphy Center for Entrepreneurship at UNT held the IDEA competition, a pitch competition to identify promising ideas. Vijay decided to submit an idea he had been tinkering with—PCs2Prosper. PCs2Prosper is a nonprofit organization that acquires retired business computers and donates them to deserving schoolchildren.*

When I handed a computer to Jasmin Machuca, tears welled up in my eyes. I stood there, pained to think about her past, yet hopeful about her future. A smile cracked her face, and I knew then that this is what making a difference really meant.

The families in front of me from the poor suburbs of Denton, Texas, had been through a lot. A single mother works a double shift at a fast-food joint to feed her four children. A child in tattered clothes sports a beanpole, gaunt stature, as if he hasn't seen food in weeks. The school itself looks worn down, as if to express the condition of the neighborhood and all its residents. Despite this, I remain reassured. Jasmin wants to be a writer, and the other children bumbling around Borman Elementary's library that day all share—with Jasmin—a common asset: unrealized potential.

From the time I was a child, my dad engrained the idea of making a difference in my mind. He didn't want me to be another statistic: someone who is born, goes to school, gets a job, has a family, and passes away. His endless, mind-numbing lectures on influencing the community eventually got to me, and soon enough, I started to pale at the thought of living life by simply "going through the motions." I yearned to make a difference in my own community that had given me so much. I wanted to be a pioneer—I just didn't know how. The familiar faces of social entrepreneurial giants such as Bill Gates and Warren Buffet continually grace the covers of *Time* and *Newsweek*, but both have years of experience, a large following, and plenty of capital. I didn't have any of these, but I didn't want to wait until I was older to begin making a difference, either. I thought, "Why can't I leave a legacy now? What's stopping me?"

In the spring of 2011, I witnessed massive slashes to my school's budget. New computers were the first things to go, which meant we'd now have to buy our own computers at home to keep up with our time's technology. Looking deeper into the problem, I found that many students from low-income homes didn't actually have computers at home (in fact, one in every seven students doesn't have access to a home computer), and this sudden realization left me with a pang in my chest. Growing up, I innocently thought that access to home computers was a given, and it was something I always took for granted, as I browsed the Internet and worked for hours on end, cursing the "slow" Internet speed while balancing Facebook messages. Technology was natural to me, and had been available to me as a resource my entire life. So when it hit me that owning computers was actually a privilege, I was disgusted with my complaints. How could I gripe while some of my less fortunate peers suffered because of this digital divide? Their educational journeys were no longer controlled by their will and work ethic; they were instead at the mercy of having access to a piece of hardware.

Around the same time as these budget cuts, I noticed my dad

working on a new laptop. I asked him, "What happened to your old one?" Apparently, while schools suffered to keep up with the times, businesses actually trashed working computers periodically to maintain their edge in technology.

The light bulb sputtered, flashed, and lit up. Clarity.

What if these working computers could be given to students who couldn't afford them? This idea was the genesis of PCs2Prosper, a company I founded two years after this epiphany. I could bridge corporate America and deserving individuals, and finally have a way to give back to the community that had given me so much, by empowering students to realize that their shot at success was bigger than they had previously thought.

Which brings us back to Jasmin. As my eyes watered, a smile also cracked across my face. Jasmin could finally be the writer she had always aspired to be, and not only would she be able to write stories that could inspire and entertain the masses, but, more importantly, she would be able to rewrite her own future.

Everybody has ideas. I've heard friends and family run into inconveniences and problems in their daily lives, only to start a sentence with, "Wouldn't it be cool if they created X so that I wouldn't run into problem Y?" Most of the time, it *would* be cool. But who's going to do it? Who are *they*?

I've learned that you and I can be *they*. So let's get started, today.

Zoe Mesnik-Greene

WHAT'S A SMILE WORTH TO YOU?

Zoe Mesnik-Greene *is a senior at the University of Washington and a student in the Lavin Entrepreneurship Program. When not working on her business or studying, Zoe loves breaking a good sweat through hard exercise, traveling, and hanging out with friends, family, and her yellow lab, Frodo.*

The story has been told to me many times . . . how I squealed with delight at scaling to the top of the refrigerator at the age of sixteen months, while my mother, in terror, grabbed me, against my will, and pulled me down to the relative safety of the floor. But playing it safe has never been how I live my life. Now as a twenty-one-year-old student at the University of Washington, I am also a passionate social entrepreneur currently building my company, StartMark, which launched its first product line, Lasting Smiles lip care, in the fall of 2014.

I do have a lofty goal: I believe that by working together, we can make a significant mark on the world by bettering consumer products, people's lives, and the global environment. How did I journey from that physically wild and fearless climbing toddler to the highly driven and single-focused young social entrepreneur that I am today?

Looking back, I definitely had a pattern of taking continuous risks to reach new achievements, despite numerous falls, obstacles, and serious injuries along the way. As a young girl, the lessons came from the discipline and commitment to gymnastics practice twenty-two hours a week. I challenged myself further in high school as I moved on to the very technical and risky sport of pole vaulting. When I raced toward the vault box and pit, balancing a weighted pole more than two and a half times my height, I had to intuitively plant it and fearlessly catapult and invert myself, aiming above thirteen feet high.

In both these highly demanding and technically difficult sports, I can now more clearly understand the roots of my perseverance and courage. There is a thread woven into the fabric of who I am that began with setting my sights on specific athletic skills in front of me, and evolved to tackling big problems in the world. In athletics, I performed hundreds of precise repetitions with the goal of perfecting risky skills with ease. Each time I made mistakes and fell, I had to pick myself up and find the courage to try again. The physical and emotional tolls along the way were overwhelming, but the joy I felt after succeeding at terrifying and risky skills was enough to engrain the importance of working hard and never giving up in the pursuit of my goals.

Nobody exemplified working hard and never giving up more than a visually impaired Paralympian long jumper, Elexis, who I had met during my senior year of high school when I lived with Olympic pole vault gold medalist Stacy Dragila while she coached me at the Olympic Training Center in California. Watching Elexis and other Paralympians train there had the most profound impact on me. Elexis told me that he doesn't let his difficulty in "seeing" get in the way of "seeing" his dreams come true. That hit me hard. I believe that there are real physical falls in life, and there are emotional falls; regardless, there is the personal choice to get up and not give up.

I learned of another kind of adversity when I was fifteen and had volunteered in a Wawa Wasi day care with young children whose parents were in prison or were street peddlers in Ayacucho, Peru. My parents raised me with the value of not just caring about myself, but doing my part to make the world a better place, and so I began in my teen years to cast a wider net, and reflect on how I could make an impact on the injustices and inequalities in the world. I learned of immense needs far and near.

Back at home in Seattle, wanting to learn more, I served on two different youth philanthropy and grant-making boards. In the summer months of my high school years, I grabbed every opportunity to work in diverse nonprofits and for-profits, including Microsoft. I took the initiative and approached service agencies and companies where high schoolers had never worked before and asked executives for opportunities to work and learn from them. I realized early on that I felt most accomplished by being creative and taking on leadership roles.

The spark that lit my fire, and ultimately led me to create Start-Mark, was a short video that I happened to view online one evening in November 2012 in my campus dorm room. I was deeply moved by the fact that 1 in 600 children around the world are born with a cleft lip and cleft palate, and that those children in developing countries who are not given surgeries to correct the abnormalities are stigmatized, cannot eat or talk normally, and often are shunned by society. I couldn't believe that a fairly nominal cost of approximately $250 could easily correct the problem and change a child's life forever, and yet so many children were not receiving the surgeries for lack of funding and resources.

I went to bed that night feeling troubled and racking my brain for ways I could possibly alleviate this problem and so many others. How could I use my interest in business, and specifically my passion for entrepreneurship, to solve world problems? I tossed in bed that night . . . thinking . . . and thinking. How could people purchase something they needed . . . that is also low enough in cost to make it an easy, purposeful, and repetitive purchase. It dawned on me. I could connect the issue of cleft lip and cleft palate to something intimate like the lips. We use our lips to smile, to eat, to drink, to communicate, to kiss . . . what could that item be? It came to me . . . a lip balm.

A lip balm is an item that you are constantly buying. I have one in my drawer, in my purse, in my car, and I always need to replenish my supply to keep my lips nourished. I envisioned a quality-made, but affordable, product. I set a clear intention in my head and heart that

I was going to make this happen. I was going to create a lip balm that also served as a social philanthropic endeavor.

Over the next few weeks, I worked feverishly. I was on the phone and Internet tirelessly. I found a manufacturer, who assured that all ingredients were organic and that the shea butter was sourced from a women's cooperative in central Africa. I found a graphic artist who designed the labels. I moved on to putting together my marketing and sales strategy as I awaited delivery of the thousands of lip balms. I was sure that selling the trial run on my campus of more than 42,000 students would be easy. However, disappointingly, after initial promises of commitment to help me sell the lip balms and after much hard work on my part preparing sales packets and materials for various campus groups offering help (including the Sales Club, the thirteen campus sororities, athletic groups, dormitories)—all the avenues I tried on campus for selling led to dead ends for various reasons.

I had put all my heart and energy into this effort, solely to donate 100 percent of the net profits earned to help these children. I was hugely disappointed, but I am not one to give up. So next, I turned my attention outside of campus. I single-handedly contacted Rotary Clubs and professional associations. I hand-prepared display bins holding fifty lip balms of two flavors and drove them around to medical and dental clinics, banks, athletic clubs, and day cares looking for interest in supporting my project. I wanted to sell the complete trial run by Valentine's Day.

With a bit of success, but still far from my goal, I dug deeper. Never underestimate the power of youth! With the help of my thirteen-year-old brother, I elicited middle school and high school kids who represented a broad range of public and private schools in Seattle to assist me. I got them excited and motivated them with prizes I managed to score from local retailers. At the end of the three months of sales, with a full academic schedule and two athletic practices a day, I sold enough lip balms to be in the positive and have an impact of $30,000 toward cleft lip and cleft palate surgeries.

The trial run had been harder than I ever imagined. However, the feedback I received from consumers was that it was the best quality lip balm they had ever used and that they really felt good about the purchase because it was benefiting an important cause. This drove me forward.

I began taking steps to develop a business model built upon social philanthropy. I plowed through marketing research studies on lip care products. I incorporated my company as a social purpose corporation, redesigned my branding, refined my lip balm formulation, and began building relationships with small-scale farming cooperatives around the world where the ingredients are sourced to support economic development in those communities. I developed a business model where every lip balm sold helps to fund cleft surgeries. My determination, passion, and hard work paid off with the national launch of Lasting Smiles lip care in the fall of 2014 with Nordstrom stores, Whole Foods, Lori's Gifts, and online retailers Drugstore.com and Walgreens.com.

My current business journey is based on endless hard work just as it was in my young days of intense athletic training and competition where I worked so hard, and sometimes fell and failed to reach my marks, but still continued to relentlessly pursue my skills. I realize now what a metaphor those athletic years were for my current work as an entrepreneur. As I move along my entrepreneurial journey, fueled by my energy and passion to change the world in big ways, I aim to not let anything or anyone get in my way of making a positive mark on people's lives.

What astounds me is that a simple idea or a short conversation can lead to monumental changes in our culture. Look for what sparks you and speaks to you and propels you forward with burning desire. While going about your day, be alert to how you can improve the world by consciously being in an innovative state of mind. Be inquisitive and try to possess an imaginative perspective on your surroundings and your emotional and intuitive reactions. Although I terrified my mother with my choice of athletic pursuits (and refrigerator-summiting antics!), it was she who instilled in me early the wise advice that I should never be afraid to ask questions or make mistakes. Never allow yourself to be complacent with the status quo, but rather drive yourself to think outside of the box and be a risk-taker. It is an extraordinary human feat to take an idea or feeling, pivot on it, and create something with it. But with courage, passion, perseverance, and persistence, *you can do it*!

Alpha Barrie

TURNING GANGSTERS INTO ANTI-DRUG ADVOCATES

Beginning at age of sixteen, **Alpha Barrie** *was the Volunteer Youth Peace Coordinator at the B-Gifted Foundation for two years. In this role, he helped to coordinate peace-promoting activities among schoolchildren within various secondary schools. These activities included debates, quizzes, interactive workshops, and creative peace expressions. At eighteen, he is currently the founder of the Youth Millennium Anti-Drug Abuse Project in his country of Sierra Leone. As the founder, he has seen and observed the problems of drug abuse among youth in post-conflict Sierra Leone. In 2014, he set up a team of young people who visited five ghettos where they have helped more than fifty-five young people learn about the harmful effects of drugs. His group has also been able to provide advice through other community programs in collaboration with B-Gifted Foundation.*

When we take the time to survey our lives and endeavors, we observe that almost all of our actions and desires are tied to the existence of other human beings. This is a clear sign that whatever ventures we start in this world should be of benefit to people outside of ourselves.

Growing up, I've slowly developed continual consolation and an un-failing wellspring of patience in the face of hardships of life, those of my own and especially those of others.

In 2010, our principal at the Prince of Wales School in Kingtom, Sierra Leone, invited the B-Gifted Foundation (a nonprofit that uses creativity and technology to address human rights, enhance peace, and promote its development) to speak to us, the students, about their mission. During his speech at our school assembly, the founder of B-Gifted Foundation presented his views on progress, innovation, edu-cation, peace, activism, and other areas of universal interest. After his speech, I was moved to go and speak with him alongside a number of other classmates who were willing to carry on his message and turn his words into action.

Talking to him after that presentation, I wasn't able to comprehend the challenges I'd face in the future fighting for the youth activism movement he spoke so fondly about. But his simplicity and sincerity had inspired me, and I felt moved and obligated to take action.

When I first told my friends and parents I was going to start what I called a "Youth Millennium Anti-Drug Abuse Project" in Sierra Leone, my home and native country, they felt a great sense of fear. For it was former child soldiers, drug addicts, etc., that I would be associating with and aiding. Many of these former child soldiers had come of age as youth in ghettos, shanty towns, and communities of the like, so con-fronting them presented a real risk. Despite what others feared for me, my inner determination to change the world by teaching my colleagues about the facts of drug abuse pushed me forward. I wanted to show them that they had the power and influence to challenge and change the future they were inheriting. I felt I could empower this group of youth who were what researchers called "at risk" of taking drugs.

Being soft-spoken and persuasive, I walked into the ghetto confi-dent that I would be given audience. I tagged along with a respectable man in that community, Borbor Kallay, who walked me around as I met youth who were smoking, drinking, and gambling. I was an intru-der in their midst, and their acts and signs clearly showed that I was unwelcome in their makeshift home. I sat down and asked if I could join them in the games they were playing and they accepted. As I sat there, I learned about some of the horrid experiences (stabbings, armed robberies, murders, and more) these youth had gone through and I thought about the dangers that I would face if they were to take up arms against me or attempt to injure me there and then.

They started to ask me if I was a journalist, or security personnel, and I said no. I was just a young person like themselves who wanted to see change in the community. I offered the gang of youth an invitation to visit the drop-in youth center where they could meet with other youth and talk about sports, computers, and music, while enjoying food, drinks, and the sharing of their unique talents. Their eyes flickered with excitement and I knew then that they were ready to take on something different in their lives away from the horrid experiences of war, gangs, and drugs.

It was at that moment in time I realized the importance of the risk I took. By putting myself out there, potentially in harm's way, I was about to change the lives of others. Since that first encounter with my troubled teenage counterparts, my mission has grown tremendously, but it's important to remember where it stemmed from. It started by trying to help others, from a willingness to give back.

Like the founder of the B-Gifted Foundation, go out of your way to try and make other people's lives better because, at the end of the day, we are all interconnected.

Brandon Wang

ON FLYING

Brandon Wang *is a student, entrepreneur, designer, and activist. Born and raised in Houston, Texas, he is a senior at Phillips Exeter Academy in New Hampshire. Since developing websites at age eight, Brandon has been intrigued by the changes that design and technology can bring, and impassioned with bettering lives through them. His team at School-traq works to make students' lives easier through organization. At Sponsr .Us, Brandon catalyzes young idea-makers through mentorship and fund-raising, and at the Project for Better Journalism, Brandon is help-ing to revitalize student journalism at high schools across the country.*

Brandon has also worked at Teens in Tech Labs in Silicon Valley, Teach For America in Houston, and the civil court of Harris County. In his free time, he enjoys tennis, swimming, and cycling. He splits his time between New England and Houston and spends time with his dog, Peanut, when possible.

I love airports.

I love the way I feel fast on moving walkways, and the zipping sounds my luggage makes when it rolls. I love stretching out at the gate as others bustle by with their lives and I calmly sip an iced latte, admiring the efficiency of infrastructure at such scale. Most of the time I don't even mind security; I always need exactly three bins and I'll tidy them in advance for the X-ray machines.

While others take a bus to high school, my classrooms are 2,000 miles away from home. I commute several times a year on a four-hour flight. Before my eighteenth birthday, I will have flown the same route at least thirty-six times. Airports have become routine and stable for me. We have a contract of respect and silence, and I follow it.

Traveling creates independence. Airports exemplify navigating without the need to make conversation. Empowerment and freedom are only a small part of the greater picture—that one is simply by oneself. I'm not extremely introverted, but the idea of plugging in headphones and walking through the terminal in my own little world appeals to me. So I do it—several times a year.

Airports are routine.

But ironically, I hate flying.

The moment I step off the jetway and into the aircraft, I am repulsed. I hate the recycled air, the cramped setting, the lighting, and pretty much everything else about the barrel I'm about to be shot through the air in. Turbulence is the worst; my mind, ever so logical, knows that with every up there will be a down. I grip the armrest tightly, seeking comfort, but everything I'm holding on to is moving.

Sitting in 24C beside a couple also holding on for dear life, one has to wonder. In our modern world, not much is better planned than a flight. With billions of dollars' worth of infrastructure and expensive monitoring equipment, the airline industry still can't negate or predict turbulence.

The unexpected and spontaneous are common aspects of our world and often permeate our everyday interactions. Flying, in an uncanny way, is analogous with our daily routines. Within the things we understand and predict really well come moments of distress, moments where things begin to fall apart despite our understanding that everything will most likely be okay—that the pilot has things under control. In those moments, the only things that can really ground us back to reality are basic: human emotions and human connection.

So I turn to 24B, to the man wearing a tartan red button-down, and introduce myself. It is spontaneous, sure, but we carry on a conversation and the color seems to come back to both our faces. The man works in IT, he explains. He's visiting his nephew who's about my age and maybe a bit younger, and as he tells me more about his career, the airplane levels out its ascent and settles into a smooth cruise.

Walking through the airport feels good to me because it is easy to step away from my surroundings and envelop myself in a small cocoon of headphones and independence. But it doesn't help when I can't rely on that social crutch anymore: when I don't feel safe, independent, or really all that lofty jammed in a chair on a flying bullet. In those times it only makes sense to turn to those around me and engage in conversation and interaction.

The eventual realization was that I didn't need to wait for an uncomfortable situation. In foreign cities I would contact local companies and startups and, amazingly, they would happily agree to invite me to visit more often than not. I once spent an afternoon at the Spotify offices in London sharing coffee and conversation with their directors, all because of a tweet. It was the earnestness that counted.

The next time I'm in an airport, I've vowed to make friendly banter with the person in the security line behind me despite my introversive nature.

That's the takeaway. Make conversation, whenever and wherever you can. Make it on the airplane, make it on the train. Make it on the bus; make it even when things are quiet. If the situation could be improved even a marginal amount with banter, then be the person that livens your surroundings with a few simple words. Be tactful, and very few people will turn you down. There's a whole world out there to discover.

When I got off that airplane, the man gave me his card and invited me to stay in touch. I've got a small collection of business cards now, actually, from people who sat next to me on airplanes. And even though I still walk through the airport with headphones in my ear, my effort to smile and start conversation wherever I can makes a difference. For me, it's about trying to be the most open person I can be.

You never know who you are going to meet, or what type of person is sitting next to you at any given moment. They certainly have a story, as vivid as yours, waiting to share when prompted. Take initiative and be the one who inquires about that story. You may find a new client, friend, lover, employer, or distraction from the crazy turbulence you're bound to encounter on any flight, and in life.

It starts with a "Hello." I'm Brandon, and it's nice to meet you.

Daniel Ahmadizadeh

CONNECTING FLIGHTS, STORIES, AND EXPERIENCES . . . THIS IS WHO WE ARE

Daniel Ahmadizadeh *is an aspiring entrepreneur passionate about serving others. He has previously worked as an associate for Uprising, a small, San Francisco–based venture capital firm that catalyzes epic social entrepreneurial endeavors. He was also an associate for a nonprofit organization, CareMessage, which addresses the global healthcare crises by designing, building, and implementing innovative mobile technology (started by a* Forbes *30 Under 30 award recipient). A student at Stony Brook University, Daniel has founded organizations ranging from a quidditch team to the first college chapter of Watsi, a global funding platform for medical treatments that connects donors with people in need of medical care and enables them to fund low-cost, high-impact treatments.*

Bonjour. Warm buttered croissants. Air France flight number 748 to John F. Kennedy Airport. "Big Apple" bound. Every taxicab reminds me of Dijon mustard. Iranian-French-Canadian Muslim living in the Bronx? White skin. Curly red hair. Freckles. Irish? Persian?! My story shocks them every time.

Thanksgiving dinners. Paella feasts. Incentives to learn how to read and write Farsi. Good friends become family.

Life goes on.

Sunny San Diego in the summertime. Lemonade stands. Living is easy. September 11, 2001. Another "random check" at the airport. That escalated quickly. *Au revoir* prep life, hello public education. "Who's this kid?" Middle school in Harlem, acting tough as nails. Let the "white chocolate" era begin.

Birth. Love. Hope. Future. Life. Brother. Clone.

Walking with some swagger. Honduran babysitter turned private Spanish tutor. Where will Dad's endeavors take us next? Madawaska, Fort Kent, Carlsbad, Modesto, Miramichi, Stamford, Phoenix, Turlock, and Lynch, Nebraska (population 269) vs. New York City. Yankees win! This is high school?! Time to have fun. Stick figures in Art. Frogs in Biology. What a breeze.

Reality check. Focus. Set a goal. Just do it. This is one big ladder. Thinking . . . She is really pretty. Her, too; what a babe . . . Focus, focus, focus!

Giving tours of the Holocaust Museum in French. Definitely worth extra credit. Ski resorts in the desert? Some fantasy world we live in. Good-bye Dubai, hello U.S. customs.

Dark room. Alone. Parents wait outside. "Where were you on January 3, 2008?!?" "School?" *"Don't lie to me!"* Holding my breath for ten minutes straight. Will I go back home? Time is indeed relative. Italy, France, Iran. Traveling opens the mind.

"This year will determine the rest of your life," said everyone. Today is a new day. "Don't go. It's not safe!" We went anyway. Persian food is just too good. Learn to drive in the streets of Tehran. Part-time cab driver. Captain of the basketball team. College application prompt: "What is courage?" "This is." Now that's a strong essay.

Met the love of my life then broke my own heart. Employee at Dunkin Donuts rejects tips from college students? Who knew a middle-aged Bengali man would change my life forever. Learning more about myself. Start. Going. Slowly. Almost there. "You can be anything you want in life, son . . . either a doctor, lawyer, or engineer," said immigrant parents everywhere.

Follow your dream. Risk it all. Fly to San Francisco on a whim. E-mail everyone you can. Learn from failure. Fall. Get up. Keep failing.

Photo apps are great, but are they really how you want to be remembered? *Democratize. Empower.* Teach people *how* to fish, don't just *give* them the fish.

What gives *you* goose bumps? Good. Do it. "Is what you're doing worthy of your life?" Yes? Start today. No compromise.

Phase one completed. An adventure awaits.

"I want to be a president/architect/photographer/astronaut when I grow up."

Why not, little bro, this is your dream . . . chase it . . . and never, ever let anyone hold you back. I love you and always will.

Kevin Breel

WHAT DO YOU DO?

Kevin Breel is a twenty-year-old writer, stand-up comic, and activist for mental health. As a writer, he has contributed to The Huffington Post *and CNN. As a stand-up comic, he's become one of the youngest performing acts in Canadian history. As a mental health advocate, he's been seen on media outlets all around the world, including CBC, CTV, MTV, and* The Today Show *on NBC. His TEDx talk titled, "Confessions of a Depressed Comic," went instantly viral online—with more than half a million views in less than thirty days. Now it's one of the most watched TED talks of all time with nearly two million views, alongside talks from Steve Jobs, Bill Gates, and Seth Godin. Bringing warmth and unparalleled insight to the topics people tend not to talk about, Kevin has become a speaker in demand at colleges and events throughout North America. In 2014, Kevin dedicated the entire year to doing an international speaking tour to talk about mental health. The tour stopped in more than fifteen states and three Canadian provinces.*

I don't really know how to answer the question, "What do you do?"

I want to say I ride motorcycles and play basketball, because I do those things. But the person asking the question always seems to mean, "What do you do to make money?" And I wish I had some cool answer.

I really don't. An honest answer would just be: I do about three different things. Sometimes I write stuff. Sometimes I do stand-up comedy. And sometimes, I speak at colleges and private events about mental health, specifically suicide prevention and depression.

None of those things really fit together at all. And I think that's okay.

I've never really identified with being an "entrepreneur." That always has sounded to me like a guy in a white T-shirt coding or starting up an app that is Kickstarter meets Yelp meets Google Maps . . . for cat lovers. I think I am more of a dreamer, who can occasionally take enough action to make some of my ideas happen. I say occasionally because it seems I'm often better at the dreaming than the doing. I guess that's okay, too.

This year, I'll probably speak more than fifty times at colleges and events all over North America. I'll probably spend a few weeks in N.Y.C. and L.A. doing stand-up comedy. And I'll probably spend an unhealthy amount of time holed up by myself on my laptop, writing a guest post for some media outlet (I've been lucky enough to do them for *The Huffington Post* and CNN), or just trying to record some of my random thoughts.

In the end, it's a process that has required me to push the skillset of my "entrepreneurial" toolbox.

I've hired a booking agent. I have a business manager. An awesome guy in L.A. named Jed does all my media and press. And I've put together a small but capable team to help me grow as a performer and as a person.

The one thing I've really grown to like about the "business" side of what I do is the opportunity it provides to see how much my impact directly relates to my income.

My manager, Josh, is fond of using the expression, "If you sell ten books, you impact ten different people. And you make ten books' worth of money. If you sell ten thousand books, you get to impact ten thousand people. And make ten thousand books' worth of money."

It's a simple way to look at things. But it also rings true.

I hope, whatever pursuit you chase, your heart is in it and you are passionate about it. But at the end of the day, everyone needs to be able to eat and provide for themselves and, later on, their families. So there has to be a happy medium between wanting to pursue your art or your craft and also realizing that, hey, this is a business.

For me, I try to put the majority of my focus into my craft. If I get better as a performer, as a speaker, as a writer, I feel the money will always follow. But I know that ultimately, it's important to be smart about the business and "branding" (for lack of a better term) of what you do. Because at the end of the day, if you're not able to create the kind of income you want, then you also can't have the kind of impact you want, either.

So the two things are, for better or for worse, joined together at the hip.

I want to close out by saying something I feel fits into the theme of youth being talked about in this book.

Three years ago, I sat at a desk inside of my high school feeling like I was wasting my life.

Every day I showed up and would spend six hours at school: reading, writing, memorizing, copying, cheating, etc. (Just kidding about the memorizing. Definitely serious about the cheating.)

And over time, I started to ask the question, "What am I going to do with my education?"

The short answer turned out to be: absolutely nothing.

Right now, I'm doing three of the most random things you could ever possibly put together and turn into a "business": writing, stand-up comedy, and speaking out about mental health as an activist.

While some foundational principles were built in school, the majority of my growth happened through actually getting out into the world and trying things. Taking risks. I gave a lot of bad talks before I ever gave one at TED that hit a million views in ninety days. I entertained a lot of small crowds before I ever filled theaters and arenas. And I definitely wrote (and still write) some horrible things before I got opportunities to write for *The Huffington Post* or CNN.

Trial and error is the best teacher.

Every time I get up onstage or stare at the blank page, I face another opportunity to try something and, maybe, completely blow it. Something about that keeps me sharp and helps me grow.

In youth comes the right amount of overconfidence and naïveté to think you can actually change the world. You get to dream big dreams and create crazy plans for total domination of the universe. But it's also the time you need to actually do stuff.

Don't just plan it out. Don't just think it. Don't just dream it. Really do it. Feel it. Taste it.

A mentor of mine once told me, "You want to have a business and a life. Not just a lot of ideas that sound good in a notebook."

Sometimes school turns us into overthinkers and overplanners.

Sometimes, you need to step out of your head and follow your heart.

I think this book is about dreaming big dreams and being brave enough to actually chase them. That's what each person's story represents. Not a list of accomplishments, but rather a sense of self that was bold enough to step outside of the proverbial box and try something that might totally suck, but may also prove meaningful.

There is something inspiring about that. We all could fail. I think that's what keeps it exciting.

I feel very fortunate to have started on this path as a young person. Why? I don't really know. I think, maybe, it's because young people have the wonderful quality of being naïve enough to think that they can actually change the world.

And I've come to realize that, maybe, that's exactly why we will.

JOURNEY

Everyone is handed adversity in life.
No one's journey is easy. It's how they
handle it that makes people unique.

–KEVIN CONROY

Samuel Mikulak

MY ROAD TO THE OLYMPICS
IN LONDON 2012

Currently, twenty-one-year-old **Samuel Mikulak** *is a student athlete at the University of Michigan, seven-time NCAA champion in Men's Gymnastics, and an Olympian who competed for Team USA in the 2012 London Olympics. He won the individual all-around title in both the 2011 and 2013 NCAA Men's Gymnastics Championships, and was a member of the five-person team that represented U.S. Men's Gymnastics in the 2012 Summer Olympics, where he and his teammates placed fifth during the team final and he placed fifth in the vault final. Samuel has been featured in a variety of media outlets, including ESPN,* USA Today, Business Insider, *the* Los Angeles Times, *NBC Sports, CNN,* Sports Illustrated, *the* Boston Globe, *Associated Press, and* Bleacher Report.

When asked what my goals were when I was in high school, I simply replied, "Make the Olympic team." This statement would transform the next year of my life into an experience that I feel fortunate to have had; an experience that helps define the person I have become. When I fractured both of my ankles twelve months before the Summer Olympic Games, the mere thought of my lifelong goal escaping me was enough for my coaches and me to set up a plan of action for the next year in order to optimize my chances of recovering and making the team. It took fracturing both of my ankles to reinforce in my mind what I wanted most in life and how I was going to get it. The injuries were only a small part of the price I had to pay for the journey that followed as I embraced the road to London.

In summer of 2011, I took part in the Puerto Rico Cup, my first international competition, as a member of the Senior National Team for the United States. The time spent preparing for this competition was more significant than most other competitions; a good performance would grant me entry to a pool of gymnasts in consideration for the Olympic team and be used to evaluate my readiness for the World Championships several months down the road. My preparation was superb and, accordingly, I was ready to compete with vigor and confidence, but when I fell short on a dismount during a floor exercise, my ankles subsequently shattered along with my goals. If it had not been for the adrenaline rushing through my bones, I would not have finished the competition and would have sooner realized the severity of my fractures. I was now face-to-face with an obstacle that would test my desire and resolve. There were no promises or guarantees I would make the Olympic team even if I worked hard to rehab and compete at my full potential, but I knew if I did not try there was no chance I would make the team.

My goal was, simply, making the Olympic team. I even ordered a rubber bracelet, which read, "Mind of a Champion," to remind me of the challenge each day. The bracelet was not enough though, so I ordered a flag of the Olympic Rings online and positioned it above my bed. More than ever, I stared at this flag, questioning my abilities and calculating my chances. They just did not seem too good. But the most relevant part of this story is that I made the conscious choice to block out all the negative thoughts before they could spread like a disease in my mind. Instead, I placed all my focus where it could help my recovery.

Making the World Championship team in October would have been an impressive milestone to the U.S. Olympic Committee. Instead, half a year passed and my recovery accelerated enough that I was given a different opportunity. I competed at the Kellogg's Pacific Rim event in mid-March, placing second in the all-around close behind Chris Brooks. At this point Brooks was a consistent gymnast and a serious contender for an Olympic team spot. My wheels were turning once again, but I made sure to retain the focus and composure that had gotten me back to where I now stood. With a rapidly growing support system, my quest to earn a place on the Olympic team became more apparent among committee members and the gymnastics community. People seemed to believe that I could make this happen, and although that was a comforting thought, to achieve personal success I could only focus on the positive and drown out all doubt from myself or others. There is no hope in letting your mind wander and become distracted by the hearsay of other people, and because of that I fastened myself to my family, friends, teammates, and community. That is where my hope lay.

The Visa Championship was the first showing where all the Olympic team contenders were on the same stage and evaluated by the same judges. By this point in my journey, my mind was a fortress, where no thoughts would enter unless I allowed them. A particular instant at the Visa Championship stood out to me as a test of my mental strength, one that could possibly have been used as a crucial decision-making factor in solidifying a spot on the Olympic team. As I prepared for the parallel bars, the equipment was being checked, the bars tightened and the springboard straightened. But when I firmly grabbed the bars I felt them shake, enough that I glanced at my coaches and shook the bars again, signaling for an emergency check. One of my coaches sprang up and quickly tightened one of the bars. Without hesitation, I jumped and performed my first few skills, the opposing bar shaking all the while. My other coach then ran onto the podium and fastened the other bar before fleeing the area, just in time for one of the more acrobatic elements I do, which would have been extremely dangerous with faulty equipment. I finished the routine with poise and confidence, and although an accident like this was completely avoidable by double-checking the bars before I began, it was viewed as a demonstration of mental strength to the rest of the onlookers.

My preparation for the Visa Championship paid off immensely and I placed third in the all-around standings, affording myself not only an opportunity to secure a generic spot on the Olympic team, but one of only two spots that would allow me to compete in all six events at the Olympic Games. Now it was a matter of going to the Olympic Trials and performing just as well as I did at the Visa Championships. For the first time, London was in my sights. The patience I taught myself to harness over the past year had paid off. Success is not a matter of giving it your all, but executing your skill in the best places at the most opportune times. Using the knowledge acquired from my coaches, teammates, and training over the past few years, I was able to find success.

Olympic Trials came around soon after the Visa Championship. I would be returning to my home state of California. As I headed to San Jose, my college teammate Jordan Gaarenstroom went to his hometown of Laguna Beach, gathered a large group of our friends, and caravanned up the coast to watch me compete for an Olympic team spot. The group soon became infamous at the Olympic Trials when they all designed "Team Sam" tank tops centered with a large picture of me doing gymnastics on the chest of each shirt. Their efforts to bring some home-field advantage to San Jose proved to be successful, and I loved the fact my friends were willing to make such a dramatic statement in a professional setting. To us, it was not about the politics of the Olympic Trials, but the feelings of excitement for the opportunity the event provided. Reinforced by Team Sam, I smoothly sailed through six events and landed myself at the top of the podium when day one of competition concluded. Unfortunately, on my last event of that day I tweaked my left ankle and was thrown into another chaotic decision. Since my ankles had posed such a powerful obstacle in my journey thus far, I knew the decision to compete or not would be handled very respectfully. After a talk with committee members and coaches, it was decided that I would only compete on the pommel horse to stay off of my feet and demonstrate my skills on an event that the U.S. team was notoriously weak on. I had to wait until the fourth event before I could perform the next day, but after an exceptional performance on the pommel horse, I had finally done everything in my power to gain a spot on the Olympic team and achieve a lifelong dream.

The following day, I was officially chosen for the U.S. Olympic team along with Jake Dalton, Danell Leyva, Jon Orozco, and Jonathan

Horton. It was truly an incredible moment that I will cherish and remember for the rest of my life. Upon exiting the Olympic team selection room, my parents and extended family, along with Team Sam, all rushed to congratulate me on my accomplishment. It was a lot to handle at one time, but the first thing I was able to do with my success was share it with the people I care about most. The success that entered my life also entered the lives of those involved in my story—my coaches, my teammates, my family. I hadn't just won; Team Sam had won.

When you are striving for something in life, realize how success will affect those around you and use that force as motivation to achieve exceptional goals in life. When you are fighting for a cause that is bigger than yourself, you will find that you have no bounds and that the journey, not only the successes, is what shapes the person you become.

Kristen Powers

I LOST MY MOM,
BUT GAINED A PURPOSE

A sophomore at Stanford University, **Kristen Powers** *is creating her first documentary,* Twitch, *following her genetic testing for Huntington's disease (HD), a neurological brain disorder that led to the death of her mother. Every child of a parent with HD has a 50 percent chance of inheriting the fatal gene, which means Kristen and her younger brothers are at risk of inheriting the same fatal disease. Kristen hopes that this film's story will spark international conversations about genetic testing, the implications of making the choice to test, as well as remove the stigma surrounding neurological diseases. She raised more than $40,000 using crowdfunding platforms to fund the creation of this film, and is currently working on the specifics of a global tour, festival screenings, and TV distribution in both the United States and the UK, starting late summer 2014. She has appeared in major news outlets like* USA Today, *has been named a "White House Champion of Change," and previously spoke at TEDxTeen.*

When I was seven years old, I had high expectations for the life I wanted to lead. I had my bucket list in hand everywhere I went.

1. Be interviewed by Matt Lauer of *The Today Show*.
2. Serve as the youngest mayor in the country.
3. Become the president of the United States.

However, an illness that seeped into my life shortly after my thirteenth birthday radically changed the path I've chosen to take.

Huntington's disease.

I didn't know what these two words meant when my family first sat me down at the kitchen table to explain the impending situation. All I knew was that my mom wasn't the same as she had been before. As days progressed, I watched as she struggled to walk in a straight line, keep her arms at her side, or even pick up a glass of water at the dinner table. Those two words—"Huntington's disease"—became the justification for her intense depression and emotional outbursts. "Brain disorder" and "no cure" were repeated over and over in my household, and as my dad consulted with relatives on the phone, I was left sad and confused. Wasn't there anything I could do?

Two long years later, I could see my mom still suffering from a swift and devastating deterioration. By my fifteenth birthday, she had been admitted to a twenty-four-hour assisted living facility, needed food specially prepared for her swallowing difficulties, and, worst of all, had lost her ability to speak. Just one year later, in 2010, we were informed that she needed to be bound to a full-body wheelchair. And a month after celebrating her last Christmas, she died alone in her room from complications due to pneumonia. She was forty-five years old.

Watching her intense deterioration left me with a ton of questions. Why was my mom different? How did this disease start? Why did she lose her motor skills? And why were we sitting by watching this happen? Why is there no cure?

By the time my mom passed, I had researched enough about the disease to know that my brother and I each had a 50 percent chance of expressing the same faulty gene that caused my mom to pass at such a young age. I vowed to never let this get the best of me. I would "stay strong" like my dad encouraged me to. I would stay positive. I would prosper.

It's what my mom would have wanted.

In the years after her death, I began to classify myself as an optimistic realist. Although some of my bucket list items had changed since I was seven, I wanted to get started early. I wanted to lead a happy and meaningful life of value, knowing that there was a 50 percent chance I wouldn't live beyond my forties.

I turned my focus to extracurricular activities in school to learn and boost my skillsets. I cofounded my high school's sustainability club and teen-led organic garden, with the goal of decreasing the environmental footprint of our school on the planet. I held the first sustainability club meeting and used every available resource to create proposals and get petitions signed to build a community garden. And while there were times people told me to "wait until I'm older" to start following my passions, I knew I couldn't. There was a possibility I wouldn't have the chance—just like my mom hadn't.

So every Saturday, a group of teenagers supporting the garden project came together to grow fruits and vegetables that we would then share among ourselves and the local food bank. In three years, we contributed 300 shopping bags full of organic vegetables and fruits to local hunger programs all across Chapel Hill, North Carolina.

As I grew more food over time with this community that became like family, I remembered the weed of a disease that took a piece of my real family away from me. I knew in the back of my mind that I might have the same seed sitting within me.

And I knew from the moment I attended my mom's funeral that I was going to test myself for Huntington's disease when I turned eighteen (the legal genetic testing age in the United States). The decision wasn't a light one by any means, but I knew that nothing could develop a thick skin like having your parent die before your eighteenth birthday. I could handle the answer—good or bad.

People warned me that knowing the results of the genetic testing would be devastating and alter my direction of life with a "burden of knowing," but throughout all my experiences I had learned to value goal-setting and prioritization as a way of living life effectively. I had already learned to cope with the fact that everyone dies, and because I knew that external factors could, at any moment, affect my life's goals and my ability to achieve them, I decided I wanted to know one way or another in order to make the most out of whatever time I did have on this Earth.

Stealing a phrase from my favorite hip-hop artist, Macklemore, I needed to "put the passion before . . . being comfortable" in order to succeed.

I am passionate about finding the cure for this disease and figuring out its role in my life and the life of others. So, rather than just simply get tested for my own knowledge, I decided to create a documentary about the effect Huntington's disease has had on my life and on the process of getting tested, and promote the cause on a crowdfunding platform. If nothing else, the film would selfishly serve as a productive distraction during a stressful testing period. To date, I've raised more than $45,000 and shared the story on hundreds of news outlets. This, I believe, will turn attention toward the gravity of the disease and help give hope to all the young people who are trying to blossom regardless of a weed in their own lives.

Through my journey, I've come to terms with the idea that we are all going to die and we have no idea how or when it is going to happen. This seemingly obvious fact is not as morbid as it sounds. Instead, it is an opportunity. To accept our fate is one thing. To embrace it and make something out of this one life we are given is an entirely different matter. The unknown is brilliant if used to propel our goals and dreams into reality. Those are foolish who wait because they "aren't old enough" or "don't have the time" or "need to work first." Those who choose to chase their dreams now, like me, will live a life fulfilled, regardless of when our time is up.

While I may not have reached the expectations of my seven-year-old self, I'm still moving forward. I recognize that some of my goals and dreams will happen in due time, but only as long as I continue to do what it takes now to push myself in order to attain that position of success. All the while, I'm making sure I lead a life that is happy, meaningful, and memorable. Otherwise, being interviewed by Matt Lauer, running for mayor, or serving as president of the United States just wouldn't be worth it in the end.

Alex Jeffery

FIND YOUR GIFT, GIVE YOUR GIFT!

Alex Jeffery is a nineteen-year-old entrepreneur and speaker from Australia. After going through many ventures, failing and learning some tough lessons since the age of twelve, Alex has become clearer on his big mission to bring our generation alive and together. Alex is the Founder of Onely Inc. and the global experience series, ONEWorld Summit. He was also named in Australian Anthill's "30 Under 30," Under35CEO's "Under35 CEO of the Month," and has spoken at corporations such as Australia Post.

It would be awesome to say that living a life with purpose, direction, and fulfillment is easy and comes naturally. It would also be awesome to say that more than 5 percent (my estimate) of the world's population is truly alive and actually experiencing self-actualization every day. If this were the case, the world would be a completely different place. Instead, most people are playing it safe, sticking to the script, and following the rules without thought as to why society functions as it does, which leaves most people in a state of complacency, automation, and process that isn't quite "living" to me.

I was lucky enough to learn early on that life has so much to offer if we are willing to make the most out of it. In fact, at eleven years old, I decided exactly what I wanted to do, what I wanted to have, and (most importantly) who I wanted to be.

We are in an extraordinary time in history. We are more powerful than ever before, and are only going to become even more limitless in the near future! With this thought process, I decided I wanted to be the most progressive and transformational entrepreneur, shifting systems and helping to move our generation to a place of abundance, love, and sustainability.

I followed this revelation with two years of research and personal development, which is now a constant part of my life each day. This meant researching people such as Richard Branson, who had accomplished what I wanted to do in life. I read all of his books, articles, and interviews with the aim of finding out as much about the way he thinks and the way he works as possible. And while I sometimes found myself overwhelmed, feeling as if I couldn't do as much as he had done, I asked myself where he was and what he was doing at seventeen years of age, and then went out and did something similar in my own projects, all while keeping sight of his highest accomplishments and the bigger picture.

You have to learn that, in order to really do something extraordinary and worthwhile, it means doing things that others will consider crazy, spending endless late nights working on your craft, possibly missing a majority of your "social" activities, and sometimes, unfortunately, damaging relationships due to time restraints and prior commitments. And while none of these things are desirable, they are often a result of chasing your own dreams. All throughout high school, I missed many birthday parties and social gatherings simply because I had things I knew I needed to accomplish if I was going to realize my vision!

However, in saying that, there is a way to truly make sure this journey is fulfilling . . . and that is to *truly* love what you are doing right *now*!

I highlighted two words there, "truly" and "now," for good reason. On my journey I have met and shared deep discussions with people who came across an opportunity to make a lot of money, and then tried to trick themselves into thinking they were passionate about that activity. At the end of the day, these people were the ones to give in when their business opportunities did not go as smoothly as planned.

This is why you need to make sure you are *truly* passionate and in love with the activity you are doing. There will be many times when you get pressured into not being so "crazy," into spending your time like everyone else does. In order to be successful, you'll instead need to reach the stage where you become so aligned with your *"Why?"* that you are able to say *no* to certain opportunities, simply because you know deep down that those extraneous things will not help you reach your personal mission. I have been offered multiple opportunities to work for certain companies, but have been able to say "no" with confidence as I knew it was not for me, and my time would be best spent fulfilling my personal goals.

I started my first real business venture at fourteen, which was when all my friends started going out and living the "social life." There were many weekends I just wouldn't go out, simply because I didn't have to go out to have a good time. I loved what I was doing. Many labeled what I was doing on the weekends as "work," and I can't remember how many times my dad said to me, "You need to get out, Al. Have some fun!" However, I didn't agree with the set societal beliefs that work can't be fun and that you couldn't turn your passions into a career. I wasn't going out on those weekends, but at fourteen, I was actually having more fun than my friends who had a "social life."

Many people will begin to tell you to "seriously rethink your 'work-life balance.'" After my experiences the past five years, what I have realized is that it is not about "work-life balance," but rather "work-life integration." "Work" takes up a large portion of people's lives and many people work with the plan to "live" after retirement. Shouldn't we live out the healthiest part of our lives, and use this to make our greatest impact? Why should you have to leave your true self and your favorite clothes behind in the morning to go to "work" five, six, seven days every week? I believe we need to find ways to live our authentic selves all day, every day. In work, play, family . . . everything!

The first, and easiest, way to do this is to find what truly makes you come alive, what makes you excited, what inspires you, . . . and *make* that your "work." You have to create the life you want to lead, and create the world you wish to live in. Think: "If money were not an object, how would I spend my days?"

After all of these experiences you will surely go through, it is true that the rewards at the end of the tunnel are totally worth it all. It is also true that it is not all about the destination, but about the journey along the way. I find it hard to believe that people can go through a mundane, mediocre life of nine-to-five work with the hope of reaching retirement (the "destination") and be able to enjoy it fully. If you have to wait until retirement to enjoy life, what have you been doing the last fifty years? Unless of course the work you do from nine-to-five is completely aligned with yourself, then that is awesome!

Throughout my journey to date, through all the mistakes and lessons I have learned, there is one thing I would like you to take away from *2 Billion Under 20*. Many people have told me (and through early experience I have come to believe) that when you look back at life, the thing you regret the most is not that you tried something and failed (although if you truly love what you do and keep trying different angles, you never "fail" anyway). The biggest regret you will have (if you don't pursue your passions) is that you didn't give it a shot.

We are all here to chase our dreams, to create something worthwhile and valuable that will outlive us.

So get out there, do what you love, make a difference, and have a hell of a lot of fun!

Ryan Orbuch

THE DAY WE BEAT OUT ANGRY BIRDS ON THE APP STORE

Ryan Orbuch *is the founder of Basil Ltd. as well as cocreator and lead designer of the best-selling application Finish for iPhone, which received an Apple Design Award in 2013. The award recognizes apps that raise the bar in design, technology, and innovation. Finish has been covered on TechCrunch,* Forbes, *CNET,* The Huffington Post, *and more. Additionally, Ryan has been featured nationally on Bloomberg TV and Fox News as an expert on teens and technology. Ryan was the first high school student hired at Techstars Boulder, one of the world's top startup accelerators. Techstars provides selected startups seed funding and intensive mentorship from accomplished entrepreneurs.*

January 15, 2013, was the first time I ever pulled an all-nighter. I had written at least one hundred e-mails in the prior forty-eight hours, lining up the final press pieces for the huge PR push to accompany our launch of Finish, the iPhone app I had created, designed, and built with my classmate and friend. Finish had been approved by Apple a month earlier, and we'd been planning our launch for weeks. I was absolutely terrified as our 8 a.m. Pacific Time press embargo lifted and the app went live in more than one hundred countries. As I frantically refreshed the App Store and the news sites committed to covering our story, I had no idea how much my life was truly about to change.

When the embargo lifted and stories about Finish hit *Forbes,* TechCrunch, 9to5Mac, iMore, and many other media outlets throughout the morning, I turned to the App Store charts and again started refreshing. I watched Finish start climbing, breaking the top eighty paid apps in the entire store and hitting number one in the productivity category less than twenty-four hours after launch. It blew my mind, and that was just the beginning.

It goes back to a few years ago, when ninth and tenth grade were extremely tough for me emotionally. I was stuck in what felt like an artificial and constraining environment, hungering to create more and make a real impact on the world. I was doing exactly what I was supposed to. My parents were happy, my grades were good, my teachers liked me, and yet I felt like I was doing zero work of significance. I knew I had to do something separate, something real, outside of the bubble of school.

Stress was everywhere during the December finals in tenth grade. I'd tried the standard school planner and other to-do list apps. They weren't useful. I'd always loved technology and design, and I began to think that fixing the personal and societal problem of procrastination might actually be doable. I spent the entire second semester of my sophomore year researching how to approach this, the psychology behind procrastination, organizing methodologies, motivation, and productivity. When summer came, my friend Michael and I jumped fully into this mission. We spent the next eight months designing and building a task management and to-do list app for procrastinators.

Fall of my junior year was also brutal. We thought we'd have everything fixed "by the end of the week," but it actually turned out to take months, and it was a hard lesson in how software worked. When we finally submitted our app to Apple, it didn't sink in right away. Had we really done it?

Yes.

I got a call from Apple the day after Finish launched in January 2013, when we were number one in the App Store productivity category. We were featured on the front page of the App Store a few weeks later as "New and Noteworthy!" Soon thereafter, I got a call from Fox News and was invited to the Denver studio to be interviewed via live satellite from New York for *Fox & Friends*. We beat Angry Birds in the entire App Store charts that afternoon. Awesomeness!

I now find myself living in two worlds on a daily basis: the world of answering press and customer e-mails, and the world in which I stress about my chemistry test like everyone else our age. I've learned the incredible value of building something from nothing and running further than I thought possible with a promising idea. Finish was one of eleven apps in 2013 to win the Apple Design Award, which recognizes apps that "raise the bar in design, technology, and innovation." While receiving the award was amazing validation, it also provided a moment to reflect and fully appreciate how crazy this journey has been so far and how it is just the beginning.

Caine Monroy

MY ARCADE

FROM CARDBOARD BOXES TO A WORLDWIDE PHENOMENON

*At just nine years old, **Caine Monroy** was featured in an eleven-minute documentary about the arcade he created in his father's shop out of cardboard boxes. The documentary went viral instantly, gaining more than one million views the first day and more than five million views the first week. Since the video came out, Caine became the youngest speaker ever at the USC Marshall School of Business, has been featured in places like* Forbes, Fast Company, The New York Times, National Post, 60 Minutes, *and temporary exhibitions at places like the Exploratorium in San Francisco. Caine, in 2014, began working on his next project, Caine's Bike Shop.*

When summer break finally came around, I was just as excited as any other kid I knew. No school, no problems. Life was good!

But summers can be long and boring in Los Angeles. It gets very hot and the floors and concrete get even hotter. The days drag on, especially for a young kid like me. Unfortunately I wasn't around many kids my age during the summer of 2011, but that didn't stop my imagination from filling the void. All I needed was a little push to get started. The only push I could find was from myself.

I spent many days hanging out at my dad's auto parts shop. It is a small shop located in Boyle Heights, tucked between a bunch of other car repair and parts shops. Being stuck in that shop, there really wasn't much to do but sit around and try to survive the summer heat.

Besides the heat, one thing around me was also in abundance. Cardboard boxes.

With nothing but time, tape, markers, and scissors, I took the first step in this journey of a lifetime. With all the time in the world and an overactive imagination guiding my hands, I knew I was going to build something I loved, but I wasn't sure what that something would be. I always loved arcades so I figured, "Why not build my own?"

My cardboard arcade-making proved good for both me and my dad. I kept busy and my dad resumed his work without being too distracted by my boredom. The shop is loaded with cardboard boxes, and with my dad constantly ordering new parts, the box supply was never-ending. The days went on and so did my building. Cardboard box mini-basketball hoops, cardboard Skee-Ball, I was able to create it all. Soon I had the arcade of my dreams, all built from material that was just trash to my dad and me just days before.

Eventually the front part of the store was lined with my cardboard arcade games. With not much room left to build new games, I started to focus on bringing people in to actually play with the cardboard box games I had created. With each incoming customer, came hope. With each passerby who didn't give me the time of day, despair. I look back and think how some people that passed by may have thought that these games were just boxes covered in colored marker, not knowing that they were actually workable arcade games. The days passed and I waited and waited. I tried to flag people down, but often times I was met with a "no." A better part of the time, the sidewalk remained empty. Nobody was walking by and I just sat on a chair for hours on end, waiting for someone to join me in these games. It got boring and part of me wanted to give up. Despite all this, I continued my attempts to draw people in.

Time went on and the heat continued to rise. I still sat in front of the shop and continued to try to bring in customers. Sometimes I just wanted to drop everything and tear the place apart. But just when I was about to rip up my cardboard creations, a man walked in who changed my life forever. His name was Nirvan and he took interest in my arcade. He told me how he was amazed at my working cardboard arcade games, and the creativity and energy I had put into making them. Someone was finally playing my games, and for that I was happy, but my excitement skyrocketed when he said he wanted to make a short film about my arcade.

At nine years old, I was flattered to have a filmmaker cover my work. However, Nirvan was ready to make this story a national sensation, and arranged a flash mob during the filming of the documentary in order to stir even more hype around the cardboard box arcade. Next thing I knew, people were pouring into my arcade. I continually received compliments left and right from people who were amazed at my creations.

And a few months later, when Nirvan released the short film, titled *Caine's Arcade,* the story went viral. Millions of people viewed the film on Vimeo (just in the first week!), and my dad's phone was ringing off the hook from media outlets like *Forbes, The New York Times, Fast Company, 60 Minutes,* and more.

It is truly amazing how fast things have changed since that historic summer. Despite all my recent adventures, speaking engagements, and press appearances, I'm still just a young kid. And what kid doesn't love to play with friends, ride a bike, and create things? However, through these experiences I have learned a lot, even at my young age.

I developed the patience to keep sitting in front of my arcade, waiting for the rare person to pass by. Imagination filled the car shop with my creations. Determination brought my cardboard boxes into the hearts of millions worldwide.

Of course I couldn't do this alone. Without the people I have around me like my dad and Nirvan, I wouldn't even be writing this. I learned how to appreciate the fact that my simple cardboard idea spread to the rest of the world, and that with the help of others in our generation and in generations before us, we can accomplish so much more still.

The journey is still continuing, and it appears to be far from over.

Payal Lal

THAT'S IT!

Payal Lal, *from India, is currently part of the first class of Yale-NUS, a new liberal arts college in Singapore. She dropped out of law school in 2012 to spend a year interning at various educational technology companies, as well as start her own company called Tutor Connect. Apart from entrepreneurship, she enjoys writing, traveling, and interacting with new people.*

As I sat in class, listening to the teacher explain what law meant to society, I felt the sudden urge to hit myself with the bulky textbooks that lay in front of me.

I was in law school, but I was not happy about it. For the past few months, all I had heard was how brilliant it was that I was going to study law. But now that I was here, it wasn't so brilliant.

In India, students go to higher education institutions to study for professional fields like law and medicine right after high school, instead of having to complete general courses like most people in the United States. Such fields are encouraged by our society as opposed to studying the arts, which is generally considered purposeless.

So not surprisingly, my family was extremely happy when I confirmed my admission into law school a few months ago. Even though I hadn't been sure about pursuing law as a career, my family's excitement had reassured me. I ended up accepting my admissions offer, more excited about the notion of learning than about the field of law itself.

My friends and family claimed confidently that I would have money, respect, and more than anything, happiness. And I believed them!

So all in all, I was an eighteen-year-old girl, living in the capital city of India, and, despite having a large part of my life ahead of me, my future had already been decided.

Sitting in classes and interacting with my new classmates, I realized that these other kids were truly happy to be here. I, on the other hand, didn't feel as happy as they seemed. I felt like I was settling for a dream that was never mine in the first place.

I asked myself why I was pursuing law. And I didn't really have an answer. I couldn't see myself being a lawyer and being happy at the same time.

I decided to save myself that regret and drop out of law school. It was a tough choice to make, considering the fact that I was giving up a seat in an amazing institution surrounded by a proactive peer group. I didn't know exactly what I would do or where I would go after I dropped out, but it was a leap of faith that I felt I just had to take.

But now came the tough part. I had to tell my family. In India, dropping out of school is looked down upon. It's mostly done by people who either can't afford to continue their education or those who don't have the ability or desire to learn. I knew it was going to be tough to explain my decision to them without sounding like I had lost all my senses. Although my parents were comparatively open-minded, they considered education to be of utmost importance, just like most Indian families.

I decided to bring this up with them the first weekend I went home. I started by telling them how law was turning out to be something very different from what I expected. The kind of education I was getting didn't seem as wholesome as I expected. The lifelong learning opportunities I thought I might have as a law student and as a lawyer turned out to be more about having a good knowledge base than a good education. Moreover, a lot of my "education" came down to doing well on tests and exams. I wanted to *really* learn and explore. There were people to meet and places to go, and so much to learn from them all! Unfortunately, "all of the above" just wasn't an available answer choice in law school.

I felt like I was being programmed into a sort of robot with nothing but preinserted knowledge that didn't help my ability to one day achieve things beyond the standard level of practice.

At first, I was greeted by wide-eyed silence as I shared my beliefs with my parents. Then came moments of disbelief. My parents thought I was just homesick, and that these silly words were just a symptom. They insisted that things would get better and that it takes a while to get adjusted to college. They tried to reassure me once more and told me to continue studying law.

The conversation ended there, with my parents dismissing me and telling me to stay home a few days longer. I kept bringing the subject up over the next few days until they realized that I was very serious about not pursuing law. They suggested completing my five-year law degree and then transferring to another professional field, but the notion of spending five precious years of my life to earn a degree I wouldn't utilize didn't seem right. I had a strong instinctive feeling that this just wasn't what I was meant to do. I wasn't sure where my passion lay, but I knew it wasn't law, and it would be a struggle for me to settle.

As I continued to insist on dropping out of law school, my parents began to worry. They felt that I had an aptitude for law and that I should continue my schooling for it. We even had a brief session with some career counselors who agreed that law would be a good profession for me. These sessions made my parents even more determined to send me back to law school. Thankfully, I couldn't start another college right away. It was too late to do that. I'd need to take a gap year now, which, according to my parents, would now completely tarnish my resume.

A lot of my extended family meanwhile openly opposed the idea of me dropping out of law school. They felt certain that it would ruin my future. My friends were also fairly aghast at the idea, but they were still supportive.

By this point, I was fairly tired of all the pressure to go back to law school. And I was exhausted by hearing my parents' futile arguments. I even considered giving in to the pressure and going back. But my instinct quickly overpowered that moment of weakness, bringing me back to square one.

Somewhere along the way, I realized that it was my decision and no one else's to drop out of law school, for the simple reason that this was my future that was in question. If I ruined it, that would be my fault. But if I ended up stuck with a degree and a job that I had no interest in, I would regret having given in to parental and peer pressure just so that "society" would approve of me. Not having that regret for the rest of my life made taking a gap year worth the risk.

There have been many instances in my life where I have argued with my parents. But there are very few instances when I have completely opposed them and actually done something against their wishes. This was one of them.

And so I officially did it. I dropped out. And it felt wonderful. Scary, but wonderful.

The world was suddenly full of endless possibilities.

I got a lot of Facebook messages, a lot of phone calls, and a lot of e-mails. Most of them from bewildered, unsure voices, wondering why I had done it. Were the professors not good? Were the accommodations bad? Were my classmates not friendly?

As patiently as I could, I explained to everyone why I was no longer a law student.

A huge task lay ahead of me. I was not in school, I didn't have a job, and I didn't have any idea where I was headed. I had to start exploring. I had to make sure that my leap of faith ended with a safe landing. I started by figuring out the education bit first, to make up for all the worry I caused my parents.

Back at law school, I expected a wholesome education and encouragement to develop a thirst for learning, neither of which I received. So I started seeking educational institutions with that kind of philosophy. In India, the education system tends to revolve largely around testing and grades, which alleviates the desire to learn, so I started looking at universities and programs overseas. A lot of universities in the United States and in Singapore seemed to resemble the model of education I was seeking. I decided to apply to those places.

Applying abroad was a hefty task in itself. I had to take the SATs and other standardized tests, write essays, get transcripts, teacher recommendations, and more. Tasks that normally spanned four years of high school had to be packed into a short span of three months.

It wasn't going to be easy.

Meanwhile, I recognized the fact that I had one full year to myself. I could revive all those moments where I wanted to pursue things but couldn't because of a lack of time. One of the things I had really wanted to pursue was a business idea that I tried to venture into with a friend a few months prior, during the summer. But when we realized that college would start too soon for us to seriously pursue our project, we gave it up. Although my friend was now in college, far away from me, I was willing to take it up again by myself.

The idea was called Tutor Connect. India has a huge after-school tuitions market, whereby tutors teach individually or in small groups to help students with their studies. But this market is very disorganized. My idea was to organize this market by formulating a company which collects data about various tutors, including their hourly fees, location, subjects of expertise, etc. Students could also rate their tutors after their sessions with them, solving the problem of finding a tutor, which is mostly done through referrals in India, a concept not very reliable and extremely time- and cost-ineffective.

I started by researching my market. In more technical terms, I started my first round of "customer validation." I picked a sample group from my target market and started talking to them about the kind of problems they faced with respect to after-school tutors.

It was extremely tough, because this wasn't an established market, and I had very little experience. Moreover, networking was tough. People around me weren't used to seeing an eighteen-year-old girl dropping out of law school and starting a company. When people asked me, "What do you do?" I wasn't sure what to tell them. I wasn't yet an entrepreneur, but I wasn't exactly a student, either. Telling people that I was on a gap year seemed to give them the impression that I was just looking to pursue this project because I had free time. My confidence levels temporarily dropped. But despite the challenges, I loved what I was doing. I felt like I had found my calling.

Slowly, very slowly, people began to see light in my logic. They began to see the bigger picture, which I had seen two months ago when I dropped out of law school. People began to admire my courage. It felt good.

But still, the majority of people who would hear what I'd done laughed at my foolishness. By this point, I stopped caring about what others said. I simply surrounded myself with people who were more positive.

In November, I started another company. This time, it was an e-commerce company. I had discussed the idea many times over the past year with my best friend from high school. We had fantastic ideas for an online store, and we really wanted to make it happen.

Even though I was loaded with work between my university applications, Tutor Connect, and the online store, I didn't feel pressured. I felt happy. I looked forward to waking up every morning so that I could get a few steps further than yesterday. I applied to the Thiel Fellowship, which awards twenty entrepreneurs under the age of twenty $100,000 to drop out of the formal education system for two years and pursue their entrepreneurial projects instead. I made it to the semifinals, which really boosted my self-confidence and gave me an amazing group of friends to talk about entrepreneurship with.

Tutor Connect did a pilot round, and my online store also had a great first season. I felt like I learned so much more from those businesses than I ever could in school. Practical exposure made it possible to apply knowledge I gained much faster and in a way that could make me money. And since I was on a gap year and didn't really have a peer group, I learned to be more independent and to interact with people of different age groups. I saw myself growing as a person.

Soon after, I started getting answers from all the colleges to which I had applied. I wasn't sure if I wanted to go to college anymore at all. I loved what I was doing, and I couldn't see a reason to stop doing it. The next few weeks involved making a decision tougher than dropping out of law school.

Eventually, I decided to go back to college. I was admitted to the first class of a liberal arts college called Yale-NUS, which opened its doors in Singapore in 2014. In other words, it's a startup in itself. Unfortunately, it meant giving up my own startups. But this was a chance to combine my love for learning with my love for entrepreneurship. It felt right.

It takes time to find what you truly love. It takes struggle. And more than anything, it takes courage. But the moment you find that thing where you can say, *"That's it! This is what I love!"*—that moment is truly priceless.

So keep going. Don't be afraid of taking wrong turns. Don't give regrets a chance.

Find what you love, and just look forward to the day when you can join me in saying, *"That's it!"*

Patrick Lung

WE ARE ALL BETTER TOGETHER

Patrick Lung is a sophomore and Morehead-Cain Scholarship recipient at the University of North Carolina at Chapel Hill. His passion lies with business-technology integration and he is currently working on reinventing the way college students approach online calendars. In the past, he has directed both a national research journal reaching every high school in the country and a volunteer tutoring organization with more than 300 students. He was the youngest person to ever intern at the Canadian Institute for Theoretical Astrophysics, or serve as a consultant for his school's Peer Consulting Team. He has represented North America for Go (a strategy board game) and was offered the chance to represent Canada in the World Mind Games. He has been a divisional leader in his St. John Ambulance youth organization and currently runs all Red Cross first-aid courses on his university campus. In his spare time, he enjoys playing soccer and basketball, getting brunch with random people, and dancing . . . or at least trying to.

School never became a second home for me. To ensure that I would always be academically challenged, my parents kept switching me into more and more rigorous schools as I grew up. While these transitions definitely helped me excel academically, they hindered me in other ways. With my shy, mild-mannered disposition, always being "the new kid" proved a tremendous challenge. My loneliness as I constantly adjusted to new social environments reinforced the notion that school was only there for me to improve independently, be it in math or at basketball. Accordingly, I spent my afternoons doing multiplication drills and my recesses playing sports that normally involved teams by myself.

This went on for quite some time before I arrived at a realization. I began to think that, just maybe, the place I trudged to every morning could become more than a combination of passively listening to a teacher, mindlessly shooting hoops, and talking to myself in my head. I began to think of school as a place where I could fit in and grow up. Previously, I saw my school community as a bunch of individuals who were in the same place doing the same things at the same time. However, when I made an effort to get involved in team sports, I saw that I had been wrong. Playing soccer and basketball with other students helped me see my classmates as active supporters of my goals, and myself as an active supporter of theirs.

Toward the end of middle school, basketball took a backseat to my new obsession with space. Even though I could not explain my attraction to everything "astro," I applied to Marc Garneau Collegiate Institute, the only high school in Canada dedicated to helping kids like me get, quite literally, "out of this world" and into space-centered careers. There, I would be surrounded by sixty of the top STEM students in the country. At first, when I was accepted, I again remained within my personal bubble, struggling to figure out my problem sets on my own every evening. Eventually, I realized that high school could also be approached with a team of friends. I began to express my passions and started fitting in with students who shared my interests. After opening up to several similarly minded wannabe scientists, I was able to bond with them over space shuttles and supernovae. Together, we competed in space station design contests, ogled through telescopes, raved about everything NASA, and finally (but most importantly) began to feel at ease with who we were.

Being with peers who had aspirations as high as my own made me dream even higher, as M.G.C.I. had promised would happen when I applied. Reaching for the top, I e-mailed forty different professors one summer, and somehow landed an internship at the Canadian Institute for Theoretical Astrophysics. There, I conducted supplementary research on star formation for my PhD mentor. But back then, all I knew was that stars were pretty. Determined, I dedicated hours upon hours to reading a graduate astrophysics textbook . . . and understanding absolutely none of it. I was sixteen at the time, and everyone else working at the facility was a senior in college or had already graduated. I was living alone at home, too, so I didn't have my family for support. After weeks of preparation, I still knew nothing about what I was supposed to do. I couldn't figure out how to program in Python. In fact, I remember spending two days just switching variables around to absolutely no effect (of course, however, not wanting to disappoint, I told my mentor that I was making astronomical progress). Finally, I cracked under the confusion, and asked the students beside me for help. With coding, it's always little obstacles that get in the way, and one student gave me the guidance I needed to get past those problems. One month later, after working eleven-hour days, I was finally able to produce a report. And it actually meant something.

That same summer, I also attended Shad Valley, a summer enrichment program far from home, filled with people I had never met before. We were quite the awkward bunch at first, but there was an infectious, inevitable friendliness in the air. I wasn't used to becoming best friends with people in so little time, so initially, I actively resisted doing so. However, living with others in such a creative and collaborative setting changed my attitude pretty quickly. In less than a month, we became a close-knit community, and while the program's entrepreneurship emphasis and startup competition redefined my thought processes, it was the family I became a part of that impacted me most. By the end of the month, I realized entrepreneurship was a lifestyle, one centered around connecting with people and supporting your peers. In my senior year of high school, I chose to apply what I'd learned that summer. My academic program was known for hard workers, and with a few of my fellow students, I helped build a volunteer tutoring organization named Top Tutors. We brought together our nerdy peers to help tutor students in surrounding underprivileged neighborhoods. As a group of 52 tutors, we worked together to provide what those schools needed, and what more than 300 students ended up benefiting from.

Later that year, the stars aligned again, propelling me into outer space, or at least all the way to the University of North Carolina at Chapel Hill, which, at 800 miles away from my home, felt like another universe at least. In this new environment and country, I certainly felt like an alien at first.

Once again, I began by studying and going to as many networking events as possible to find resume-boosting opportunities. Only later did I realize that organizing group study sessions and chatting with random students were, as they had been in past years, better alternatives. I rekindled that interactive, entrepreneurial spirit, and I quickly made friends who helped me realize that my time in college could be both productive and enjoyable. Two years later, I realize that stepping outside of my comfort zone to build a community was the most important thing I've done at UNC.

Two months into college, however, I had bigger problems. I was having trouble choosing a major, and was losing motivation to work hard. I needed a change in mindset. I heard about the Thiel Foundation Summit, an idea-sharing meet-up for society's young nonconformists and entrepreneurs alike. I flew to New York City alone, rented a flat with a dozen strangers, and listened to their stories. Together, we realized we weren't alone in receiving resistance from our surroundings, and that forging our own paths would be easier with a support network (sound familiar yet?). Since that fateful weekend, I've been back to the Summit twice, and each time I go, I'm inspired by the entrepreneurial teens I meet. Just witnessing their progress in changing the world is the best motivation one could ask for.

Looking back, I'm surprised that everyone welcomed me with open arms, in many stages of my life. Although the power of collaboration was something I had experienced time and time again, attending the Thiel Foundation Summit finally made me realize that working effectively with others was the key to my success thus far, as well as the reason I'm able to write to you today and share some of my story with you. If there's anything I'd recommend to you, reader, it's this: There will always be people who want to join you in your journey.

Let them. It turns out life, like everything else, is better together.

Ben Lang

BAD BREAKUPS

Ben Lang is a soldier in the Israeli Defense Force by day and serial entrepreneur by night. Currently, he is the founder of Mapped in Israel, which provides data and reviews about members of Israel's high-tech entrepreneurial ecosystem. Previously, Ben served as a growth hacker at lool ventures, and has worked at or founded a handful of other tech startups. Ben is also a regular contributor to Forbes, Business Insider, TechCrunch, Mashable, *and* EpicLaunch, *and is a member of young entrepreneurial communities YEC, ROI Community, and Sandbox. He once survived a summer in Silicon Valley spending only $250. He has run a half marathon, and organized hackathons. When he isn't fighting for his country, starting businesses, or contributing to some of the most established business media sources, Ben speaks. He has recently spoken at the MIT Forum, Tomorrow Israel, and IDC University among other places.*

A few years back, one of my best friends and I decided it was time for us to build a startup together. We had worked together on a few smaller-scale projects during our early teens, and now, we wanted to take it to the next level and build something that could actually make an impact.

At my high school we had built an internal note-sharing site in tenth grade. Almost everyone in school used it to share notes before tests and finals. Honestly, without this site I never would have passed high school, and the success of that project pointed to the larger opportunity I had to build something even better with my friend.

I thought it made sense to build a similar platform for all high schools to use. This way, students in other schools could benefit as much as I had from this service.

So my friend and I joined forces to build what we called MySchool-Help. We knew almost nothing about building a startup, but we figured we would learn along the way.

A few months later I heard about a program called Teens in Tech. I decided to apply for the incubator knowing that I probably wouldn't end up getting in.

A few weeks later I was surprised to find out that we were actually accepted!

I told my cofounder that we had the opportunity of a lifetime to go to Silicon Valley for the summer. We had both just finished high school and it seemed like the right move. After a good amount of arguing I decided I was going and he decided he was going to stay in New York. We agreed that he would work on MySchoolHelp at night.

I moved out to Silicon Valley and fell in love with the startup world. I would work 24/7 on improving the product, meeting the right people, talking to customers, and more. My cofounder and I started disagreeing on more and more things. Long distance wasn't working well. And the fact that I was much more committed to this startup than he was caused problems.

Eventually the situation became bad enough that there were threats of getting lawyers involved. This was all pre-revenue. It didn't end well and we destroyed the startup and our friendship at the same time.

The reason I wanted to share this story is just to show how important it is to choose the right team, for your personal life, for your mentors, and for the companies or projects you will go on to create. Choose to surround yourself only with people you know will commit to your personal and professional success 100 percent. Choose people to surround yourself with that will challenge you, support you, and bring you to new heights, not send you crashing and burning to the ground. If not, you could be headed toward the same situation I experienced with MySchoolHelp, and lose an opportunity (and a friend) in the process.

Brittany McMillan

SAVING THOUSANDS OF LIVES (AND INSPIRING MILLIONS) THROUGH SPIRIT DAY

Brittany McMillan *is an eighteen-year-old equal rights activist from Surrey, British Columbia. She is the founder of GLAAD's Spirit Day movement, and has made several lists for her work including* The Advocate's *2012 "Top 40 Under 40" and* The Daily Dot's *"Top 10 Online LGBT Activists in 2012." She has also been a runner-up in* Canadian Living's *Me to We Awards (in the Social Action category) and* Seventeen *magazine's 2012 "Pretty Amazing Contest" (which 2 Billion Under 20 co-author Stacey Ferreira won in 2013). She has also been honored to walk the red carpet at the GLAAD Media Awards in 2012 alongside celebrities like Shay Mitchell, Dianna Agron, and Mario Lopez. In addition, she was asked to speak at the Media Awards and present an award to Facebook. Upon graduating high school, Brittany was presented with the Stephen Godkin Humanitarian Award for her anti-bullying efforts.*

I was seven years old when my parents got divorced and from then on, my family life was pretty hectic. My parents argued a lot and to this day, they still fight every so often. As the oldest of two children, I was forced to act as a mediator between the two, and often asked to relay some not-so-nice messages between my parents. A couple times, my parents got into physical arguments. One time in particular, when my parents had just recently separated, the fighting got so bad that my little sister started crying and I had to lock her in the bathroom and separate them myself. Other times, my parents just flat out embarrassed me by arguing (loudly) in public places, like my school or the grocery store.

Needless to say, family life wasn't great. There was a lot of moving between houses, a lot of arguments, and a lot of tears. Most of the time, I didn't get along very well with either of my parents or my younger sister. As I got older, those relationships with my family members only grew more strained.

For a long time, school was my safe place. I had lots of friends and great teachers who were always there for me throughout my family troubles, but coming into high school, my friends got split up between two catchment areas. Most of my friends ended up going to a different school than me and for the most part, the ones that stayed either turned to drugs, dropped out, or found new friends. For the first time, I felt completely alone at school.

High school only got worse when I started getting bullied. One summer, one of my very close friends from elementary school suddenly stopped talking to me. He wouldn't give me a reason why, just said he didn't like me anymore. Then, when we started high school, he would accuse me of gossiping or spreading rumors about him when in reality I had been the one fending *off* the rumors about him, defending my former friend. After that, his older sister approached me in our school cafeteria with all of her friends. She proceeded to call me names, yelling at me and embarrassing me in front of everyone. Until she graduated, she and her friends would elbow me into lockers. Sometimes I would try to avoid them, but they'd go out of their way to make sure I got shoved. The situation got even worse when their mom got involved. From a mutual friend, I learned that she had started telling other parents not to let their children be friends with me. She told them I was a bad role model. Me! Student council member since grade one, straight A student, and devoted Christian. It became apparent that just like home, school wasn't a safe place for me either.

As a result of the family troubles I'd been dealing with my entire life and the recent evolvement of bullying at school, I began to feel depressed. I felt so alone and overwhelmed that during the summer of grade eight alone, I tried to kill myself three times. And for the next few years, it seemed that a day didn't go by that I wasn't considering suicide. In fact, most days, I thought about it more than once. All of my elementary school years, I had depended on school to be the place where I could feel safe and happy. School was where I knew with all my heart that I was loved and cared for. It was the place I could go to get comfort during especially hard times at home and it was where I could be praised and appreciated for my actions, whereas at home those feelings were few and far between. The loss of such a place was devastating. I spent a lot of time alone and feeling sick. Some days I would go to school crying because I hadn't slept or eaten properly in days, and my bones ached so deeply that it hurt to even breathe. I used to ask God why He was doing this to me. I'd always been told that God had a purpose for everything and I didn't understand why He was making me suffer.

But then came the start of change. In October 2010, I was on a blogging site I'd recently joined called Tumblr. It was on Tumblr that I read about several teens who had committed suicide due to homophobic bullying. For one week straight, it seemed like every time I logged in, there was another death. As a student council member, I had fought for different causes practically all of my life. I'd collected items for charity, I'd raised awareness for environmental issues, and I'd helped to build wells and schools through fund-raisers. After reading about the suicides and battling thoughts of suicide myself, I knew that this was the next issue I would tackle, the next thing I had to do to make a difference in the world.

Having been depressed for the three years prior to that October, I'd known firsthand what it felt like to want to die. I knew how sad and lonely and angry you had to be to feel like the only way out was to just off yourself. I had lived it and I felt outraged for these teens who were bullied so badly they felt the need to commit suicide. At least for me, my depression was partly genetic. Several people from both sides of my family have had or do have depression, meaning that I am more susceptible to developing depression as well. The knowledge that how I felt was partially impacted by my DNA made it all the more difficult to imagine how badly others were being bullied that they had actually succeeded in killing themselves.

So I created Spirit Day.

Spirit Day is a day where people all around the world wear purple to stand up to homophobic bullying and show support for the LGBT (lesbian, gay, bisexual, transgender) community. The first Spirit Day was held on October 20, 2010, right after I'd read about the suicides. I asked people via different social media outlets (i.e., Facebook, Tumblr, and Twitter) to wear purple and stand up to homophobic bullying. To my surprise, the idea caught on and with the help of GLAAD (Gay & Lesbian Alliance Against Defamation) more than two million people worldwide ended up wearing purple, including celebrities, faith groups, organizations, and schools.

The following year, I had no real plans to run Spirit Day again, but once more, after reading about more suicides in September 2011, I decided to hold Spirit Day round two. That year, more than three million people around the world wore purple. In 2012, I spent Spirit Day with GLAAD in New York and more than four million people wore purple. As a result of Spirit Day, I've had the opportunity to do so many amazing things. I've been featured in magazines, met celebrities, been interviewed on TV, traveled and made speeches, and I've been able to receive tons of incredible feedback from teens who have participated or been helped by Spirit Day. It's a wonderful feeling.

2012 was a life-changing year for me. It was the year I graduated; it was the year GLAAD invited me to come speak at the GLAAD Media Awards in San Francisco; it was the year I interned for GLAAD; and it was the year that I made the top five finalists in *Seventeen* magazine's Pretty Amazing Contest. At the GLAAD Media Awards, I was able to share my story with an audience of more than 700 people and I also got the chance to present an award to Facebook. As a finalist in the Pretty Amazing Contest, I was flown to New York to spend a week doing interviews, photo shoots, and just general hanging out with the staff of *Seventeen* magazine. At my graduation, I was presented with the Stephen Godkin Humanitarian Award where the sponsors presented a speech about me and my graduating class gave me a standing ovation. It was incredible.

Surprisingly, 2012 was also the year my depression worsened but then got better. At the start of my junior year of high school, I had developed anxiety. When I got a panic attack, my heart would pound and my body would shake and my head would ache. I would start sweating and crying and hyperventilating all at once and afterward, once I'd calmed down, I'd have to go home because I felt faint and ill. I spent a lot of time in the counselor's office that last year of school, unable to handle the social aspects of my classes. For whatever reason, idle chit chat about things that didn't seem important to me (the latest celeb gossip or what sorts of crazy shenanigans had taken place at so-and-so's party) would set off my anxiety, as would my increasing workload. However, things slowly started to get better. Toward the end of first semester, I was formally diagnosed with depression and given medication, which helped a lot. From there, the thought that kept me going was being the founder of Spirit Day. As the creator, I realized that I had to be a role model for teens suffering from depression and dealing with suicide.

Even though the bullying was no longer a problem and my family issues had subsided a bit, I was still fighting depression. I knew that I had to stay strong because people looked up to me. By creating Spirit Day, I had set an expectation for people to persevere in the face of depression and suicidal thoughts. In a small way, I had also helped people understand that even though life seemed tough at the time, by holding out, it got better. Mostly, I asked myself, "What kind of anti-bullying role model would I be if I let the bullying end my life?" To help combat the depression, I started trying to think more positively, which was a lot more difficult than it sounds. Every night I would pray and give thanks for three things that happened in my day and I started writing a blog about it. When I was upset, I wrote about it in a journal instead of keeping it inside (which would result in me being cynical or bitter during the day, and a sobbing mess at night). And even though it made my anxiety creep up, I forced myself to go out and be with my friends. All of those things combined have made a huge difference.

Today, I am well on my way to achieving my life-time goal of being an elementary school teacher. I took a break from living with my mom, which has helped our relationship way more than any counseling appointments ever could. I also don't have as many anxiety attacks anymore without the stress of high school drama and unproductive classes. I start post-secondary school in September 2013 and I currently work at the day care I used to attend as a child.

Yes, I still have anxiety and I still have depression, but I'm much,

much happier. I no longer feel weighted down by my depression because I don't allow myself to wallow in negativity. As silly as it sounds, thinking three optimistic thoughts a day actually helped, as did learning to consider if what I was about to say was positive or negative (and of course the much harder task of learning to keep quiet if the thought was indeed negative). I've also been fortunate enough to have the incredible opportunity to share my story with others, a story that with each telling allows me to feel like I've taken another step forward and away from my depression. For anyone suffering from depression or anxiety, I truly believe the best thing you can do is let people know. If you share how you feel, you can get the help you need and you can also give yourself room for breakdowns. There is nothing more relieving than needing to take a breather and knowing you can take it.

I've been through a lot but I thank God for every moment of my struggles. If you remember, I had originally asked God why I had to suffer and now I know the answer. Without my experiences with bullying and suicide, I would not have created Spirit Day. Without Spirit Day I would not be at the place I am today, a place where I feel free to be the person I am—a survivor, an activist, and a complete nerd. I am so, so thankful and I love that I get to help save lives through Spirit Day. To think that five years ago, I was trying to end my life and now I can't wait to enjoy the next day of it.

Erik N. Martin

ANOREXIA NERVOSA AND
ABRAHAM LINCOLN

Erik N. Martin *is a geek. Such a huge geek is Erik that his life was saved (really!) by the video game* World of Warcraft. *By playing* Warcraft *and learning to lead a guild, Erik discovered how failure, a concept we often fear when we should embrace it, can be defeated with tenacity, resilience, and kindness. Erik is now a student at the University of Maryland, College Park, creating his own major in new media and global civics. He serves as a specialist on Student Engagement and Games at the U.S. Department of Education, and is a youth innovation adviser for Dell. Passionate about the role of youth in shaping the future of education and technology, he has been spotted emerging from his gaming cave (his room) to speak at venues including UN headquarters in New York, TEDxRedmond, and Georgetown University. Erik is slowly but surely working on the writing of a largely irrelevant fantasy novel.*

When the room cleared and the doctors left, I walked over to the bathroom to begin my three-minute cold shower. These were the times of day I hated the most, walking into a room with a mirror in my plastic women's hospital gown. Looking in the mirror, I knew the reflection didn't lie and I only felt guilt.

At fifteen years old, I had disappeared from high school entirely. All my friends had been told that I was dangerously ill. My family visited once a week. And the only person I felt I had left to trust was myself, but soon I had shattered that trust right down to my malnourished bones.

Standing there naked and weak, I said it out loud for the first time. "I am horrendously anorexic." I heard my own heart beat against my ribs. It was slow, around forty beats a minute. Deathly slow. It was tired, and I was tired.

"There is nowhere lower I can sink."

"There is nowhere left to run."

"There is nothing left to fight for."

"I am broken. Truly, entirely, mind, heart, and body; broken."

I hated failure. I wanted control. But I no longer had it. My thoughts were no longer mine. They were property of a disease that almost consumed me.

I tried to recall the factors that had contributed to this mental disease and brought me to stand here in this hospital gown. A doctor who told me my cholesterol was dangerously high. Being made fun of for my weight and accepting a deep self-resentment for my "imperfection." A fear of coming to terms with my sexuality. A failed attempt at committing myself to a greater cause, and failing to rally others to support it. A need to fix something. A desire for agency in my life.

I would run for miles on end, surviving on less than 300 to 500 calories a day. I pushed myself with sheer willpower not to stop. There was no such thing as stopping. I deleted it in my head as an option. It was a feeling unlike any other, as if I were burning my soul for fuel every step. For miles, and miles, and miles. And most nights when I got home from my run, I would lie awake in bed as my muscles cramped in agony from running and an empty stomach.

My former teacher, Mr. Metcalf, was the one who may have saved my life. One day after school, he saw my mom and apparently told her that he was worried about me. He said he didn't see the same spark in my eyes that used to be there, and wanted to make sure everything was okay. That's when my family started to catch on, an intervention I did not welcome.

I vividly remember the fights I had with my mother, father, and, most precious of all, my sister. The feelings of fear, resentment, anger, and my family's inability to understand such a devilish, dehumanizing disease are all sharp memories that I try to block out. I considered running away. I considered suicide. I wanted to escape.

In the hospital, as always, I tried to make light of the whole deal. "Fun stuff, right?" I told my reflection before hopping in the shower. Turning the handle on, the cold, heavy water greeted me. At home I would take cold showers morning and night to burn calories. At home, I would hide from my family so they didn't offer me food. At home, I had distanced myself from love and care and nourishment.

I turn the shower handle off. I close my eyes. The regret was indescribable, but in that moment of stillness I managed to find a spark. I clung to it desperately.

Part of the spark was taking a good hard look at all the facts, and myself, and recognizing I was wrong. I was wrong to abhor myself so much and wrong to act so abhorrently on it. Another part of the spark was thinking about the kind, caring, and disheveled people I lived next to in the hospital. It was hard to imagine our bright, brief friendships were sewn together by something as awful as anorexia. It was hard to imagine that we wouldn't all make it out of there. And part of it was luck, perhaps, that my mind found some hope and willingness to fight this enemy of a disease in that moment when I could not imagine finding it before.

That night I gave up fighting for the enemy. I decided to give in to what my parents, sister, and doctors had been saying all along. I began the much more difficult fight to face myself and my disease—to get better.

It was an uphill battle, but a month later I was permitted to leave the hospital and return to all the people and things I had left behind. I had a second chance, something that many who fight anorexia nervosa do not receive.

When I got out, I saw an Abraham Lincoln quote stating, "Do I not destroy my enemies when I make them my friends." What he did not perhaps realize was that these words apply even to the enemies within us.

Shortly after leaving the hospital, I underwent round two of mental battle royale by coming out as gay. But I went on to find an amazing community of support by leading a *World of Warcraft* guild, which revived my spark once again, and strengthened my resolve into a fierce fire.

And still, to this day, I stay up at night, reflecting on how lucky I am to still be alive. Most self-reflection is inconstant, rarely predictable, and frequently uncomfortable, yet absolutely necessary. We are, after all, frequently wrong, and ultimately at our best when we admit our faults.

I believe people can overcome almost anything, but also that the things most worth overcoming require the help of others and a strong community of support. I believe in resilience and giving hugs to the people you care about; you never know what internal day-to-day battles they fight. So as they search within themselves to find the endings to their own battles, let them know you'll be waiting for them on the other side. It could be the difference between life or death.

Ash Bhat

WHY TRY IF YOU'RE GOING TO FAIL?

*At sixteen, **Ash Bhat** is one of the most sought-after young program-mers in Silicon Valley. He has built his reputation as a winner and top finisher at dozens of hackathons nationwide. He built iSchoolerz in the summer of 2011 to bring students accessibility to school resources, and to bring numerous tools like school planners and ID cards to their mobile phones. Today iSchoolerz boasts tens of thousands of users. He interned at Kiip during the summer of 2013 as an iOS developer and has been featured in publications like* Business Insider *and* CNET.

You're going to fail.

Statistically, there's a very small chance that I'm wrong.

Why try then?

The journey.

Oftentimes, the journey defines a person. It's said that the journey is more about the experience than the outcome. This is true not just for adventures in the wild and fond memories, but for entrepreneur-ial ventures as well, or anything else worthwhile in life.

If you don't enjoy the journey, don't get started. There's only bad news and a hard road ahead if you don't love what you are doing.

However, let's say that you do thoroughly enjoy the journey. I can firmly say that, although you may not end up as monetarily successful as you'd like, you will enjoy what you do, and thus be happy and successful in that regard.

But, let's be honest. You still want to be monetarily successful and change the world. How can one optimize his or her chances?

Persistence.

You wouldn't be the first to notice that some of the most successful people in the world have been extremely "lucky." We idolize and lionize those who are successful and often say very little about those who weren't as "lucky." For every success story, there are a hundred stories about failure. However, it isn't really luck that separates who is successful from who isn't. It's persistence, and the lessons failure will teach you time and time again are the same ones that will one day allow you to achieve your goals.

Even the most genuinely talented people are statistically likely to fail at some point. Let's take the percentage of success to be just 1 percent (a fair estimate considering the entire world revolted against the "1%" just a few years ago). Although I'm pulling this out of thin air, it will go a long way in demonstrating my point.

Throughout various experiences I've had, I've developed an understanding for overcoming the odds with a theory we'll call "1 percent times 100." Try something one hundred times, and the chances of success are higher because you've given yourself one hundred chances to reach that 1 percent. This is true for more reasons than just statistics.

With every venture and journey, each has some degree of takeaway. Although most end with failure, you may learn how to program in a specific language, create the right connections, have a clearer picture of a market you're looking to sell to, or realize a major problem that needs to be solved. The more journeys that you have, the more takeaways you accumulate. Thus, with every venture, your experience and talents increase, making you a more likely candidate to succeed the next time you set your sights on the next "1 percent."

This further demonstrates the difference in perceived success rates between a seasoned serial entrepreneur and an anxious first-timer testing the tightropes of entrepreneurship. The seasoned entrepreneur is going to have the right connections to angel investors, venture capitalists, journalists, talent, and more, while the newbie will spend time understanding that these things are necessary and will begin working on creating opportunities that may allow for these things to occur later on.

Something that I haven't been able to explain through experience is the change in luck that comes with experience. Starting up and learning the ropes, I could never catch a break. The endeavors that I would have just started had competitors immediately that made my products obsolete. My customers would run into problems that would keep them from using my product. I would never be able to book a meeting.

That all seemed to change with time. Two years down the road, I seemed to have uncanny luck that put me in the right places during the right times, consistently getting me the right connections and opportunities. The breaks that I wished had been possible a couple years back were finding their way into my life at a surprising rate.

In my case, I started with a project called iSchoolerz at age fourteen. I was developing free apps for high schools across the country, but apart from the high school I was attending, I had no clients. I did everything in my power to get in contact with schools. I would spend hours a day scavenging schools' websites for e-mails of principals and writing page-long e-mails of what I was offering. Hours and hours of work, with no response.

However, I did learn from that process. I learned how to write e-mails and hustle. Move forward to today, I have dozens of high schools approaching me, setting up meetings, offering me money to build the same apps, and the situation has gotten to the point that, alone, I can't service all of them.

I began hacking and computer programming at hackathons once I started my sophomore year of high school. From my experiences hustling, pitching, and building new potential business ideas, I gained new levels of creativity. This, along with speaking and technical abilities, became invaluable in creating the right connections, building and pitching the right hacks, and seizing the right opportunities.

These skills led me to, among other things, become the youngest hacker for Hackers@Berkeley, win several major hackathons, intern at an innovative company called Kiip, and in the process learn and network at an increasingly exponential rate. I even got to spend time with Steve Wozniak, the cofounder of Apple!

If there's anything to take away from my experience, it's that things pick up. The catalyst for success is hard work, and while the beginnings of any journey can be tough, it's up to you to get the snowball rolling. If you are on your journey for the right reasons and understand the chances of failure associated with your efforts, as well as the fact that the more times you fail, the closer you get toward success, then you are on the right track. The momentum that you create will carry you forward and eventually help you achieve the rest.

Ariel Hsing

RALLYING MY WAY TO THE OLYMPICS

Ariel Hsing is an eighteen-year-old American table tennis player who competed in the 2012 London Olympics. Hsing became the youngest U.S. table tennis national champion in history in 2010 at age fifteen. She repeated as champion in 2011 and 2013. She was also a bronze medalist in women's team and women's singles at the 2011 Pan American Games. During her junior career, she was ranked as high as fourth in the world in both the cadet (U-15) and the junior (U-18) age group. Ariel has been featured around the web in places like USA Today *and* The New York Times *for her relationship with billionaires Warren Buffett and Bill Gates, who she kindly refers to as "Uncle Warren" and "Uncle Bill." The two even flew to London in 2012 to watch her play live at the Olympics.*

The first time I saw my parents cry was when I made the 2012 U.S. Olympic team. They said the tears were not for me, but for all the athletes that had sacrificed so much more than I did but never made it to the Olympics.

My parents are very loving, except when they are playing Ping-Pong (or table tennis). I can still remember all the yelling and killing sounds from our garage when my parents tried to beat each other. Whenever I tried to take a peek, they would simultaneously shout *"Get out!"* Naturally I thought, "Wow! This must be the coolest activity in the whole wide world!" So, one day when my parents couldn't find a babysitter for me and had to take me with them to the Palo Alto Table Tennis Club, and when I first held that small wooden paddle in my hand, my face turned red, my breath became shorter, my hands turned sweaty, and it felt like I had won a championship already.

That feeling has never gone away, even to this day.

One difficult part of being an Asian kid is that your parents tend to use you as a trophy to brag about to other parents. "Annie was so busy with school that she barely has time to practice the piano . . ." But, what they won't share is that they forced poor Annie to play piano three hours a day, every day of the week. All of that is translated to "My daughter has such good genes that she doesn't have to work hard, but is still better than your kid!" Luckily for me, my parents never had high hopes for my athletic achievements, and we all know that's because I run like a duck! To comfort ourselves, we had to believe that talent doesn't matter much, and that hard work is what truly counts. "Michael Jordan is the best basketball player ever," my father would say, "but he sucks at football. Do you know why? Because he worked his butt off for basketball!" Tiger Woods's story naturally followed. "Tiger Woods was the youngest winner ever of the Masters, and he started playing tournaments at the age of two. But you know what he said? He said he was not as gifted as other golfers, so he had to try harder!"

With this talent issue settled (at least in our eyes), we had to identify who were my strongest opponents. Of course, it was the Chinese; they have the best facilities, trained a minimum of six hours a day, and even gave out Ping-Pong graduate degrees! Hence, I started making an annual pilgrimage to China to train with the best in my craft. For every summer since I was eight, I would visit a different club in China, and I would try to outwork everyone else in each and every training session. My shirts were always drenched with sweat, the blisters on my feet had their own blisters, and a few times the heat inside the gyms got to me, forcing me to rush outside to throw up, and then rush back in to continue training.

The four-minute mile barrier was regarded as humanly impossible to break until a medical student, Roger Bannister, broke it in 1954. In the following weeks, a guy named John Lander broke that barrier again, and then four more runners accomplished the same feat later that year. Did all these athletes suddenly become physically stronger, or did their running skills dramatically improve? I don't think so. I think it's because their outlooks changed, the standards rose, and they no longer believed the four-minute mile was an impossible barrier to overcome. Going to China did the same thing for me. Even if the training didn't teach me to swing a paddle perfectly, it made me believe that if I worked hard enough, I could beat anybody, maybe even the Chinese.

Anything that is meaningful in life is never accomplished by just one person. There were three forces that carried me to the Olympics in 2012: my coaches, my support group, and my hard work. I was very fortunate to be under the care of many great coaches in the United States. Coach Dennis Davis was the first one to import high-level Chinese players to train with U.S. kids. This kind of treatment was unthinkable in China, even though many players like me had taken the reverse pilgrimage in order to improve our skills. The main support group I had was my parents. My mom sacrificed her beautiful garden to build me a Ping-Pong room to save time in commuting. My father studied my game so hard that I think he deserves a Ping-Pong PhD. I tried to do my best not only physically, but also mentally, in order to keep up and make their sacrifices worth something. I would watch clips of a single swing hundreds or thousands of times until it burned deeply in my brain. I would ask my mom to play loud music and throw balls at my feet during training to strengthen my concentration. There are so many people that helped me during my journey to London that I can't thank each one of them individually, so I'll often thank God instead.

It might sound cliché to quote Thomas Edison in saying, "Genius is 1 percent inspiration and 99 percent perspiration." But I am glad that I made the decision to ignore my comparative lack of talent and focus on the amount of hard work I put into my craft. What if I was wrong? What if one indeed needed the talent that I didn't necessarily have to be on top of the table tennis world? I would still have a healthy body from all the physical training. I would still have a sharp mind from all the mental training. I would still have all the dear friends I made from competitions. And when a new challenge comes, you know I'll just dive right into it and not worry about whether or not I'm actually ready to take on that challenge. Either way, through hard work, I'll end up becoming a champion.

Stephen Ou

MY JOURNEY
BEFORE PROGRAMMING

Originally from Kaiping, China, eighteen-year-old **Stephen Ou** *has been programming since 2009. He is the creator behind seven web applications—the hugely popular iTunes Instant, Artsy Editor, OhBoard, and more. His work has been featured widely online and offline, including Forbes, The Huffington Post, The Atlantic, TechCrunch, Mashable, and The Next Web. Besides working on his own apps, Stephen also does freelance programming. He serves as a consultant for a Fortune 1000 company. Additionally, Stephen does interviews occasionally to help inspire other young minds to start programming and selling online. He began attending Stanford University in the fall of 2014.*

My childhood experience was quite different from that of my American friends. I was born in China, and only moved to the United States in 2008. When I stepped out of the plane at San Francisco International Airport, a whole new world suddenly opened to me. But there was one big problem—the language barrier. I had to spend my first year in the United States simply learning how to communicate with classmates and friends. There were many times where I didn't understand the person I was talking to, and the misunderstanding created many awkward encounters. To overcome this problem, when I went home every day, I pushed myself to learn fifty new vocabulary words each night before going to sleep. It is through learning a new language that I realized the power and importance of resiliency and a strong work ethic.

These two attributes have played a big role in my entrepreneurship career and my life. I experience obstacles constantly. However, if I give up right away, I know I am not going to accomplish anything. The same applies to my work ethic. When I work, I give 100 percent of my attention and efforts to the tasks at hand. I focus on whatever I am doing and get it done. Many young people seem to give up or procrastinate easily because they don't see an end goal. Set yourself mini goals, work until you accomplish them, and after awhile, you will achieve something big.

GETTING STARTED

While I was still having a tough time socializing and fitting in with a new group of friends, most of my free time was spent at home browsing the Internet. One day, I randomly stumbled upon TechCrunch, a prominent technology blog, and was instantly fascinated by how simple technologies could make people's lives better. I continued to do some research and found out that the main skill required in building these simple technologies was computer programming. I knew this was something I could learn in my free time and excel at, because I had already put myself through a similar learning curve with English, and I was really passionate about using technology to solve problems around us.

As I followed the industry for few more weeks, the success stories of young entrepreneurs inspired me to start something on my own. I thought, "Since there's nothing to lose, why not just get started?"

I brainstormed for a bit and settled on the idea of making a site for social quizzing. By learning how to code through actually building something instead of reading books on the methodologies behind computer science, OneExtraLap (a website for people to create and take quizzes while competing with their friends) was born.

STRUGGLES AT THE START

Building OneExtraLap wasn't easy at first. Since I didn't know anyone who could give me programming advice, I had to figure things out myself. I searched for code samples online, copied them to my local server, ran the program, and learned what each line did.

When the code worked, I was happy. But a majority of the time, the code would contain some sort of error and I would again begin the lengthy process of learning that I had become so accustomed to undergoing. The problem-solving skill I learned was very useful in all my future projects, because, when I built my own applications, I always had to figure out solutions to any problems I saw along the way, whether it was how to find users, how to market my apps, how to fix bugs, etc. When I had to fix a problem, I tried different ways to deal with it. When I figured out the solution, I then knew what to do the next time, and repeated that process.

LAUNCHING

With a perfectionist mindset, I made sure every line of code was indented correctly and every pixel was aligned accurately.

On August 8, 2010, after nearly eight months of hard work and two major revisions to the website, I released OneExtraLap to the public. People who had been following me via Twitter and my personal e-mail list loved the site. They explored what I had created and gave me high praise for taking initiative and building such a fine site in only eight months.

I still remember those few weeks vividly in my head because of all the praise and encouragement I received. After two years in the United States, I finally finished something I was proud of. At that moment, I felt like I could take things further and that OneExtraLap might have a great future!

SOLVING A REAL PROBLEM

After the initial influx of traffic, people's enthusiasm started to gradually decrease. With constant user feedback, I came to the realization that, as a social quizzing website, OneExtraLap didn't solve any problems people had. It was a fun site to play around with, but for people to come back to use it constantly and for it to generate revenue, the site had to fulfill people's needs.

This was the biggest business lesson I learned along the way. The best ideas will still fail if no one has a use for them. Now, every time I start a project, I do basic user research to see whether or not my ideas solve people's problems or fulfill people's needs.

And that was how my second project was born—iTunes Instant. After Google released their instant search feature where users would get immediate results after typing in a query, I thought it would be really helpful to build a similar feature for iTunes. The native iTunes app on Mac and PC was slow and cluttered, so I decided to build a web interface to display clean search results quickly for iTunes. I made the design and wrote all the code in around three hours, and launched it on a Saturday night.

PITCHING TO THE PRESS

The following day, I wanted to spread the word as soon as possible. My main strategy was to tweet highly followed tech folks like Robert Scoble, hoping that they would evangelize my new product. Soon, many people fell in love with the simplicity and speed of the site and helped spread the news about iTunes Instant.

The site ended up generating 10,000 visitors in less than twenty-four hours.

On Monday, I woke up at 5 a.m. to write several personally addressed e-mails to technology bloggers asking them to check out iTunes Instant. I honestly didn't expect anything from them considering how many e-mails bloggers receive on a daily basis. After sending those e-mails, I went to school as usual. But when I took out my phone and checked my Twitter stream, I realized the site was going viral. Mashable, a prominent tech blog, had posted a feature story about iTunes Instant that morning and the story was being syndicated all over the web. In the next couple of days, iTunes Instant was featured on *Gizmodo, The Atlantic, Fast Company,* and more. The site's traffic skyrocketed and many polite, wonderful people sent me thank-you notes for building something that made their lives easier.

Obviously, building something shouldn't just be done for getting press. It's important to remember that what really matters are your customers and users. However, it's nice to receive some recognition for all the hard work, and that attention can turn into great opportunities later on.

BUILDING ON TOP OF SUCCESS

Don't give up. Grasp every chance like there's no other. Throughout the crazy week with iTunes Instant, I got several requests to do additional work for other companies, one of them being Warner Music. Of course, I wasn't going to let them go. I took the job and started getting into free-lance work. Not only was I satisfied with some of the side income I was making, but I also learned how to effectively communicate with clients. This process indirectly helped improve my English quite a bit as well.

Besides work opportunities, I also received many interview requests from various blogs and magazines. I began to share lessons I learned along my journey, and answered questions about myself that really helped me discover what I believed in both personally and profes-sionally.

Overall, it has been a tremendous ride with ups-and-downs, and I think the big takeaway for you, the reader, is to not worry about what people think of what you are doing. Starting something extraordinary at such a tender age is not a common scenario in today's society (or not yet, at least), and there certainly will be people who discourage you along the way. However, understand that this is your life and your journey; therefore no one's opinions should determine what you ulti-mately do. As long as you believe in what you want to accomplish, work resiliently every day and soon you will prove the naysayers wrong.

Corey Freeman

I'M A BLACK, LESBIAN, FEMALE, COLLEGE DROPOUT, OCD, INTERNET ENTREPRENEUR

*Eager to get started as an entrepreneur, **Corey Freeman** has been helping others with their online presence since age fourteen. Developing WordPress websites for her parents, and then for clients around the globe, she began a personal branding journey that would continue strong right into her twenties. Corey has run countless websites and worked in a multitude of online fields such as freelance writing, consulting, technical writing, video production, search engine optimization, and web design and development. She continues to add to her "Do-It-Yourself" arsenal with the goal of making the Internet easier to understand for everyone. After being introduced to Headway Themes in 2009, she became a specialist in the Internet's easiest WordPress framework. With her launch of Headway101 in January 2012, Corey has been teaching small businesses and individual professionals how to build their own websites through extensive training materials and expert consulting services. At age twenty, Corey is the president and CEO of "Corey Freeman International LLC" and dreams of becoming a philanthropist and public advocate for equality and social acceptance. She is currently developing a YouTube talk show from her desk in Raleigh, North Carolina.*

My name is Corey Freeman, and I'm a black, lesbian, female, college dropout, OCD Internet entrepreneur. That, my friends, is a lot of labels. But I like labels. Even if they're diagnoses. Which I happen to have.

Medically speaking, I have general anxiety, as well as depression and obsessive-compulsive disorder (OCD). The trauma-based kind, not the kind you're born with. Think *Monk*, not Emma Pillsbury from *Glee*. I obsess over things, have weird quirks, and talk to myself a ton. Sometimes in public. I also have nightmares about dirty bathrooms, and an intense fear of insects. Anything with more than four legs just isn't natural.

I started blogging and building websites after moving to North Carolina at age ten because I had trouble making new friends. My best friend from New Jersey showed me Geocities, a simple drag-and-drop webpage builder owned by Yahoo!. After making startlingly ugly websites about myself, which included my unfinished writings, I was hooked. I've created blogs, forums, membership sites, webcomics, and even hand-coded beta versions of "the next big thing." I never did launch that thing. . . .

In August 2009, I learned about Headway Themes, a WordPress theme framework that made it easy for anyone to make a custom WordPress design. I took to it pretty intuitively, and built a website called "Headway Hacks" (eventually rebranded as "Headway Hub") that attracted the attention of the original theme developers. In November 2009, I was hired as their first official support moderator because of my abilities.

But, to go back a few years from that point, what I now affectionately call the "brain crazies" began around age fourteen. My parents separated, Mom moved out, I was just entering high school, and I was less than a year away from realizing that I had a thing for girls. My body was changing, my world was changing, and something buried deep inside my brain was starting to take over.

I wasn't a popular kid in high school. I was always sort of a weird child, with high energy and a tendency to talk way too much. I'm pretty sure the only reason I had friends was because I was in the band program, and even then it was about being great at playing my instrument, not my stunning personality. The more things developed with my parents' divorce, the unhappier I became. I wasn't really a joy to be around.

I can summarize my high school experience as sleeping too much, going to band practice, and feeling completely and utterly alone. I had a few friends, and my family was incredibly supportive, but the kind of rift an ongoing parental separation creates in a child is almost indescribable. I didn't feel like I had anyone I could talk to. And the undiagnosed OCD I was walking around with at the time meant I could spend hours and hours feeling guilty or upset about something I had said to someone or someone had said to me, or even something "stupid" I did, like tripping over a picnic table or forgetting to hand in a homework assignment.

And then my dog died, on my mother's birthday, and everything went dark from there.

Fast-forward a bunch of sleeping and yelling and crying to junior year, when my first girlfriend broke up with me and told me she never wanted to talk to me again. I was devastated, and in that devastation, I got a bottle of Drano from Home Depot and stared at its green, slick contents in front of my bathroom mirror. The smell was nasty, but I was pretty sure I could get it down once I started.

I didn't drink it.

A friend I told had me pulled out of class the next day and sent to the school counselor. I tried therapy for a while before I headed off to college, where the brain crazies followed.

I joined the freshman class of 2010 at North Carolina State University, ready to major in business administration and fulfill my true calling as a powerful corporate force for good. And then I found out I liked learning, not paperwork. And in contrast with what my family had told me, I didn't shine in college. I was just as awkward and alone as I was back in high school.

I told an acquaintance about my recurring suicidal thoughts and once again found myself tricked into talking to a counselor. This time, the therapist I spoke to suggested I try taking an antidepressant. Having felt depressed for a few years now, I decided to give it a try.

They gave me Prozac, and two other medications I don't remember the names of, but that didn't really do much. The Prozac helped just a little, though, and I began to feel more productive as my obsessive thoughts quieted down.

With my newfound "brain silence," I preferred to place my priorities on hanging out with the few friends I could round up and trying to impress the girl I'd fallen for. I skipped classes, avoided homework, and only barely passed my first semester.

At the same time, I was also becoming the go-to expert for Headway Themes. I moderated the forums, built websites, did screencasts when my roommate was away from the dorm room, and tried my best to manage the tide of e-mails sweeping in everyday.

Then I was dumped, again, and things began to go downhill once more. In April 2011, I asked my friends to drive me to the hospital so I didn't hurt myself. After I returned from the hospital, I quit my job as a support moderator at Headway Themes, and sold off all of my Headway-related websites and assets to their company.

I was academically suspended after failing my math class second semester, and although I took a summer class to pass it, I eventually became overwhelmed by the idea of college in general. On October 14, 2011, I officially withdrew from NCSU. Formal education isn't for everyone, and it turns out it definitely wasn't for me.

I now think of dropping out as the best decision I've ever made, but it wasn't an inspiring time in my life. My parents were upset and decided to all but cut me off financially. They told me I had to figure out how to pay my own bills by the time my lease was up or I'd have to move back home. I spent months barely able to cover the cost of food or toilet paper. McDonald's became my best friend, and running a business became a life-or-death scenario. Despite the viewpoint of general society, I didn't think moving back in with my parents was an option if I wanted to keep my sanity.

There was no planning; I just took what I knew I was good at and decided that if someone had paid me once, they would pay me again. Sadly, this sink-or-swim decision was hardly an overnight success.

A regular client went from paying to not paying to only paying values he made up off the top of his head. The last straw was when he called me from another continent just to help him fix his personal Internet connection.

I also tried joining a startup with a promising regular salary, only to find my hours cut from forty a week to just two within two weeks. The owners hired me without knowing the full extent of my skillset, wasted time explaining tasks I was already trained to do, and then began asking me to do every job under the sun except the one I was hired for. I quit pretty quickly, because there's more money in hustling for clients who respect you than accepting regular pennies from "startups" that don't.

What was eventually "Headway101" started as "HeadwayExpert .com," with the intention of cramming my authority down the throat of anyone who would listen. "Hire me because there's nobody better" was my sink-or-swim sales pitch.

My return to Headway coincided with their release of Version 3 of their product, and so I started a website with the goal of working with the latest release only and charged for any service I could provide. Consulting, design, development, maintenance, fixing random stuff, whatever. All my tutorials were free with the intent to drive traffic and rank as high as possible on popular search engines. More eyes, more money.

The return to Headway Themes also meant a return to therapy. I met my current therapist just before I dropped out in October 2011, and it was through her that I somehow made it to where I am now. I actually canceled a lot of appointments due to "illness" and skipped a few because I didn't want to go until I built up a relationship with her. Without that impartial, persistent voice, I wouldn't have made it. Before her, I'd had four therapists. One who talked mostly about her own son, one who looked like Christian Bale, one who used the "tough love" approach a little too much, and one who was old enough to be my grandmother.

I had business help from people I'd met mostly on Twitter along my journey, including one of the top UK marketing bloggers and several WordPress–inclined colleagues.

Ironically, a personal argument with the cofounder of Headway Themes actually meant they were uninterested and against me for most of the start of my website. But I eventually apologized for the tiff, and now we work together fairly well. In the long run, it pays off to put away your pride and have an adult discussion.

In February 2012, I wrote an 11,000-word e-book on the new version of Headway (it's outdated now, unfortunately) and gave it away for free to grow my list. As the traction for my site continued to grow, I realized that I had accidentally become both a Headway Themes expert and a blogging expert. In between napping, building websites had become my "10,000" hours, Gladwell-esque experience.

February was also when I started on my medications again, after my best friend told me it was her or my depression. I learned that what I'd been given by my first psychiatrist, which was tweaked by the second, was nowhere near as "aggressive" as an approach required for treating years of depression. She wiped my medical slate and gave me one pill of Paxil. That little pill laid me flat for seven days while it adjusted in my system, and suddenly there was a wall between me and the black hole of my depression. I could breathe, I could focus, and I could work.

Speaking for myself, I'm now a superfan of psychopharmacology. Paired with therapy, of course.

The ultimate choice to move my business to a paid membership site, a choice that now pays my rent, was half whim and half knowing that I didn't want my previous overwhelming experience from Headway Hacks to carry over to Headway101. I wanted to be an expert, but not a free one. In the end, it turned out to be a genius move. The freedom of passive income now makes me a true believer in so many things. Blogging, authority, the power of your own skilled hands, and endless possibilities.

I'm by no means cured of my brain crazies, but they're part of my appeal now. I've learned how to own my downsides so that nobody can use them against me. And I've also learned that whether you're the client or the provider, it pays to know what the hell you're talking about. Especially if someone's brain is on the line.

Above all, you just have to keep going. Because more likely than not, everything is going to be okay.

LEARN

Do not be embarrassed by your failures,

learn from them and start again.

-RICHARD BRANSON

Conrad Farnsworth

FARNSWORTH FACES HIS
FATE OF FUSION

Conrad Farnsworth *is a nineteen-year-old college student attending the South Dakota School of Mines and Technology. At the age of seventeen, in his garage, he built and operated the first nuclear fusion reactor within the state of Wyoming. He has been featured on Fox News,* The Huffington Post, *and RIA Novosti. Currently, Conrad is working in conjunction with another* 2 Billion Under 20 *contributor—Siouxsie Downs—in an effort to usher in the next generation of nuclear reactors.*

December 1, 2011. I'll never forget that date. It was the day that I became the first person in the state of Wyoming to successfully unleash the full potential of the atom. The feeling was unbelievable . . . but I had more work to do.

I had invested a little less than two years' worth of work into this incredible device. The path to fusion was paved with bad ideas, mistakes, near-death experiences, friends, failures, and new opportunities. The end result was exciting, but not nearly as memorable as the experience I gained while building my nuclear fusion reactor. This is the important part to remember.

My journey toward achieving nuclear fusion began shortly after my freshman science fair. The project I had entered was absolutely pathetic. It landed me in third place . . . out of only three people in my category. I had put minimal effort into the project, yet expected to win. When I found out that I was unable to compete at the state level, the frustration sent me over the edge. Every project that placed higher than third place was allowed to participate in the state fair.

That evening, I vowed to outdo myself and everyone else around me. I was going to be the first person in the state to build a nuclear fusion reactor.

Work started with research on the subject. I joined what would now be known as the ".net" or fusor.net. From there I posted my first inquiry on fusion, asking what kind of material I should build my fusor out of. This is where I gained a very close friend. Will started his journey just a little before I started mine. He was incredibly friendly and was more than happy to help me help myself, absolutely refusing to "spoon-feed" me the answers to my never-ending barrage of questions. This turned out to be just what I needed. Learning to answer questions by myself was an invaluable skill Will taught along the way.

Another skill I picked up was networking. Will had actually reached out and connected with me, and was my first real connection in the world of people who studied and practiced nuclear fusion. Throughout my quest, I learned how to professionally communicate and network with others. This helped me obtain several parts and supplies, and also allowed me to hone my "people" skills, which were previously lacking.

Soon, I had the luxury of interacting with others, but still had to figure out how to do everything myself. When forming the mental image of fusor 2.0 (the one that actually worked), I knew I wanted to construct everything by myself so I could create the reactor that I wanted. The entire reactor was supported on a tube steel frame that I designed and constructed. My father donated 120 feet of steel tubing to my project (for which I am very grateful, because steel tubing is incredibly expensive). With the design still in my head, I slowed down and drew out everything to avoid errors in my construction (and thus save money). I then cut the steel into weldable segments and began construction. I never thought I would learn how to weld during my adventures into the realm of high-energy particle physics, but it turned out to be another neat experience.

Oftentimes, I get asked how much my reactor costs. The grand total for the reactor ended up being around $4,000 . . . or the entirety of my savings. Deciding to go financially independent on this project was an incredibly good idea. It gave me a feel as to what it's like to work with a budget. I know I only have "X" dollars, and I know the parts will cost "Y." It sounds like a skill that is common sense, however it really teaches you what to spend the big bucks on and what to skimp on. For example, I could spend $50 to $100 over the course of a project on copper vacuum gaskets that guarantee an ultra-high vacuum and are relatively cheap, or I could spend a little bit more on gaskets that are reusable but end up being more cost-effective at the end of all my experimentation.

I also learned a tremendous amount through a correctly proportioned balance of doing and reading. I often joke around and tell people that, "I don't read good." Aside from the grammatical inconsistencies, I honestly don't read very well. This was a double-edged sword as I was more than able to learn something by doing, but completely unable to avoid mistakes by learning through reading. This proved to be costly for me when I ordered several unnecessary items for my project and ended up having to scrap a $100 vacuum pump. On the flip side, a person could read about fusion and fusors and know everything about them, but have absolutely no idea how to operate the 7/16–end wrench and ratchet required to tighten a flange. As you go after your own goals, you'll learn not only best practices, but best principles as well.

In the end, it's not whether or not you are successful, but whether you learn anything in pursuit of your goals. Greatness and success are just by-products of a project in which a person learns.

Mohnish Soundararajan

WHAT KHAKIS AND COOKIE FLAVORS TAUGHT ME ABOUT LIFE

Mohnish Soundararajan *has worked with numerous controversial* New York Times *best-selling authors, including Robert Greene, Ryan Holiday, Dale J. Stephens, Charlie Hoehn, and more. In addition, he's also worked with Silicon Valley and St. Louis startups and nonprofits. He's currently working with a suite of book companies founded by Tucker Max and Zach Obront to help authors launch their platform, publish amazing books, and get those books famous. He's written for various media outlets, including Medium and Thought Catalog. You can find more about him at www.mohnish.net.*

About a year ago, I almost died.

"Hey, dick, let me in," I said. Of course, I knew how these things went. It was the classic "lockhimoutofthecaranddriveoff" maneuver. It was late, there were girls in the vicinity, and the conditions were perfect . . . why not make a scene? With no shits to give, I jumped on top of the car, Rambo-style. As I gripped the roof, I felt a jolt and the car started picking up speed. *Well fuck. He didn't know I was on the roof.* Within seconds, the car started to cover more ground, and the pace started to quicken. "Hey!" I yelled. No response, and the car started hitting twenty. Then thirty. Then without thinking, I smacked the windshield. My friend slammed on the brakes. I flew off and hit concrete.

Holy ouch. Not my finest moment.

Flash back to a few months prior. I was in student council. The dress code was khakis, but I was wearing jeans, because badasses wore jeans. Unsurprisingly, for a full forty-five minutes, the entire council started pontificating about cookie flavors. Chocolate. Shortbread. Banana-nut-pineapple-explosion (I don't really know). I remember thinking, "Man. I've never seen anyone so passionate about cookie flavors. *I'm not even that passionate about anything.*" And then, like an awkward cartoon piano, it hit me. "What exactly am I doing here?"

The guidance counselors of America (God bless their souls) told me what I was supposed to be since day one. Doctor. Engineer. Dentist. Make good money so you can buy girls pretty things and they'll let you have their babies, or however that worked. If you check off the boxes in life, you'll do *okay*. I was in all these clubs, doing all these activities, and I realized that, just as much as I did with the cookie flavors, I couldn't care less about any of this stuff. Like, nada. In the end, I was in school, but despite how busy I was, I wasn't doing anything that mattered to me.

Fact: I want a lot out of life. Just like you. But I looked around at all the guys who did exactly what they were supposed to do, and I realized that when I saw their lives (average, plain, normal, terrible comb-over), I didn't want that. Maybe other people do. But I know I don't. Especially not the comb-over. *Ew.*

So I ran for the hills and, instead, found keys.

I've never gotten a PhD. But from what I hear, for a tuition fee (a huge one) you get to learn from the professor, the guy who knows a lot more than you do. You get keys to the lab and you get to experiment in it. And you, because you're associated with the good name and prestige of the university, get a leg up. You can point and say, "Look at all the cool stuff I've done." In effect, swag is transferred and you build up a body of work over time.

This isn't too different from what I did; the only difference is that my professors covered my costs. Instead of receiving most of my education from high school, I learned a majority of what I know from the

Hard Knocks University of Life, and instead of enrolling in another impractical class rooted in theory, I enrolled in "the real world." I realized that this was a strategy I'd be using again, and again, and again. And, at first, I had to actively look for opportunities; they never, ever fell into my lap.

For startups, the first time I got keys to the lab was when I entered a shady pizza place. It was Entrepreneurs Meetup night, and the woman who was in charge of the whole thing gave me this weird hug that was almost sex. I walked it off, and started talking with people: locals with summer camps, IT backgrounds, etc. Then, Rasheed Sulaiman showed me a product of his tech startup on his iPad . . . I still remember how beautiful the user design interface was. I cornered him awkwardly and said the magic words. "For free, if you guys need help, I'm there." That was the start of a beautiful summer. I read books. I read blogs. And most of all, I got the chance, without paying a cent, to learn under Rasheed and experiment in his "lab." I did whatever I could to pump value to his company, and simply by association, I got street cred. I was slowly becoming the Drake of startups (or, at least I like to think so).

A few months later, I stumbled across Ryan Holiday's blog. He was a marketing strategist for best-selling authors and countless companies, including American Apparel. "He seems cool," I told my sister. I shot him an e-mail, basically saying in the most nonpathetic, nuanced way, *"I'll do anything for you."* He accepted my ask and gave me keys to another laboratory. I got to trade off the fact he was insanely reputable, and worked, through him, on marketing projects for various best-selling authors. I learned the tools of the trade, under his hand, and did so at a high-profile level. It was fun, and there's no better way to feel like a baller. And the best part? I didn't have to pay him a dime to learn under him and the authors he serviced. In fact, I started getting checks. Large ones.

I repeated this process over and over again and started learning more and more. More books, more experience, meeting more new, interesting people. And before I knew it, I became a completely different person. I wasn't in student council or a myriad of clubs, but I didn't have to be, because I was doing work I cared about that affected real people. The stakes were higher and I liked them that way. Now, I can say I worked for best-selling authors and high-growth startups. However, after seeing a glimpse of this road, I've learned that nothing is set in stone. It is fact that I'll continue reinventing myself.

That's how it works.

Falling on concrete was like falling on my face. Actually, scratch that. *I did* fall on my face. But it came to me. I was reckless. I was stupid. And, I was bored. There's nothing like *almost dying* that'll make you encounter your own mortality and realize that your time on this earth is very limited.

While I brushed it off in front of the guys and gals as "not a big deal," I was closer to death than I really needed to be. Truth is, I don't have a lot of time. A subway bus might run me over. A moped might fall from the sky. A unicorn might impale me while I'm crossing the street. I don't worry about these things; it's just that hitting concrete makes you realize that you don't have a lot of time. And, the thing is, I wouldn't want to waste it choosing cookie flavors and rocking khakis, either.

If you completely forgot to the read the cover of this book, there are a lot of kids under twenty years old. And the crazy thing is, they're all sitting at home, reading and doing things they'll never actually apply (what's the point of memorization when you're just going to look it up on Google and forget it right after the test?). And, no matter how much we try to pretend, they hate it. Back in the Renaissance, arguably the greatest innovation boom in history, apprentices learned under a master for free. They weren't paid, and they didn't have to be paid, because they got keys to the lab and their costs (food, clothes, etc.) were covered. And the crazy part? They didn't have iPhones or Snapchat or MacBooks. They created great things and made lasting work with their bare hands, and without Candy Crush.

People can choose to do great things. They can also choose to refuse education on a one-size-fits-all platter. They can choose to learn and do work with the best, for the best, for projects and people that matter.

However you decide to go about teaching yourself, it is up to you to get an education.

Javier Sandoval

WHAT I LEARNED
FROM THE SEVENTY-SOMETHING-
YEAR-OLD BACHELOR

Javier Sandoval *began working at the Clarion Content consulting company at age sixteen, and one year later rose to vice president. He became a QuestBridge Scholar for Brown University, but left after a couple of weeks to join startup Fanzo in the Seattle Techstars program, where he was the second youngest person to ever go through the program (behind Zak Kukoff, another 2 Billion Under 20 contributor). When he's not working on Fanzo, consulting, or teaching at Brown, he's finishing up his first novel,* Penelope.

It's surprisingly clean. The walls confess, "bachelor." They're white and naked, void of family portraits. A whiff of tobacco smoke, wood, leather, and cologne is in the air; then seems to fade as I slide onto the couch. Even though he's since removed the plastic covering, I remember this couch from Grandma's. I wait for him to remove his shined shoes and dress coat; I don't remember him dressing so nicely. A pile of tiny tidy books sits next to me, and I lean over to pick one of them up. The book, thin enough to carry around in a jeans pocket, reads, *Conversation, Manners, and Eloquence.* I'd be less surprised if I had found the Bible—and it's well known that he knows no God.

He sits across from me and runs his hand through his paper-white hair. It's full and thick; he takes pride in it and keeps it well trimmed—like his fingernails. "She found me interesting," he begins to explain about his forty-two-year-younger girlfriend. He's never spoken to me man-to-man before, so I lean in to trap all his words. We finish discussing her, so I inquire about the books. The only thing my father has ever told me about my grandpa is how he often came home, stumbling through the doorway drunk, messy, and defeated. These books tell an opposite story, and I wished to listen.

He looks at me, his eyes a soft green, but his stare a hard gray, and says, "I found myself alone. My friends left me, my family left me, even liquor left me because I couldn't afford it. It was my fault; I make no excuses. But that day I realized the only thing I actually own is myself. No family, no property, just my pride. I decided to better myself, to invest in myself." He started by learning, by reading self-help books, then by leaving behind his drinking buddies. His eyes jolt at the mention of his friends; separating himself from what he's always known must have terrified him. "I'm still learning," he confessed apologetically. It's the closest thing to an "I'm sorry" I've ever heard from him.

Although our family refuses to take him back for all of his previous abuses, he now impresses others. His neighbors have elected him Neighborhood President, young women beg him to tell stories, and the old men at the park brag about knowing him. Everyone refers to him as the "Professor" now.

Leaning back, with no familiar plastic squeak, I give him my respect and vow myself to change. He's right: People, respect, and objects come and go, but you're stuck with yourself. So make something positive of yourself.

Michael Costigan

HOW I'M TURNING MY AUDIENCE INTO A PLATFORM

*An internationally recognized speaker, **Michael Costigan** has connected with thousands of students across different countries and cultures. He has received numerous honors for his work and was recently named "Young Business Leader of the Year" by the National Financial Educators Council. As a thirteen-year-old, he set off to start his first business, madFusion. Written off and rejected by many for being too young or too inexperienced, he rose above skepticism to become what many said he never could. Now, years later, he strives to help teens facing the very same issues he faced. At twenty, he relates to young people as he shares their experiences—their insecurities, their struggles, and the reality of growing up today. Michael has been featured on ABC, CBS, FOX, and NPR. He is a TEDx speaker and an active contributor to Entrepreneur .com and Inc.com. Michael has worked with groups of parents, educators, and nonprofits to influence people from around the country to help teens lead their generation. He also manages business development at TeleSign.*

WHAT DO I DO?

As a young entrepreneur, I'm often asked to clarify what my business is. No, I don't own a tech startup, run a flashy online retail site, or offer to optimize people's search engine rankings. I'm a youth leadership specialist, and I've been speaking professionally for three years now. I've spoken to audiences ranging from 50 people to 5,000 people, around the world, sharing stages with leading experts at numerous youth conferences, the Young Leader's Gulf Forum, and even TED. I help teens find their passions and discover their futures. Throughout this adventure it quickly became apparent that I needed a way to stay engaged with students and educators after I finished speaking at an event.

The great thing about public speaking is the way in which it lends itself to creating a platform. A platform for one's ideas online, over e-mail, in a book, or even on traditional TV and radio is of high value. Most successful speakers want some sort of a platform, a place where they can continue to share their message and ideas for all followers to hear. For most speakers, though, this stops at a Facebook page, Twitter account, or blog. While all of these are essential to having a platform, they won't necessarily make you a widely recognized expert on your subject matter. To borrow a term from one of my mentors, Josh Shipp, what many of us really want to be is "content celebrities."

PERSONAL BRANDING 2.0

Each year, hundreds (if not thousands) of individuals create an online presence and attempt to share their own advice for the betterment of other people's lives (or, as it sometimes appears, just to hear themselves talk). The self-help industry in the United States generates somewhere between $11–12 billion a year, which puts it on par with the private cloud market.

Hate it or love it, self-help is probably here to stay. And I'll be the first one to say it can be sleazy, disingenuous, and sometimes full of scams. Often when we think self-help, we think late-night infomercials, mail-order weight-loss programs, and endlessly scrolling sales pages on the web. Sure, this stuff might make its owners quite a bit of cash, but it's not the type of personal brand I am building.

We live in times where education is becoming democratized: where advice, strategies, and even positions are being sought after by highly specialized subject-matter experts rather than formal institutions, scientific journals, or talent searches. If you don't believe that this is happening, you need only to look at services like Skillshare, which allow anyone to teach an online class and charge for it, or Wikipedia, or experts like Ramit Sethi (author of *I Will Teach You to Be Rich)* who are hired to consult for Fortune 100 companies without ever having operated one. Some people see these changes as alarming, a threat to intelligent progress or a lowering of standards. I actually don't believe any of that is true, and this phenomenon isn't new. The U.S. government has been appointing noncareer diplomats without any "real" foreign policy experience to high ambassadorships for years, and almost all Fortune 500 consumer brands have turned to celebrities who are in touch with their target demographic for sales ideas and incentives at ever-increasing rates.

ACHIEVING THE LEVEL OF SUBJECT-MATTER EXPERT

Today's digital world makes it easier than ever to educate oneself, test out ideas, and sell services. If I want a great logo for a new product, I don't look for someone with a BA in Graphic Design; I look for someone who has an awesome portfolio online, and someone who is respected in the design community on Twitter and Facebook.

For speakers like me, this means I ought to hone my craft, meticulously study my market, and break through traditional media barriers to inject myself into the national spotlight.

There's no special day when I will wake up and be a subject-matter expert. Rather, the term is one I hope will be bestowed upon me by those I interact with—the media personalities who interview me, the authors who publish my ideas in books, and the thousands of people who follow my advice to execute their own strategies that will enable them to overcome struggles and live out their passions. There comes a point when these things happen, when thousands of written words make up solid advice on a variety of life topics, when hundreds of speaking engagements reach hundreds of thousands of people, and when my experiences helping people become documented success stories.

ESTABLISHING A PERSONAL BRAND

By no means is there an official how-to guide for establishing a personal brand with an overarching platform, but here are some of the essentials.

You must choose a niche that you can focus all of your energy on. It is very important that the area you decide to become an expert in is one that you are intensely passionate about. If you never had to "work" another day again, would you still find yourself devoted to learning about this topic, desiring to help others with the knowledge you obtain?

Your niche must be simplified down to something for which there is a market. For example, if you want to become an expert on organically grown Colombian coffee beans, you might be better off tabling that for a specific article and focusing on becoming a "Coffee Expert" in general. Testing the market can be challenging, but things like Google Trends can be very revealing and show you whether or not people are searching for the area of expertise you hope to offer. Generally speaking, it is best to find sizable niches.

You must find a mentor in your field (someone who's already doing what you want to do, or similar enough that you can learn from them). A real mentor is at least five to ten years ahead of you in your field and has a sizable following. They're someone respected in your field and certainly someone who comes up in conversation with people in the same circle. I would suggest that you look for someone who has significant control over the market and who influences its standards and direction. Reaching out to this person can be complicated, but then again, you want to be sought after, too, one day, right?

Your materials must make you look five times more expensive than you actually are. Everyone judges books by their covers (you did before you bought this one) and they judge personal brands that way as well. If you have low-budget-looking materials, whether that be a website built with GoDaddy's site builder or YouTube videos shot in your bedroom, you won't get very much traction in the market. If you look like you should cost 20 bucks an hour, that's how much people will expect to pay, so aim to look instead like you're worth 1,000 bucks an hour and charge something less than that.

You must execute like crazy. I know everyone says this and that it's self-explanatory. But really, starting your own business is a challenge, and I honestly believe starting your own self-sufficient personal brand is harder. I've done both. Once you have all of these foundational items taken care of, your career is going to grow very slowly through manual campaigns. To fast-track your success, you must partner with people who are better known than you and get them to say positive things about you, co-author books with you, or direct client overflow to you. Don't approach people until you know you are ready or you risk alienating yourself from them and those they influence.

The rest is sort of a crapshoot . . . really. I've seen some speakers go from zero to six figures in a year and others struggle for three years. I was somewhere in-between. It can be frustrating to look at industry experts and see their success as so much beyond your own, but it's also important that you remember to study their first steps. Many say it takes ten years to become an overnight success and I believe it's true.

MINI FAILURES AND MINI SUCCESSES

You will have both. Throughout your journey as an entrepreneur/developer/speaker/doer/general badass (yes, feel free to use that as a business title and self-description after reading *2 Billion Under 20*), there will be roadblocks. Sometimes big ones, the kind that require you to pivot your business in a different direction. Roadblocks can be good; the sooner they come up, the better, because you would have run into them down the road anyway. Keeping a solid perspective will be your saving grace.

Not everyone is an entrepreneur. Not everyone should be an entrepreneur. I think that this is a view that should be more widely expressed. You know if you're the type of individual who will never be satisfied no matter how much you're paid or how well you're treated, as long as you're working to support someone else's vision. Almost all of us will fail at some point. Having been in this space for awhile now though, I can confidently say that those who have no fear of failing repeatedly, who are able to always get back up and try something different, usually do find success in their own way. However, if you're not an entrepreneur, these same rules still apply! All of us should learn what we are passionate about, and create our "brands" and "businesses" accordingly.

Peter Solway

WHAT COMPETING FOR A TENNIS GRAND SLAM TAUGHT ME ABOUT CHARACTER

At fifteen, **Peter Solway** *was traveling the world on a bootstrapped and self-sufficient budget as an international teenage tennis prodigy. After a year of touring and competing nationally (in his country of Australia) and internationally, Peter sustained a back injury that jeopardized his future tennis career. However, he quickly discovered the same passion and skills he had been cultivating in his sporting career served him equally well in business and entrepreneurship. By his first term in his final year of high school, Peter secured the importing contract for Arkon, a manufacturer and global supplier of car, home, and office mobile mounting solutions. At just seventeen years of age, he had outperformed his competitors, many years his senior, in the bid to be the company's Australian master distributor and online presence. He has started three businesses in his teens.*

Since I was old enough to remember, I had a competitive drive to be the best I could be. Failure was not an option. Naturally, since both my parents were tennis players, they introduced me to the sport at a young age. From the moment I touched my first racquet, I had one goal:

become the world's best tennis player, and win a Grand Slam (Australian Open, U.S. Open, French Open, and Wimbledon).

I used to watch the Grand Slam tournaments imagining it was me who'd just won those events. I practiced incessantly, and by the age of fifteen, found myself constantly taking time off from school to compete in tournaments and pursue my dream of being the best in the tennis game.

The International Junior Tennis Tour was my first international tour. My parents and I flew from Australia to New Zealand for a three-week tournament. After a grueling three weeks of sweat and near tears, I was excited to rank well enough to skip past the qualifying round in the next stage of tournaments. I knew this would allow me to focus my energies on the important stages of the upcoming tournaments and progress through the rankings faster.

But when we returned home, my parents sat me down for a heart-to-heart conversation. They knew I loved tennis, but flying internationally to compete was costly, and money didn't grow on trees. They told me I wasn't going to be able to continue competing. I stayed up all night thinking about how a lack of paper with green coloring could be a hindrance for people pursuing their dreams, but I didn't want that to be me. I wanted to compete. I needed to.

The next morning I asked my parents to have another conversation about the topic. My solution was to travel alone, rather than having them come along. I knew the cost of the tickets was the most expensive piece of traveling, and only having one ticket rather than three would cut that costs by two-thirds. They hesitated, knowing that I was fifteen years old at the time, but after seeing how determined I was to compete, they agreed.

I started planning more ways to cut the costs while I was on the road. I stayed in dingy hostels that only cost $10 a night and budgeted all my meals so that I was getting proper nutrition but cutting costs wherever possible. All in all, I was able to cut my personal costs in half, but I soon realized that wouldn't be enough.

I started looking for external funding. My parents and I reached out to coaches, friends, other tennis parents, and anyone we could think of who might be able to put us in touch with sponsors, grants, and other venues of support.

Every day, I filled out application after application and attended lots of meetings to try and secure enough funds to continue pursuing my dream. After much effort, I received two very supportive grants from the Revesby Workers Sports Club and the Peter Bullfrog Moore Foundation that allowed me to travel all over the world to compete.

Now that I didn't have to worry about money, I was able to work extremely hard and increase my world junior ranking to 550. Every couple of weeks, I sent my supporters updates that resulted in follow-on grants and additional support from their communities. And as my game became better, I grew more confident in my abilities and ended up renegotiating better racquet and gear sponsorships that led me to bigger and better tournaments.

But just a couple months later, my world came crashing down.

After a career-ending back injury, I was told I would never play tennis in the same way again. I could no longer compete. Everything I had worked so hard to achieve—beating the obstacles on the court and off of it—was over.

Was it all for nothing?

Spending a couple months to reflect on that question, I realized how formative these years were for me. I learned the value of a dollar. I learned about selling myself, my vision, and my passion, starting with my parents and working my way to corporate sponsors. I learned how to raise money. I learned about resilience. And most importantly, I learned what it takes to pursue something wholeheartedly. These lessons alone allowed me to go on to launch three businesses in my teens, and they will continue to serve me well for the remainder of my life.

You must be willing to play the game at any cost. You must be willing to make sacrifices, and you must be willing to sweat. At the end of the day, the lessons you learn, whether you realize it or not, will be applicable to other areas of your life. You can never truly fail, and you can always set your sights on winning the Grand Slam of another field if an injury, setback, or drop-off stops you in your first line of pursuit.

Fletcher Richman

"THE STARTUP OF YOU" AS A STUDENT

During his sophomore year in college, Fletcher Richman stumbled upon startups and was delighted to have already found what truly made him happy. He proceeded to completely immerse himself in the vibrant startup community of Boulder.

While in school, Fletcher got engaged in as many ways as he could—helping run the first ever TEDxCU and creating his own entrepreneurial club. After that, he was focused on building a bridge between the local startup community and the university by creating Spark Boulder, a nonprofit student coworking space. He and a few other students helped raise $140,000 to start the space, and it has helped hundreds of student entrepreneurs get involved in the local community since. Fletcher also has been involved with PivotDesk, a local startup, for more than two years. He started as an intern and taught himself web development, and now that he has graduated he works as a growth engineer—building internal business intelligence and analytics tools, as well as traveling the country to grow out some of PivotDesk's market presence in emerging startup communities. Locally, he's the organizer for Open Angel Forum and Boulder Beta.

Note: This is a perspective on how and why to get involved as a student entrepreneur through the themes of The Start-up of You *by Reid Hoffman and Ben Casnocha. It is an amazing read and I highly recommend it.*

In today's world, the skills and mindset of entrepreneurship are incredibly important for everyone, especially students. A college degree no longer guarantees you a stable career. Developing entrepreneurial skills gives you a great advantage in finding a job, creating your own job, or even pursuing your passions outside of entrepreneurship. By considering your life to be a startup that is in permanent beta (meaning you are always trying to improve), there is a clear set of steps you can follow to develop and improve yourself and your future.

1. DEVELOP A COMPETITIVE ADVANTAGE

Why it's important.

The first step is understanding yourself. You can start by understanding your assets, aspirations, and the market realities. *Assets* include hard assets (money, physical possessions, etc.) and soft assets (skills, experience, connections, etc.). *Aspirations* are defined by a simple but hard to answer question: Who and what do you want to be? That one question is something that many people are still trying to find the answer to, so don't worry if you don't know yet. *Market realities* are what people will actually pay you for.

Finding your competitive advantage is a constant reevaluation process, and arguably the most important step.

How I did it.

This is a step I'm still working on, and probably always will be. I've gone from a major in environmental engineering to one in electrical engineering, and then electrical and computer engineering, expanding and changing my competitive advantage each time. I have developed new assets to match my changing aspirations, which are moving to fit today's market realities. As a college student, my focus isn't on acquiring hard assets, just soft assets. When I started in school, I thought that the most important assets were concrete abilities like being able to solve math problems. What I have realized is that these skills give me an ability to execute, but I'm much more interested in the ability to explore and create. Therefore, I have focused my schoolwork and my life around becoming a disciplined explorer by developing a strategic and defined methodology for innovation.

2. PLAN TO ADAPT

Why it's important.

It's easy to just do the bare minimum of what it takes to get a degree, and not take advantage of the opportunities at college. Staying on track to graduate in four (or five) years is important, but you also need to be flexible about what you do while at school. You have a unique opportunity as a student to try a wide range of student organizations, internships, and hobbies while at college. A great way to test your competitive advantage is to find experiences that match your aspirations and get involved. By prioritizing learning during these experiences, you can grow your soft assets to match your aspirations. The best part about these experiences in college is that it's easy to quickly change where and what you spend your time on. As a student, there is no expectation of long-term commitment for almost anything you get involved in, which is a significant advantage in broadening your experiences.

How I did it.

As soon as I got to school, I started looking for ways to get involved. My freshmen year, I joined several student groups and got a part-time internship. I've shifted multiple times between various student groups in energy, leadership, and entrepreneurship. I continuously move toward groups that ignite my passion because I have found that the more passionate I am about something, the better work I do. One great example is the student group I took over, the Active Entrepreneurs at the University of Colorado. Two graduating seniors passed the club down to me with no members. I realized there was no group working to connect all the student-led startups on campus, so I built a website and started to bring them together. I got a $1,000 grant from AwesomeBoulder to put a giant whiteboard in the middle of campus and have students write ideas on it. I also started a weekly coworking session for students to get mentorship. Outside of school, I have been involved in internships in government, corporations, and the startup world. Internships are the perfect opportunity for a low commitment experience, so I'd recommend taking advantage of that and experiencing several different industries. I've been involved in clean tech, IT, and power systems, and real estate as well, and these varying experiences allow me to have a unique viewpoint on daily challenges.

3. BUILD A NETWORK

Why it's important.

The people you know are one of your most valuable assets. People can help provide resources, information, and opportunities. The people you surround yourself with are also a strong influence on who you become. By spending time with people you want to be like, you can change yourself to get closer to your aspirations.

How I did it.

The quickest and easiest way I saw to build my network was to use online tools. All of these services are free, and provide ways to expand my network and reinforce relationships.

I set up a Gmail account, and forwarded all of my e-mails to it. This made e-mail a thousand times easier and more efficient. I created a Twitter account, and followed all the groups and people I got involved with. Twitter is often an easy way to reach out to other entrepreneurs, and is a great promotional tool. I created a LinkedIn account. LinkedIn is a powerful professional networking tool that allows for easy introductions, and is valuable for understanding the history/background of people in your network. Add me as a connection if you want; I am happy to introduce you to any of my connections. I made an account on Meetup. Meetup helps you find local events and groups in areas that interest you. Boulder has an amazing variety of events. I made an account on Quora. This is an invaluable learning tool filled with a constantly growing knowledge base. I followed people like Jimmy Wales, founder of Wikipedia, and topics like startups, venture capital, and everything else that interested me.

4. PURSUE BREAKOUT OPPORTUNITIES

Why it's important.

To find and pursue breakout opportunities, the first key is curiosity. By exploring your areas of interest, you can tap into networks of opportunity and better understand how you can contribute.

How I did it.

I see attending and volunteering at events as the best way to satisfy my curiosity, meet new people, stay in touch with previous connections, and keep up-to-date on opportunities. I attend meet-ups, speaker series, and other entrepreneurial events as much as I can. Every time I go to an event, I seem to make a new connection or make progress in a way I never would have expected. I even got my current internship at PivotDesk by attending a pitch event they were at and following up with an e-mail letting them know their site was broken on tablets. Their VP of engineering offered to sit down with me for lunch, and a few weeks later I was hired as their first intern (and later as a full-time employee).

After attending many events, I started to help organize them as well, following the "give before you get" mentality of Boulder. Volunteering helps build my personal brand, while also giving me direct connections to influential people. I helped organize an event as part of Boulder Startup Week. After the event, I ended up meeting David, the lawyer who would become the first sponsor and key supporter of Spark Boulder. They helped us financially, did pro-bono legal work, and provided a foundation that allowed us to raise $140,000 in community support to create a 5,400-square-foot student coworking space. He's also now one of my good friends. It's incredible to think that none of that would have happened if I hadn't helped organize the event.

5. TAKE INTELLIGENT RISK AND TAP NETWORK INTELLIGENCE

Why it's important.

Once you find opportunity, you need to take action. Although it may seem like a lot of risk, I encourage you to just go for it. Start a new organization, build a prototype of your idea, or go do whatever you have always wanted. Once you get started, you have a chance to really utilize and accelerate the network and the knowledge you have been building.

How I did it.

I have found that pursuing the things I am passionate about leads to the highest likelihood of success. People can tell if you are genuine and passionate, and it is inspirational. It makes people want to see you succeed. Being active as an entrepreneur also helps you "make your own luck." Although many paths to success seem like luck, you have to put yourself out there to get into those lucky situations. I could give you specific details on how I took action, but they may be hard to apply to your situation. Instead, the following are a few of the tactics I use to maximize network intelligence and generate more opportunities.

I use online tools to stay in touch with people I meet. When I meet someone, I try to get a business card or phone number and follow up with a short e-mail and request to connect on LinkedIn. I also use tools to reach out to people I don't know; specifically through Twitter, LinkedIn, Quora, or by guessing their e-mail with Rapportive.

I seek out opportunities to connect like-minded people and groups when I recognize similarities or synergies. Just by knowing the people in your network, I can create opportunity through a simple e-mail or Twitter introduction. It might be for an internship opportunity, volunteering, or just to connect like-minded individuals. This is an easy way to gain credibility and people's trust/thanks.

I follow and promote interesting new companies and organizations on Twitter. Early stage companies appreciate a mention, follow, or retweet. Twitter can be used in a variety of ways: to give feedback, to connect, for promotion. Be creative!

I follow the practice of "give before you get." I try to give back and help others whenever I get the chance. At first you may feel like you can't do much, but people are often just looking for some feedback on their idea/product. By just taking a few minutes to try it out, you can provide them with an incredibly valuable service and maybe some ideas to improve their own company. This practice applies to any situation, improves the community as a whole, and will always come back to benefit you.

I don't pass up opportunities. I took on any challenge, big or small, until I was so busy that I had to prioritize.

(Note: These suggestions are very much opinions. They have worked well for me, but take them with a grain of salt because everyone has different strengths and weaknesses and therefore needs different strategies.)

And that's it! As you may have noticed, none of these steps have an "end." I just constantly iterate these steps, and they seem to complement each other more and more as I grow older.

So with that, I say welcome to the 2 Billion Under 20 community! The best part about being in this community, startup communities, and other similar groups, especially for a student, is that everyone is willing to take their time to help you out. Don't be afraid to seek out someone with whom you are interested in talking. Offer to take them for coffee. You will be surprised at who will say yes (pretty much everyone). Keep in mind that these are just the first few steps! What you do from here depends on what you are interested in. Whatever you do, it is important for you to focus on opportunities that fit within your skillset and aspirations.

Brett Neese

I COULD HAVE RUN AWAY . . .
BUT I DIDN'T

*Professionally, **Brett Neese** is the director of partnerships at Student-RND, a nonprofit, which aims to help high school and college students from across the United States fall in love with code and increase the diversity of young people in the technology industry. He's a passionate advocate for youth and plans to spend the rest of his life expanding opportunities for young people and defending students' rights.*

Personally, Brett loves music, writing, and traveling—he spent most of 2014 circumnavigating the globe via crowded airplanes, cramped boxcars, and tilting ships, and loved (almost) every moment of it. His Twitter handle is @brettneese.

Walking into the coffee shop that day was hard.

I was to meet an individual who I knew very little about. A colleague suggested I e-mail him—a colleague who I only knew through an exchange of about twenty e-mails. But I was determined and ambitious. I emptied my pockets for this trip, purchasing a Greyhound ticket and making room arrangements overnight through Airbnb. It was my first trip out of town on my own; I was in the real world.

And I was scared. I wasn't on a community college campus anymore. If something went wrong, I had nowhere to turn. I had passed my opportunity to bail. I was moving forward, for better or for worse.

As the clock neared our meeting time, I fidgeted. I resorted to using Foursquare to confirm that the individual who responded to my initial e-mail was the one I was staring down across the room. It was, as best as I could tell, and I hastily made my way over to his table.

Apparently, he had our meeting scheduled for the day prior and, by chance, happened to again be working out of that particular coffee shop that day. Because of this miscommunication, he had to run to a board meeting merely minutes after we started talking. I did manage to spit out what should have amounted to something resembling an elevator pitch, although the point was lost in my "freshman anxiety." I had obsessed about this meeting for days. I was driven and it was fate; I was going to be successful. I was anything but. While shaking extensively and attempting to vomit some words that made sense, my brain effectively shut down. The next time I saw him, only weeks later, I didn't even recognize him.

For whatever reason, I expected to walk out of that meeting with a $1 million seed round because that's how startups worked, right? The genius kid hustles his way to meet an influential investor and pitches a mere (but genius) idea, the investor connects the kid to lots of money, a company is formed, and the kid buys a Tesla and a giant house before proceeding to become exponentially rich and powerful. They turn his life story into a movie, starring either Justin Timberlake or Ashton Kutcher, and he lives happily ever after.

Unfortunately for me, that didn't happen. As I later learned, that never happens. Overnight success sometimes takes many, many, many sleepless nights and many, many, many failures.

For several weeks, I was destroyed. I had let myself down. I had screwed up. I had bet my entire life at the time on that meeting. I had convinced myself that this was how startups worked. I learned some hard truths very quickly. And, adding salt to my wounds, the individual wasn't actually an investor, and wouldn't have been in a position to write me a check even if I had pitched him perfectly.

I don't know why I didn't run away from the startup community and leave the entire crazy experience behind me like a sane and rational person would have. Except that maybe I was riding on a wave of angst and bravado that nobody could destroy, not even myself. I came back. I had some unfinished business. I wanted more.

I was not sane and rational. I could have run away. But I didn't.

I came back many times. I crashed in random lofts and in strangers' spare bedrooms. I attended meetings, meet-ups, conferences, startup weekends and startup fairs, and had coffee meetings and lunch meetings (and dinner meetings and brunch meetings). I seized every opportunity I could. I made my way across the state and across the country. San Francisco, Omaha, Minneapolis, Chicago, New York City; if there was something to be learned or someone to meet, I was there. Budgets were tiny and, for a long time, based entirely on my part-time minimum wage college job cleaning test tubes. But I had to be everywhere. I had to connect with everyone. I had to learn everything. I had to do whatever it took.

I'm not successful. I haven't started a major company or raised a bunch of money. I can build things, but I'm not exceptionally good at it. I've thought a lot about this. How could a guy who has failed so many times continue to get as many lucky breaks as I have?

Over time, however, I've developed a deep appreciation for simply how much I've grown. The people I met two years ago are now personal friends and colleagues. Some of my closest personal moments and milestones have been shared with them. My comfort zone has slowly expanded from the days of shaky coffee meetings to hosting and speaking at my own events. I've slowly created entirely different definitions for what success and failure are and mean to me.

But growth takes time. Learning takes time. It won't happen in one day. It may not happen in two years. And it takes many failures. But it happens.

Failure is only failure if you make it failure, and it's not the polar opposite of success. In a world that seems governed by immediate results, it's hard to truly appreciate the amount of knowledge to be gleaned from every failure and mistake you make. This, for me, has been one of the hardest lessons I've had to learn.

As I've grown older, I've begun to appreciate and treasure all of my experiences over the past few years, from the crazy ones (the time I had to walk ten miles to speak at an event in Omaha because I lost my wallet) to the sad ones (the day I was fired from an internship). They were all scary, weird, just a bit crazy, and, in many cases, incredibly uncomfortable.

If you're reading this, you'll likely experience similar phenomena at some point in your life (if you haven't already). You'll go through uncomfortable, embarrassing, and just plain crazy experiences. You'll be let down. You'll fail yourself. You'll fail a lot, actually. And you'll take it very personally.

Just don't go away.

While it's easy to think of these moments as failures, they're the exact opposite. If someone is bothering to criticize you, it's because they want to help you. Reading this won't make any of those moments of failure any easier. But it's your failures, crazy stories, and uncomfortable moments that you'll later find invaluable.

Today, the individual I met for coffee that dreadful day has become a fairly close friend, and he remains an incredibly important mentor. I may have embarrassed myself, but that was the true fate of our meeting and, as I later learned, we both knew it. Had I not bombed that meeting, or had I not recovered from the fact that I had bombed that meeting, the experience would've wound up as an erratic anecdote, an oddly colored thread on the quilt of my life. Instead, I decided to allow myself to learn from that moment. I now consider it one of the defining moments of my life. There isn't one path in life, and there are a lot of lessons that can only be learned by failure, so don't go away.

Nick Liow

THE STEREOTYPE OF A
SOCIALLY AWKWARD PROGRAMMER

Nick Liow *is a nineteen-year-old who is working to challenge copyright laws and build ways for creators to give to the public domain while also getting paid for their work. Originally from Vancouver, Canada, Nick skipped high school and began attending the University of British Columbia at fourteen to study computer science. He has previously built a handful of computer games and has interned for Electronic Arts (the makers of some of the world's most popular video games). He was awarded a Thiel Fellowship in 2013. He recently raised more than $40,000 through crowdsourcing for his new game,* Nothing to Hide, *which is an anti-stealth game that has been featured in* Forbes, Popular Science, *and* Opensource .com *among other media outlets.*

"So, um . . . here's the game I made . . . on my own."

"*That's great, Nick, would you like to talk more about it?*"

"If . . . if you don't mind."

There's some truth in the stereotype of the "socially awkward programmer."

Two years ago, I took a year off from school to fly down from Canada to the Bay Area for an internship at Electronic Arts (the makers of popular video games like *The Sims* and *Madden NFL*). On my first day, I introduced myself to our studio with zero confidence, as if I was afraid of myself. But every Friday, I was asked to show my week's work to the team. And with each passing Friday, I improved in presenting my work and myself.

By the end of my internship, I became confident in both my technical abilities and people skills. Or rather, just confident enough to be dangerous.

During the summer, I made a game-creation tool using my new-found programming prowess. My project garnered interest on a game developer forum, and it opened me up to constructive criticism. It stung for a bit, but it was much needed. With the forum's help, I made the tool bigger and better.

Confident up until that point, I took the project further. I launched a crowdfunding campaign on Kickstarter, thinking to myself the five fateful words: "How hard could this be?"

For every day of my Kickstarter campaign, I pestered my friends, cold-called dozens of blogs, and spammed my favorite forums and communities. I mentally strained myself for thirty days straight, soured some friendships, and was blocked or banned by people I admired. The Kickstarter *barely* succeeded, but at what cost?

The experience left me drained. I was convinced I would never be cut out for entrepreneurship. By the time school started up again, I was left with few friends; all my friends in school had moved on to the next year while I took my year off, and all my colleagues from Electronic Arts were in a different country.

I was alone with the one person I was most afraid of . . . myself.

A few months later, I visited that same game developer forum where it all began.

I helped others with technical problems, gave them constructive feedback, and shared my ups-and-downs with them. A forum regular recognized me from all those months back, and asked why my project had halted? It turns out he once had a project similar to mine and was an alumnus of WebFWD, Mozilla's startup accelerator program. He liked what I was doing, and wanted to connect me with the director of WebFWD.

My old self would have sheepishly said, "Thanks, but no thanks." But this time, something sparked in me. Maybe it was ambition for where I wanted to be, or anger at where I currently was. Whatever it was, I dropped all my courses the next *day*, and met with the director and asked to join the next WebFWD cohort.

He said yes.

Social skills aren't like technical skills. You can't just memorize a bunch of tips and tricks. It's about fundamentally *changing who you are*. In true techie fashion, I shall summarize my findings in list format.

Always get outside feedback. Not only can feedback help you test and refine your work, it can help you come up with new ideas. If you avoid or ignore constructive feedback, that's not "sticking to your vision," that's vanity.

Help others because you want to. Not just because you *shouldn't* expect anything in return, but also because you *literally can't*. There's no way of knowing who your best connections will be. I've contacted dozens of journalists to no avail, but it was one guy on a forum who got me into WebFWD.

Connect with others, for your own safety. Startups are stressful, and as young as we are, we have to be careful. We need to support each other, and be there for each other when it all becomes too much to handle alone (and it *will*).

A few weeks ago, I flew down to the Bay Area for my WebFWD inauguration. I met up with my former mentor from Electronic Arts, to catch up with each other, for old times' sake.

"Hey, Nick! How's that game-creation project you're working on?"

"It's going great! Would you like me to talk more about it?"

"If you don't mind."

Victoria Chok

CHOICES

Victoria Chok *was trained from the age of four professionally in ballet until injuries forced her to convert her passion into a hobby. She channeled her efforts into establishing a charity at fourteen to promote local artists to expand their creative works of art. The group's impact connected around 500 local artists to showcase their opportunities and at the same time fund-raising more than $100,000 for various charitable causes. She is currently the senior vice president of Nspire Innovation Network, Canada's largest nonprofit organization building leaders in a business and technology space. She leads the national team to create diverse initiatives, conferences, mentorships, and events—reaching more than one million people across North America. She was recognized as a "Global Changemaker" by the British Council; a "Global Teen Leader" with the We Are Family Foundation; and named one of Canada's "Top 20 Under 20" by the Youth in Motion. She is also an adviser to Pearson Education and a global ambassador with the International Association for Volunteer Efforts. She has held various positions at Royal Bank of Canada, Thomson Reuters, and Google. She is currently completing a Bachelor of Science with a major in geology at the University of Western Ontario. She will be joining PepsiCo as a financial analyst upon her graduation.*

Exhausted, I lay sprawled on a cold metal chair at the edge of the café in my local community center. My three remaining campers, whose parents seemed to "lose" track of time every Friday, alternated loud screams that irritated every bone of my tired body. It was a long week of work as a camp counselor and, as a recent high school graduate, the last thing on my to-do list was spending my Friday evening baby-sitting. Irritation was an understatement.

"Is this seat taken?" asked a middle-aged woman, her sweaty fore-head revealing that she had just finished a workout. I was not in the mood to yield a seat, even the one taken by my backpack, but I knew she was here to stay, so I reluctantly cleared the extra seat in order not to be rude.

"Excuse me?" she continued.

"Now what?" I thought. "I gave you what you asked for. What else do you want from me."

Once again, trying to be polite, I acknowledged her question.

"Do you have a phone charger I can borrow? I seem to have forgotten mine."

Great, she wants more.

As luck would have it, I forgot to put my charger away earlier, and it was in plain sight.

There's no getting away from this one. Maybe I'll be left in peace after she charges her phone.

Then, the unthinkable happened.

One kid . . . two kids . . . where was the third?!?

In the midst of talking to this mystery woman, I lost track of the third camper, and I knew his mother would be here any minute! In a frantic attempt to locate him, I left the other two campers with the woman using my charger. She was bound to the station with her device anyway. Luckily, I found the third camper hiding in a corner not far away.

Upon my return, I cringed as I realized my mistake in leaving the other two campers with an unvetted stranger, but to my surprise, they were both gathered around the "phone charger borrower," whom I later came to know as Joyce. This would be the first of many surprises from her.

"What's success?" blurted the youngest camper. This question obviously has a complex answer, one which I wasn't prepared to explain to a four-year-old.

"That's a very good question. What is success?" prodded Joyce, looking directly at me. I could sense it; she was turning my campers against me.

"Well . . . it's different for everyone. I guess, for me, it's whatever makes me happy," I replied uneasily. Right then, the campers' parents arrived to pick them up before I faced further interrogation.

"You know, I completely agree with your definition of success." Joyce seemed to be quite interested in this question. Right when I was about to go home and sleep, too. Darn. I decided to continue humoring her while I waited for my ride.

I described to her that my driving principle was happiness. Before every action that I take, I ask myself, "Will this make me happier?" Suddenly, this thought-provoking discussion energized me. Maybe Joyce wasn't so bad after all.

After what seemed to be an hour-long discussion, I learned that Joyce *was* quite an interesting person. She graduated from the same university that I was attending and pursued a career in finance. However, she felt unsatisfied that she was fulfilling the expectations of others and not her own. After much thought, she resigned and pursued a career in modeling. She possessed a certain air of eccentricity that made her story all the more appealing. It felt like I was watching a movie—each word that escaped her mouth kept me on the edge of my seat.

As we wrapped up our conversation, she mentioned that she was a strong advocate for the performing arts. A light bulb suddenly flashed in my mind. I was organizing a charity talent show in a week, and one of my guest judges had suddenly withdrawn their commitment just a couple days ago. This was my opportunity to keep in touch with Joyce and check something off of my to-do checklist.

A few e-mails and phone calls later, Joyce agreed to be an honorary judge for the performance. She also volunteered to be a guest speaker for our organizing team, since I just couldn't keep her inspirational story a secret.

The speech she later presented was nothing short of a revelation. She began with the question I was asked by my four-year-old camper. "What is success?" Joyce cleverly used this point to begin sharing her story, and listening to her past would soon become a defining moment in my teenage life.

The fluffy narrative of finding the inspiration to change careers was just the beginning. Her real story consisted of growing up in poverty and living through an unsettled separation, and an abusive relationship, where her children were forcefully taken away from her. Chills shot down my spine and tears formed in my eyes as she went on to describe her past in vivid detail. You could hear a pin drop in the room; everyone was listening intently.

Then, she shared four words that have become my guiding quote to date.

"Happiness is a choice."

During our first encounter, I would have never known about the many hardships she currently shared with us. The agonizing emotional pain from her troubles left her depressed; she only found sanity by biting a pencil to force a smile. She lost the ability to speak for years and lost the desire to live. In spite of adversity, after a few years she picked herself back up when there was no one else to rely on. At this point in her speech, there wasn't one dry eye left in the room.

A week later, Joyce performed phenomenally as a guest judge for the charity talent show. The event was a success and the crowd loved her enthusiasm and charisma. Only a few knew she hid her tears with a smile.

Her story left me thinking for days. Never have I felt so compelled to be positive. Joyce's story contributed to a seismic shift on my daily outlook. I spent many sleepless nights thinking about her shocking experiences, and how she still remained optimistic after all that she had been through. My memories of that day are as vivid and fresh as they were four years ago when I first lived them.

Shortly after the charity show, I sent a thank-you note to Joyce and an invitation for her to attend a formal celebration dinner. One day later, no response. One week later, no response. One year later, no response. I haven't heard a word from her since August 2009.

She did leave me with undoubtedly the best piece of advice I have ever received. We cannot control what position or situation we are placed in. However, our reactions to our surroundings are a choice. They are what define us.

And for that insight, I thank you, Joyce.

May we cross paths once again. You are the reason why I always carry a phone charger with me.

Tessa Zimmerman

THE THREE LESSONS FOR SUCCESS

Tessa Zimmerman has taken the health and wellness world by storm with a self-empowerment model for students called ASSET: Awareness, Self-Efficacy, Science of Happiness, Exploration, and Touch and Connection. In 2010, she started a blog called TeenSanity. She anticipated that only her parents would read it, and was greatly surprised when tens of thousands of visitors checked out her blog. Along the way, she found her voice in the wellness industry as the teen speaking up for what teens need, not what adults think they need. Taking everything she learned from mentors, books, and workshops, she created the ASSET model at sixteen. Today, Tessa blogs weekly on her site, iamtessa.com, has her own segment on FTNS radio, runs workshops, and speaks at schools. She was a member of Watson University's inaugural class. You can normally find Tessa interviewing health experts like Kris Carr, creating new recipes, meditating, or reading a book on business. While she appreciates open doors, she much prefers to bust down brick walls.

At thirteen I was diagnosed with four disorders: severe anxiety and panic disorder, post-traumatic stress disorder, obsessive-compulsive disorder, and depression. I was tired of being paralyzed by my own fears. I couldn't go to the grocery store without having a panic attack. I was obsessed with being perfect. I couldn't get more than four hours of sleep on a school night. My therapist told me I would live at home for the rest of my life. But a little voice, very faint, told me I could do much more than that. I could turn my life around. The voice inside my head insisted, and I listened to that slight bit of courage. By the time I was sixteen, I had a successful teen health blog. Now at age eighteen, I have a teen self-empowerment company. I give talks at schools, go on the radio, and facilitate workshops. I balance school, a healthy lifestyle, and a company. It's not always easy, but the pain I went through as a child motivates me to erase that suffering for future generations. I've got the motivation, but keeping it up can be tricky, especially when there seem to be a billion brick walls in my way. The most beautiful thing about these brick walls is they come with the best lessons. There are three lessons, in particular, that have changed my outlook and the success of my business.

LESSON ONE: TRUST YOUR GUT

My business could've been much less successful if I hadn't listened to myself and trusted my inner voice. In fact, I wouldn't have a business or courage or confidence at all, if it weren't for listening to the inner voice of Tessa. Now there are actually two voices in my head and in yours, too. There's the ego or fear voice. Then, there's your actual voice, the one that can jump over the obstacles, lead you to the best decisions, and help you to gain confidence within yourself. Now this may seem "out there," but know that in life, you're going to have to learn to listen to your own voice. When you listen to fear, you'll make unconscious decisions that often have great consequences. Fear guides us away from our authentic self, our best self. When we are not operating as our best selves, how could we possibly have a successful business, career, or life? Listen to yourself. Be guided by your intuition. Trust yourself.

LESSON TWO: LOVE FAILURE

When my mentor, Roman Price, told me to "befriend failure," I thought he was nuts. How could failure possibly be a good thing? It shows I am weak and stupid. I immediately brushed off the idea of befriending failure. I would not add it as a Facebook friend, or send it a Snapchat, so why would I have it in real life? Then things started to not go "my way" and I experienced . . . failure. Doors closed to opportunities and it caused me great distress. For days I'd be miserable, and I have a self-empowerment company. I mean, I needed to get my shit together! Failure in my business led me to believe I was a failure. And that just felt awful. (Let me tell you a secret: The ones who run self-empowerment companies . . . we need the most help!)

After multiple times of going down this failure track, I realized I needed a new approach. So I returned to my mentor, and of course he told me to "befriend failure." I thought, "Gosh, Roman, I was hoping you were going to offer me a different theory." But he didn't and I was forced to look at my challenges with new eyes. Instead of hating failure, I asked myself, "What did I learn from this experience?" That's when the failures turned into successes. I started to learn how to shift my company in the best direction by playing with different strategies. If something didn't work, instead of beating myself up, I tried a new tactic. When an opportunity closed, I looked at how I could find a better one. Failure isn't failure if you treat it as a stepping-stone to success. Love your failures, and you will grow yourself (and your company!) far beyond your expectations.

LESSON THREE: BE RESPECTFUL
AND *ALWAYS* BE HUMBLE

Being a teen entrepreneur, it's easy to get "big in the head." Sometimes you think you're better than anyone else. Like, "I run a company, take AP courses, and just biked ten miles while updating my tweets and checking my e-mail." That attitude is exactly how you will fail. No one (your parents, friends, future employers, business partners, etc.) wants to work with someone who thinks they're perfect, acts arrogant, and makes people feel bad about themselves.

Here's how to be respectful:

Show your gratitude. Say "thank you" when people take time to talk to you. It doesn't matter if they own a small business, are homeless, or on the *Forbes* 30 Under 30 list. They will remember you by how you treated them. Whenever I meet someone, I bring them a gift, just something little to represent how grateful I am for their time.

Be humble to your elders. They know far more than you because they have more years on you. Remember that!

Respect includes treating yourself well. If people who put you down surround you, then you need to step up and respect yourself. This can be a huge misconception when people are trying to push you. There are people who will push you and help you to grow, but if people are telling you "you suck," get out. You don't deserve to be treated like that and it will only hurt you and your endeavors.

There are many ups-and-downs in this teenage world, especially for those who go wholeheartedly after their passions. I'd be lying to you if I told you it was a piece of cake. I've had people tell me I will never make money doing what I love, or ask my favorite question: "What qualifies you to do this?" A trusted partner walked out on me. Events have flopped. Speeches have fumbled. But today I stand confident in my business and it's because of these very lessons that I am a success today.

Romain Vakilitabar

LESSONS LEARNED FROM SURVIVING IN THE SAHARAN DESERT

*After a bad accident where he almost lost his life, **Romain Vakilitabar** decided he would pursue a journey worth living. Since then, he spent years building a business doomed to fail, wrote a children's book communicating climate to younger audiences, and traveled the world with Unreasonable at Sea helping social entrepreneurs scale their business globally. Now, taking the experiences he's learned, Romain is the VP of marketing and global expansion at Watson University, a new university model that brings in fifteen of the most promising next generation leaders to Boulder, Colorado, where they learn the skills needed to solve the world's toughest intractable problems. He's lived in the townships of South Africa and was voluntarily homeless in the streets of Scandinavia in order to test the dogma that "need is the mother of all invention."*

"Come on Romain, be reasonable, you haven't really failed. In fact, you have gained a world of knowledge and experience." It was along those lines that my father offered his words of reassurance after I lost my grip on a business I had tried so hard to keep alive. At the time those words were as useless to me as a broken umbrella in a hurricane.

I was living in Boulder, Colorado, as a college dropout, struggling to revive my baby, a failing business. It was a business I had started in my freshman dorm room, which had grown to include a small team. And though recently I had felt on top of the world, things soon slipped out of my hands. After a string of terrible decisions, I was left without a cofounder and without my team. The best thing I had ever created was dying because of my naïveté, my lack of humility, and my inexperience.

Conflicted in a world where failure meant "doom" and "the end of the world," I packed up a bag and decided to run far away from what I saw as a shameful situation. My journey was long, filled with being the target of scams, being beaten up and stolen from. But accomplishing my goal of reaching the Saharan Desert to witness true simplicity and peace made all the adversity along the way inconsequential.

Lying on the Saharan Desert floor, I found a thin layer of sand crusted over my eyes when I woke up from a deep, uninterrupted sleep. Uninterrupted except for once, when I opened my eyes to view the brightest set of stars that had ever blanketed me. Awaking was the needed affirmation that none of what had happened the previous night was a dream. The campfire was now ashy. Miniscule particles from what was a blazing fire were taken with the desert wind somewhere. And though the fire was stifled, the lessons I learned from the Saharan nomads still burned strong within me.

Sprawled atop the cool morning sand of the Saharan Desert, I thought about the five lessons of the desert illuminated by the philosophical words of the desert nomads—words that charred through my "thick skin" and brought me back to my failure as an entrepreneur.

1. BRING ENOUGH WATER AND DON'T FINISH IT UNTIL YOU HAVE FOUND A NEW SOURCE AND HAVE TASTED ITS WATER.

To the desert nomads, this is a literal and figurative lesson in rationing and in being careful to not waste any resource. As water is indispensable in the desert, revenue is crucial for business. One of the most obvious mistakes I made as an entrepreneur was never identifying a clear revenue stream. Although I tapped into different markets and was making money, I abandoned them prematurely to find other markets where the revenue would flow in more copiously. I had identified a new source, but I did not "taste" it before abandoning my work in the markets I was currently dealing with. Never abandon those people to look for others who might pay more until you are absolutely certain the new market will pay more.

2. YOU CAN SURVIVE JUST FINE WITH THE ABSOLUTE MINIMUM.

The people of the desert have perfected this. More baggage means more weight, and more weight means more difficulty moving through the desert. They know what is absolutely necessary for survival; the rest is an inconvenience. Their supplies included water, food, wood, and blankets used to protect the food from sand, for staying warm at night, and as a saddle for their camels.

As a new business owner I focused too much on the business bling, like flashy business cards, uniforms, and superfluous equipment, which distracted me from the business that I really needed to take care of. Though we spent close to nothing in comparison to many startups (only because we were poor college students), our focus was directed at rather insignificant things. It was as if our desert tribe spent time and money purchasing neat desert uniforms or costumes, but forgot to buy water or save money to cover the food for our next journey. I learned how little I really needed for my business to succeed. In fact, it wasn't much more than Internet access.

3. YOU NEED TO HAVE PATIENCE.

When the conditions are not perfect, the desert nomads do not travel. It requires an incredible amount of patience to stay put, especially during Saharan windstorms, knowing that the longer one stays, the faster vital resources will be depleted. However, survival depends on patience. If you try to go too far, you will lose reference points and therefore lose your way. Patience is also tested when the water supply runs short. Nomads subsist one day at a time through the abominable heat, knowing that they will eventually find a new source to replenish their supplies.

My biggest weakness as a business owner was my lack of patience. I expected results to flourish overnight and I lacked the endurance to take one step at a time, understanding that each step would lead me closer to reaching success. So I stopped walking and let the heat wipe out my startup.

4. YOU HAVE TO KEEP REFERENCE POINTS.

When you are surrounded by only sand and sky, it is easy to get lost. And though desert nomads tend to have great sense of direction, getting lost in the unchanging background happens. The desert constantly changes when the wind blows. Thus, it is prudent, in fact imperative, to keep reference points so that when you do get lost you can track back to the last place of navigational familiarity.

The desert's reference points seem to be akin to key performance indicators (KPIs) in the world of business. It is important to have the right metrics of success, so that when times get rough, tracking back to the last point of business stability is possible. As an entrepreneur, I never set benchmarks and my goals were too long-term. When money ceased to come in, we were not sure how to adapt. Business changes almost as quickly as the wind blows, and it is imperative to know how to find your way through the changing landscape without getting lost.

5. THE DESERT DOES NOT ACCEPT EGOTISM OR INDIVIDUALITY.

Life in the desert is one of calculated risk, and there are many ill-fated decisions that can lead to one's demise. There are many uncertain situations such as questions of direction or availability of water. The desert does not accept egotism because when you are egotistic, you do not make cautious or calculated decisions. By the same token, individuality and thinking that you can survive on your own, without your tribe, has the same effect in our everyday lives as egotism in the desert.

My business failed because I was not willing to consider the thoughts and recommendations of others. I believed that my ideas carried more weight because the business idea was mine and the company was started in my dormitory room. I was egotistic and I equated the praise of my idea to praise for my business. As a result, I did not look at my business pragmatically. I expected customers to line up. And when they didn't, I blamed the difficulties on others, feeling I could manage better on my own. Not being pragmatic about my business and failing to appreciate the tribe that was working hard alongside me led to the demise of the startup.

My travels around the world helped me cope with the anguish of failure as an entrepreneur. I learned lessons in entrepreneurship everywhere I went: in small Vietnamese villages, cacophonous streets of India, and in poverty-stricken townships of South Africa. But it was living in the desert with desert nomads that shed light on all of the mistakes I had made as an entrepreneur. I'm still not sure if I was hypnotized by the campfire or whether these realizations came to me because the silence of the desert leaves a lot of room for thought. Maybe I had not yet gotten over my failure as an entrepreneur. But as I woke up with the sun and its complimentary heat lying on the soft mattress of sand, I realized that the desert and its tribesmen had answered all of my pressing questions for me.

I thought back to my father's words of reassurance after my business had failed, and I realized that failure does not represent "the end" as I had concluded at the time. It took six months traveling around the world to understand that. It took living in the Saharan Desert to understand that failure is just the start.

Zak Kukoff

FIVE MINUTES

Zak Kukoff is an eighteen-year-old social entrepreneur, and was the youngest person to ever graduate from Techstars, one of the world's top tech accelerators. Zak is the founder of Autism Ambassadors, a nonprofit that builds friendships between students with special needs and typical students in more than twenty-five schools throughout the United States and abroad. He also writes for The Huffington Post's *education section and helped organize both TEDxConejo and TEDxYouth @Conejo. He previously founded the education-technology startup TruantToday. His work has been featured in* The New York Times, *Tech-Crunch, Bloomberg View, The Next Web, and other well-known publications. He has also been honored by the Clinton Global Initiative and NBC Education Nation.*

"Five minutes."

That's how long it's going to be until I find out who was voted "Startup Most Likely to Succeed" at President Bill Clinton's Global Initiative Conference. I've spent all day in a building overlooking Lake Michigan, competing with four other CEOs for the opportunity to pitch my company to President Clinton. The winner would pitch live at the closing event, which is starting in just a few minutes and is packed with the kind of people who make the news every night.

I don't know what scares me more: winning, or not winning.

I shouldn't be nervous. I've spent hundreds of hours this summer practicing and refining my pitch for my company TruantToday, a truancy prevention system for schools worldwide, with my mentors at Techstars in Boulder, Colorado. The voters in the Clinton Global Initiative breakout session loved what they heard, especially the part about our pilot program projecting six-figure returns on its next-to-nothing investment. But now the aides are tallying up the votes, and my head and throat have that sensation of fatigue and dizziness I usually get right before I break out into a full fever. I'm trying to remind myself that, regardless of what happens, it's an honor just to be here on a day when most of my friends back home are in SAT prep classes or are flipping channels on their TVs.

In the corner, the aides have finished tallying up the votes. One of them, a young woman who looks somewhere between my age and the ages of the other CEOs, stands up and clears her throat.

"Okay, we have a winner . . ."

I stand up in my seat, thanking Scott Case (the founding CTO of Priceline and the current CEO of the Startup America Partnership) for his gracious introduction. It's all on me now; the entire room, including the former president, seems to shift its focus in my direction. I fall back on my practice and recite our elevator pitch from memory. A heartbeat or two, then applause.

The few months immediately after my sophomore year of high school were some of the busiest of my life. Between Techstars, the Clinton Global Initiative, and the NBC Education Nation Innovation Challenge (where TruantToday was voted as the "teachers' favorite" company shown at the conference), I racked up more frequent-flier miles than I knew what to do with and pitched my company more times than I previously thought possible. But one of the biggest lessons that I learned (repeatedly, I might add) is the importance of practice and preparedness, specifically, that practice makes permanent. Every time I practiced my pitch (multiple times per day), whether it was in front of friendly mentors, possible investors, or known critics, I solidified it and became more comfortable with it. The level you practice at directly determines the level at which you can perform at anything in life. And whether you're presenting to a friend or a former president, you can only do as well as you've practiced.

Arshdeep Sidhu

RUNNING WITH OPPORTUNITIES

Arshdeep Sidhu is a recent grad from the Ivey Business School. An experienced event organizer, he planned two of Canada's leading undergraduate technology conferences: Canadian Undergraduate Technology Conference and National Business and Technology Conference. Most notably, he led student engagement at OneProsper International, a non-profit that empowers small farmers in India with drip irrigation systems. His interests are in marketing and data analysis in retail and payments, having interned at Blackhawk Network, a prepaid payments company, and ConAgra Foods, a consumer-packaged goods company.

I love serendipity. Some of my most memorable experiences have been happy accidents or moments initiated from a "hell, why not" approach to life. It was a similar impulsive moment about two years ago that got me involved with a little-known nonprofit that had just launched a few months prior, OneProsper International. Its mission is to eradicate world hunger and poverty through the provision of drip irrigation systems to small farmers in developing countries. These systems provide water straight to the crops' roots, thus more efficiently using scarce water and more effectively growing an abundance of food. I instantly loved the mission and got involved.

Over the summer, going into my first year of university, I developed the model for the organization's university clubs and recruited more than fifteen of my friends and their friends from three universities in Ontario. Two of the clubs launched that September, and the third launched in January 2012. Following my early success and dedication, I was appointed to lead student operations by the executive director of OneProsper International in October 2011. I gave myself the fancy title of "President of the Student Strategic Team" and began planning for growth.

In addition to the university clubs I launched, the organization established four high school clubs in Toronto. Once I started to oversee the student division of the organization, I tried to get in touch with the representatives at those clubs. Initially, the high school members would not return my e-mails or messages on Facebook. After several attempts over two months, I finally was able to connect with everyone and receive status updates. In summary, the clubs were dysfunctional. They had the skeleton of a club, with people and positions, some ideas for events, and official recognition by the administration. However, there was no execution of their ideas. To make matters worse, the university-level clubs were forming similar characteristics to the high school clubs. I thought it was a lack of structure and support, so I worked on developing better communication methods and providing guidance for the executive teams, but after a few months there still was no impact.

As the school year came to an end in April 2012, I slowly started to "trim the fat" until I was the only student involved with the organization at a leadership level. I relaunched the clubs initiative with better frameworks, support networks, confidence, and (what I hoped would be) a better strategy. I focused on recruiting very talented and skilled people to the Student Strategic Team, and when faced with excuses regarding their prior commitments, I told people what Eric Schmidt told a young Sheryl Sandberg once. "If you're offered a seat on a rocket ship, don't ask what seat." This helped build the foundation for our future growth.

Our next leap came when we launched a creative social media video recruitment campaign in August 2012. Our team of five people made short, thirty-second video shout-outs for OneProsper International, with links to apply to be a part of the organization. They also made a longer informational video to appear in the description. We got friends who we thought were influential in some way in the community to do the same thing. A combination of timing, determination, and creativity made this campaign a huge success! More than fifty students from across two provinces applied to launch clubs at their schools.

Over the next year, we got more than 100 students actively involved in leadership positions, established a club presence at nine different campuses in Ontario, and also enlisted a high school Youth Council in Toronto. Most importantly, our initiatives changed the lives of more than 20 small farmers and have engaged more than 500,000 students through fund-raisers and youth-empowerment conferences. It has been quite a journey, but I believe we have only scratched the surface of the potential for this organization. We are currently organizing a conference with an aim to inspire more than 1,000 youth in person to solve world problems, pilot testing city-wide dodgeball tournaments at the middle school and high school level in the cities of Hamilton and Ottawa, and are planning to expand outside of Canada. From my experience I would like to share three of the most important things I've learned so far.

1. EXECUTE

I have a bad tendency to overthink, overplan, and daydream about how things might potentially develop. This wastes way too much time, and most plans never come to fruition exactly as you plan them anyway. The best alternative is to develop a strong vision and then just execute. React as needed; the strategy may change, but the vision should be big enough that it remains the same.

In September 2012, the high school teachers union in Ontario decided to strike over contract negotiations and sent a strong message that Ontario should cut all teacher involvement with extracurricular activities. With no teacher supervision, sports teams, school dances, and clubs, among other things, would vanish. We expected the provincial government to come and swiftly resolve the issue, but it dragged on for another five months, which was basically the entire school year. This was something the Student Strategic Team could never foresee, much less plan for. However, our vision was focused and we worked on alternative ways to achieve our goals. We launched regional committee models and encouraged students to host events outside of school during this time period.

2. EXCEPTIONAL PEOPLE NEED GUIDANCE AS WELL

The main reason that operations of our high school clubs in Toronto and university clubs were dysfunctional was because there was a lack of early guidance for the club executive teams. I believe we had exceptional people on the teams who wanted to create an impact, but there is often a myriad of other initiatives that members are involved in that can easily take priority when faced with early roadblocks. It is always difficult to start a new project from scratch, at any level. This is why it is often advisable to get a mentor for those attempting ventures with little prior experience.

I adjusted for our lack of guidance, and now we have Youth Coordinators that liaison and support (at most) three clubs or committees each. The Youth Coordinator is able to share ideas from other clubs, provide insights, and help direct anything from hiring an executive team to demonstrating how to successfully wrap up an event. Moreover, this improvement has increased communication throughout our operations and has cultivated a better culture in a virtual team that is often divided due to distance.

3. RELATIONSHIPS MATTER

My biggest priority has been recruiting talented students and keeping them passionate about the cause. When I first started, I began by reaching into my network. Luckily, I enjoy interacting with many people from a variety of different backgrounds, so it was not too difficult to get a few friends together at the beginning. Very shortly after,

I began to ask for favors, then more favors, and even more favors from other friends. I have realized it is a lot easier to ask and get things from friends than strangers. This taught me the value of building relationships early on, always looking to help others first before asking for help, and always appreciating favors, no matter how big or small.

Through building strong relationships I was able to secure strategic partnerships with some of the largest youth-oriented organizations in the province, such as DECA Ontario, Nspire Innovation Network, and the Ontario Students' Trustees Association.

However, none of this would have ever happened if I hadn't taken the chance to get involved with an unfamiliar, new nonprofit that I had stumbled upon a few years ago. Serenity brings opportunities but you need to be able to take risks (hell, why not?!) and get uncomfortable because that's when the magic happens.

Aaron Kleinert

FINDING BALANCE AS A HIGHLY RECRUITED STUDENT ATHLETE

*At seventeen, **Aaron Kleinert** is one of the top soccer players his age in the country. He is one of the Olympic Development Program's pool of 150 players from which they pull to create the national team. He is currently the captain of ODP's Region 3 Team, and was previously the captain of Boca United's nationally ranked football club as well as Boca Raton High School's nationally ranked team, before opting to join Orlando City S.C. MLS Youth Academy team in August 2014. He has been featured on TopDrawerSoccer.com among other websites, won tournaments across the country at his team's center defender position, and is currently being recruited by some of the nation's top Division 1 soccer teams.*

Balance is defined as comparing the value of one thing to another. This requires assessing the potential and necessity of each variable and adjusting the scales accordingly. Life itself is a challenge of balancing and pursuing the most important elements individually needed to fulfill your own niche on the planet.

Having soccer in my life has continually improved my ability to weigh situations on and off the field. I began playing soccer when I was eight years old as part of the Boca United Football Club. After realizing the opportunities I had moving forward with the game, I minimized appearances on other sports teams, including basketball and football. This was tough for a kid who just wanted to constantly run around and play. By making this decision, even as a young eight-year-old, I began considering my future as a serious student athlete and, potentially, professional player one day.

Going into middle and high school, the nights became longer with training and academics. In a household focused upon high academic standards, having athletic ability didn't mean studying was forgotten. Scheduling was always a priority, from hours of training at the gym and on the field to studies and homework. Every day after school, I'd be forced to sit down on the couch with textbooks next to me to review math lessons, and I would not be allowed to continue with soccer until homework was completed or specifically scheduled to be finished later that night. School was never a challenge, but if I was going to spend six hours a day in a general classroom setting learning information, I was going to strive to retain the important facts and thought processes we were supposed to learn from the experience.

While high school is a time for experimentation and socialization, as an athlete my course varied. Regimens of workouts and soccer drills replaced movie nights with friends and family weekend getaways on longer school breaks. Professional athletes, as well as aficionados in other walks of life, say it takes 10,000 hours to perfect a particular craft, but why limit myself to only 10,000 hours? The beautiful game of soccer is bigger than just twenty-two men running on a field for ninety minutes; it's a development of character and responsibility gained through victory and defeat, actions and reactions. Tactical soccer skills relate to the real world, from time management to making on-the-spot decisions and assessing their consequential outcomes.

Like my role model, Cristiano Ronaldo, has stated before, "I am not a perfectionist, but I like to feel that things are done well. More important than that, I feel an endless need to learn, to improve, to evolve, not only to please the coach and the fans, but also to feel satisfied with myself. It is my conviction that there are no limits to learning, and that it can never stop, no matter what our age." As a serious student athlete looking to one day turn professional, both on and off the field, balance has become the key lesson learned from which all my success derives.

Christopher Pruijsen

BIRTH AND REBIRTH AS A BURNER . . .
IT TOOK A WHILE TO GET HOME

Christopher Pruijsen *was the youngest-ever president of Oxford Entrepreneurs when he attended the University of Oxford, where he enrolled at age seventeen. He cofounded AMPION (formerly StartupBus Africa) after having cofounded Founderbus UK in 2012. AMPION now operates in sixteen countries in Africa.*

Currently, Chris is cofounder and CEO of Sterio.me, which reinforces learning with interactive and prerecorded audio lessons—accessible via any type of phone—no Internet or smartphone required. The Sterio.me technology enables learning across literacy, language, and data/device barriers. It was named by Fast Company *as one of the "10 Most Innovative Companies in Africa."*

On this flight back from San Francisco to London post–Burning Man, I feel again reborn as the man I always have been.

I understand that sounds pretty cryptic, and so does the title, but I hope what I have written below will shed some light both on those statements and my values and thought patterns as a human being. Take from it what you can. Quite frankly, I am grateful that you have taken the time to hear my story of radical self-expression.

My life started in 1993 in Rotterdam, Netherlands, and it was only soon afterward that I painfully lost my father when I was only two and a half years old. He was ruthlessly murdered, which is a story for another time, but the event shook the very foundation my family had previously stood on. It was not long before I became a ward of the state and grew up in state child care (orphanage from ages six to nine, and again when I was thirteen). With conflicting emotions toward my mother during those years of hardship, I was not an easy child. I couldn't find any intellectual fit with my immediate family and became aggressive due to an unstable home environment.

After a decade of despair, changing schools, fighting the foster care system, and endlessly exploring the world around me in search of true meaning and a mode for self-expression, I somehow, fortunately, ended up at Oxford when I was seventeen. Throughout my years there, I was wooed by big banks offering $70,000 starting salaries, which in the Netherlands is twice the national average family income (and a higher multiple of my family's income to date). But in 2012, upon receiving offers for investment banking careers at several big banks, becoming disillusioned, and experiencing the possibility of a more entrepreneurial path of life through the Global Entrepreneurship Summer School (GESS), the Kairos Society, and Oxford Entrepreneurs, I recognized my calling was actually not to work for banks and bureaucracy, but to create an impact as part of the entrepreneurial ecosystem.

What I have found is that, since the moment in April 2012 when I started on this path, my group of close friends has become much richer in personality and much more expansive, spanning not only countries and nationalities but also industries and generations. I started to connect more with people as I became less pitchy and arrogant and, in Burning Man terms, I became more inclusive as well as more participative in life. I started thinking less about my needs and desires and more about those of others. I went from orphan to adopted member of this larger global and entrepreneurial ecosystem. I had finally found a home.

At Burning Man there were 68,000 people this year. All these people spend a tremendous amount of time, money, effort, creativity, and love in order to create an experience in the desert for just one week a year. At the festival people wear whatever they want (if anything at all). There are classes every day on anything you can imagine, from AcroYoga to fire spinning and massage. There are massive parties, day and night, but also speakeasy venues, live music, and an incredible wealth of collaborative art experiences. People don't exchange currency for any of this, but merely ask you to participate in the festival by gifting something to the community in return for the gifts you receive from others, such as art, volunteerism, or experiences of your own for the community to interact with; everyone contributes. There is no capitalist exchange.

I've learned equally throughout my life and from Burning Man to think about my role in the world as well as the relation the world has with me. As I write this, the very real insecurities of being alone and by myself in this world come back to haunt me, but are quickly replaced by feelings of warmth and comfort as I think about my values and about the concept of happiness. I'd challenge you to think about what your friends mean to you, what you value in a friend, and about friendship itself. Think deeply about love and interconnectedness. As an orphan, trust me when I say that these are some of the things that matter most in life.

The journey you create for yourself may be hard. Despite your own potentially unsettling "start" or upbringing, you are defining your own path instead of following in the predefined footsteps of others. But once you discover who you are, a community of like-minded individuals all around the world will appear and open up to you, taking you in as one of their own.

You then will have found that ephemeral sense of belonging, a true intentional community. And trust me, nothing in the world provides a more profound sense of happiness and security than the sense of belonging that comes with a tribe.

Eric Arellano

ONE DROP IN A SLOW OCEAN

Eric Arellano *is seventeen years old and has founded two projects dedicated to providing clean water to the developing world. The Clean Water Utility Project, his more recent venture, partners with city governments to give residents the option to check "yes" on their water utility bill to automatically donate $1 every two months toward clean water in the developing world. In 2009, at age thirteen, he cofounded Just Dig It, an organization created "to provide access to clean water in the developing world, beginning with Ghana, West Africa." Before shifting its focus to the Clean Water Utility Project, Just Dig It raised more than $30,000 and provided clean water for nearly 1,750 Ghanaians through fundraisers and donations.*

Change is slow. Yet progress is constant.

Of course, as a young thirteen-year-old boy I couldn't comprehend the former. Trapped in the bubble of affluent suburbia, I couldn't begin to fathom that, in this day and age, 900 million people still couldn't get a glass of clean water. World Vision, a nonprofit fighting all aspects of poverty, held an event at my church which made me aware that in the time that I had taken my seventeen-minute shower that day, 51 children had died from a water-related disease. I was, and am, outraged.

Luckily, this anger was matched with a message from my former youth pastor that week pointing out that we, the youth, are the future. Inspired by the work of other young entrepreneurs like Zach Hunter, who started Loose Change to Loosen Chains at age twelve (a program combating modern-day slavery), I decided at thirteen that I would stand up to this water injustice. I reached out to five of my best friends and we decided to form a nonprofit, called Just Dig It, with the goal of raising funds for clean water wells in Ghana, West Africa.

We started small, selling cookies, brownies, and water on the corner of our neighborhood street. This $200 fund-raiser was quickly followed by more events and some very generous donations. Contrary to my brother's original doubts, we had raised more than $3,000 within two months, which was enough to purchase a small well.

Our fund-raisers continued and were soon matched with a partnership from my church's Youth Ministry. After raising more than $20,000, we were invited to visit Ghana in August 2011. While we helped at a health clinic and played with children, our primary goal was to see the impact Just Dig It had on rural Ghana. After witnessing the putrid water previously consumed by the village of Wusuta-Sakakyere, we partook in the opening ceremony of Just Dig It's well in the village.

I did not experience the stereotypical mission trip where a six-year-old African girl emphatically hugs me in thanks for my work. Yet I could see the impact we had left as six teenagers from Pleasanton, California. I could see the polluted water the villagers no longer had to drink. I could see the gratitude of a chief and his village. And I could see my vision for the future.

Big change had happened; I thought we were limitless.

I began to think larger and shifted my attention toward the potential impact that an entire community could make. I realized that Just Dig It had raised funds like most other organizations, relying on large donations from the best endowed. Why not instead utilize the entire community, regardless of contribution size, to solve one of the biggest problems facing the world?

With that mindset, I developed the Clean Water Utility Project. The idea was to work with the city of Pleasanton Water Utility Department to ask Pleasanton residents to donate $1 every two months toward clean water in the developing world. Water bills would include a short description of the project and a checkbox where residents could sign up to automatically donate $1 every two months toward clean water. It is estimated that with 75 percent participation, we would raise about $60,000–$75,000 a year.

In love with the idea of uniting the community through small donations, I shared this plan with everyone I knew. After a few short months of revisions, my three friends and I felt we were ready, so we met with Mayor Jerry Thorne to present the idea. Praising the initiative, the mayor explained that it could be implemented through a city council vote, which he predicted would be easy to pass. Tied in with my earlier Just Dig It success, the mayor's words created an idealistic vision of presenting to the city council within two months and having the project implemented by the end of the year.

I was wrong. We had our presentation materials ready, but I decided to contact Becky Hopkins from the Pleasanton Youth Commission to see if she could help us. She warned us that it might take up to two years before we could even get the city council to vote on the measure. She also advised us to do more preliminary work, through meeting with city staff, before presenting to the city council. I realized change with the Clean Water Utility Project would take a lot longer than with Just Dig It.

And it has. Fortunately, things are going faster than Becky predicted, but we have still had our fair share of setbacks.

What I have recently discovered is that, despite these delays, progress has been constant throughout. We have developed solutions to the policy issues that arose in response to our plan. We have been in communication with potential partner organizations, and Becky Hopkins has even become our ally and advocate in the city government. With everyone's help and persistence, it is now expected that our dream will soon become a reality.

It took more time than I would have liked, but progress is marching on.

Nowhere has this lesson of change been more evident than in my personal life. While I had been lobbying for progress abroad, I was surprised to discover that change had suddenly become the epicenter of my own life. You see, I wasn't raised in the most liberal background, despite my upbringing in the San Francisco Bay Area. I got a detention in the fourth grade for calling a peer gay (I know, I'm ashamed, too). My parents put up "Yes on Prop 8" signs all over our lawn in 2008. We were to love the "sinner," but condemn the "sin."

Naturally, there were issues in our house when I began to question my sexual orientation. The process to accept myself was slow and painful. After years of homophobia and "dating" girls, seemingly to prove my "straightness" to both my peers, my family, and myself, I decided enough was enough. I wasn't comfortable with it at first, but in September 2012, I accepted that I am gay.

I had hoped my parents would immediately make that same acceptance. Terrified of the consequences, I came out to my parents in November of the same year. I'm very fortunate that unlike other LGBTQ youth, my parents did not disown me. I understand their religious and political convictions, however, and their disappointment still hurts.

It turns out the popular cliché from the YouTube videos is true: "It Gets Better." My dad has come around, and my mom is getting there. Gone are the days of hurtful comments, replaced with mere discomfort. Still bad? Yeah, but definitely a lot better.

So why did I just tell you about both my professional and personal life? I am not trying to discourage you from making a difference. Change can be rapid. In fact, it was at the beginning of Just Dig It. And when it is, the results are very exciting and rewarding. Instead, think about how you will respond if and when positive changes don't occur right away. I am still coming to terms with not instantaneously getting the results I hope for both personally and professionally, yet my experiences have led me to believe that with persistence and time you will eventually reach your goals.

The other thing I would like you to think about is the power of the individual. We live in a world of more than seven billion people, so how could one youth possibly make a noticeable difference? Like all of us, I, too, have grappled with a sense of insignificance. I've questioned whether Just Dig It made a noticeable difference because the project seems small compared to the monumental scale of the global water crisis. However, a quote from my favorite novel, *Cloud Atlas,* has extinguished these doubts of our potential: "My life amounts to no more than one drop in a limitless ocean. Yet what is any ocean, but a multitude of drops?"

Change is often slow. Yet progress is constant. Will clean water be universal by the time I graduate college? No. By the time I die? Maybe. Regardless, progress promises that the day will eventually come when my ultimate goal is realized. This slow pace is frustrating, but it is important to remember the meaningful change one can make. If my individual drop has had such an impact, imagine the ripple effect of 2 billion.

SUCCESS

Eighty percent of success is showing up.

—WOODY ALLEN

Jack Andraka

JUST IMAGINE WHAT YOU COULD DO

Jack Andraka *is a Maryland high school student who, at age fifteen, created a novel paper sensor that detects pancreatic, ovarian, and lung cancer in five minutes for as little as three cents. He conducted his research at Johns Hopkins University and is the winner of the Gordon E. Moore Award at Intel's International Science and Engineering Fair. He's also previously won the Smithsonian American Ingenuity Award and was Mrs. Obama's guest for a State of the Union Address in February 2013. He has spoken at TED Long Beach, and more than eleven TEDx events, including one at the Houses of Parliament. He is the youngest speaker to have addressed the Royal Society of Medicine, and has been featured on* 60 Minutes, The Colbert Report, ABC World News Tonight with Diane Sawyer, *NPR* Marketplace, Popular Science, *BBC, and Al Jazeera. He was also featured in the award-winning documentary* You Don't Know Jack *by Morgan Spurlock. Jack is currently working with a team of teens on the Qualcomm Foundation Tricorder XPrize and speaks at conferences across the world about open access, STEM education, and universal Internet availability. He's also been on the national junior wildwater kayaking team and has won awards at multiple national and international math competitions.*

Looking back, it seems as if I was always destined to be a scientist. My earliest memories are of me tinkering with a small artificial river to see how changing width and depth of the water flow affected velocity and discovering the drowning machine effect of the miniature low-head dams I created. Of course I didn't know at the time that I was creating experimental designs and holding one variable constant and changing others to discover what happens. I just enjoyed the process. As I entered middle school I started competing in science fairs. At first I was terrible! I completely memorized a speech and practiced it relentlessly until I was word-for-word perfect. That was to say "perfect" until something broke my train of thought or a judge asked a question in the middle of my spiel. Then it all fell apart and I had trouble getting back on track.

My problems persisted until I realized that a presentation was similar to the musical theater performances I enjoyed participating in. Mistakes happen, but the show must go on and it's a better performance if the presenter is actively engaged and excited about the work. One day a mandatory theater rehearsal was scheduled for the same day as an important science fair. I had to make a decision that would affect my course in life. I had to do some hard thinking about why I enjoyed each activity. I made a pros-and-cons list and discussed it with my parents. Finally, the lure of asking questions and discovering answers no one had seen before was stronger than my desire to act, so I turned my back on the stage and entered wholeheartedly into the world of science.

I investigated areas from retrofitting low-head dams for safety, to discovering the effects of nano vs. bulk metal oxides on marine and freshwater organisms. Then one day a close family friend, who was like an uncle to me, passed away from pancreatic cancer. At the time, I didn't even know what a pancreas was, and pancreatic cancer was something I had never heard of. Sad and confused, I turned to the Internet to learn more. Unlike kids in previous generations, who had to rely on a few outdated books they may have been lucky enough to find in their local libraries, I am fortunate to have been born in the computer age. I went online and started reading through the information I found on Wikipedia and Google, and what I found really shocked me. More than 85 percent of pancreatic cancer patients were diagnosed late, when the patient has less than a 2 percent chance of survival. Pancreatic cancer also has an abysmal five-year survival rate, making it the cancer with one of the worst prognoses.

I wondered, "Why are doctors so bad at detecting pancreatic cancer?"

What I discovered was eye-opening. Today's "modern medicine" is relying on a sixty-year-old test that lacks accuracy and only detects 70 percent of pancreatic cancers. And at $800, the test is pricey. Most insurance policies don't cover it, which means it's not an option for low-income patients. This ultimately means your doctor would have to be almost entirely sure you have the disease to order this test.

I was sure there had to be a better way.

So I began setting up a list of scientific criteria that this kind of test would have to pass. It would have to be inexpensive, rapid, simple, sensitive, selective, and minimally invasive. I was confident I could meet the requirements, but I wasn't exactly sure how.

During my research I learned that one reason the test hadn't been updated was due to the daunting nature of the search. For example, when we test blood today, what we look for is a cancer biomarker, or higher levels of specific proteins in your bloodstream. While the process sounds straightforward, it's anything but. The reason finding this biomarker is so difficult is that the liters of healthy blood in our body are already abundant with proteins, so trying to locate these tiny increases is incredibly difficult. It's like attempting to find a needle in a haystack, only worse. Picture instead trying to find just one slightly different colored needle in a stack full of nearly identical needles.

The way I began identifying a potential biomarker was to sift through an enormous database of 4,000 proteins to research each one and evaluate its validity as a biomarker. Thankfully, on the 2,000th try, I finally located the very protein I was looking for!

The protein I found online is called "mesothelin" and it's just a run-of-the-mill type of protein . . . except if you have pancreatic, ovarian, or lung cancer. Then it's found at extremely high levels in your blood. The key here is that it's found at these higher levels before the cancer is actually invasive, very early in the disease when a patient has a close to 100 percent chance of survival. Once I had identified a reliable protein to detect the cancer, I shifted my focus to detecting this bio-marker, and thus pancreatic cancer.

My breakthrough came in high school biology class. I'd brought with me a scientific journal article that I'd been wanting to read forever, on single-walled carbon nanotubes. These nanotubes are so fascinating to me; they are really long, thin pipes of carbon, and are about 1/50,000 the diameter of your hair. They also have incredible properties (like extraordinary conductivity) that make them superheroes of materials science. So while I was reading this article I was thinking of ways to link nanotubes' sensitivity to an antibody that only reacted with mesothelin.

Then it hit me—I could have a network of these nanotubes with the antibodies in it and it would react specifically to mesothelin, changing its electrical properties based on the amount of mesothelin present. In other words, I was pretty sure I had found a method that could one day detect pancreatic cancer.

And just as I had this epiphany, the teacher walked up and took the article away!

Thankfully, after class, I was able to persuade the teacher to give me back the article and that's when I began to investigate this promising idea.

The next step for me was to get into a lab to do research, so I typed up a budget, timeline, materials list, and procedure so professors could see I meant business. I then e-mailed those documents and my findings to 200 professors that had anything to do with pancreatic cancer at Johns Hopkins University and the National Institutes of Health.

And then I sat back waiting for positive e-mails to pour in. . . .

But over the course of the next month, all I received was rejection after rejection.

Many of the e-mails said, "This idea will never work!" and "You're not old enough to be in a university lab. The legal age is sixteen." Clearly, the professors did not have as high an opinion of my idea as I did.

Out of the 199 rejections I received, there was one lukewarm "maybe," so I headed in that direction.

Three months later, I finally met with the "maybe" professor. Over the course of an hour-long interview, he called in other specialists to ask more and more questions. By the end of our meeting I had answered every single question.

And subjecting myself to interrogation paid off; I finally landed the working space I needed.

It was shortly after I started working in the lab that I discovered my "brilliant" procedure had something like a million holes in it, so over the course of seven months I painstakingly filled those holes. The result? One small paper strip that had 100 percent cancer diagnosis. Success!

Through this research I've learned a very important lesson: through the Internet, anything is possible. Theories can be shared, and you don't have to be an expert with multiple degrees to have your ideas valued by others. It's a neutral space where what you look like, gender, or age doesn't matter. It's just your *ideas* and work ethic that count. Redefining relevance for me is about looking at the Internet in a whole new way, realizing that there's so much more to the Internet than just posting duck-faced pictures of yourself online or watching furry cat videos. The Internet gives you the tools to be a scientist at any age!

My hope is that the Internet continues to grow as a forum for people to connect and collaborate in solving the pressing problems of our generation.

So if I could develop a cancer test from information I found online . . .

Just imagine what you could do?

Simon Burns

WHAT IS THE DEFINITION
OF SUCCESS?

Simon Burns grew up in Winnipeg, Canada, where he studied finance and learned to code. He moved to Silicon Valley the summer of 2013 to head growth at QuantConnect, a financial technology startup. He then joined Jason Calacanis's LAUNCH media company in San Francisco where he led business development efforts for the LAUNCH Festival and their various media properties. Following six months of working in media at LAUNCH, he combined his skills in media and financial technology to run communications for Robinhood, the mobile-first commission-free stock brokerage. From Simon's work, Robinhood has been featured in CNBC, Bloomberg TV, Forbes, TechCrunch, and various other outlets while growing to 275,000 signups in two months.

Success, in our modern society's definition, is contextualized in terms of influence, authority, and capital. A similar trifecta of elements is key for the recipients of success to reach it. By pure definition, success is the result of performing successfully, repeatedly. This definition is of no coincidence; humans by nature are exceptionally good at perceiving patterns. Success, as can be said of intelligence, is a measure of the

level at which one can reproduce a positive attribute. If one can reproduce successful outcomes long enough for other humans to recognize
this pattern, it defines us.

Many have stated that "intelligence is nothing but sophisticated
pattern recognition." The accompanying texts in this book are written by young adults almost certainly within the highest strata of intelligence, be it spatial, emotional, athletic, mathematical, or any of
the other forms of intelligence that are known to exist. Also, I would
venture to say that they are among the most sophisticated in recognizing patterns. If I were to deliver a message in this story that went
only as far as to simply describe the characteristics of the patterns I
have thus far recognized, I would be being disingenuous and of no service to the reader.

Before I begin my story, it should be said that, unlike the dictio-
nary definition, success is arbitrary, subjective to its environment and
to what its surroundings dictate. When I look to measure my own
success, I remind myself of my life's goal at the age of ten, which was
quite simply for the name "Simon Burns" to be read in a history book.
That was it, to have my name in a book that told the story of this era,
as Rockefeller and J. P. Morgan defined their age and Carnegie his. I
wanted to help define my generation. This attitude precludes following society's prewritten scripts, accepting authority, and having idols.
It is a clear, precise, and ambitious goal.

I still don't know in which area of the history book I will find myself. But at any moment of self-reflection one passes through before
making major decisions, I think of the direction that will have the
highest probability of bringing me to that goal. Too many who make
up our generation overlook the small building blocks that make a generation. We grow up receiving gold stars from our parents for learning the alphabet and are incognizant of the fact that we are driven by
social media, which has led to the gamification of our lives with hash-
tags and LIKE buttons. Let us all make our lives build toward a greater
goal, the goal of defining innovation in our era, and doing so as a unified
generation so that all of our names can be read in the history books
of tomorrow.

What I've said so far is essentially a prologue to inform you that
my own view on the events of my life is at best mistaken, biased, and

egotistically cherry-picked. If I had chosen the safe way, first I would have probably decided to become a lawyer, most likely vindicating the "1%"! And one day, the time would have come to hand over my knowledge to the next generation of lawyers, informing them of my insights and experiences much like I am with you through this text. The message from that old experienced lawyer would be that risks are not worth taking.

Instead, the message from the nineteen-year-old me writing here is one of the virtue of fearless ambition. And this is for your benefit, as Frank Lloyd Wright expressed, "When anyone becomes an authority, that is the end of him as far as development is concerned." Following this logic, my wisdom could very well be reaching its parabolic height in the near future. This is great for the reader but a concern to the writer if there is no way to combat jadedness but to keep educating oneself, staying forever in tune to the innovative narratives in modern society. As people grow old, the rate at which they change does as well, and their ability to shift and understand a new narrative is weakened. Too often, groups cause individuals to abide by the opinion of the crowd which, if you are smarter than average, will undoubtedly bring you down. All this is to say that, by definition, being unique, smart, and successful are traits out of the ordinary.

These cultural factors are created not born; apathy and structured obsolescence of careers is developed, not inherent. When asked, 45 percent of students in fifth grade said they wanted to change the world. I would be depressed and shocked to read how many persons aged thirty, forty, or even sixty would say the same. We all reside in the same human condition, have the same drive to combat existential threat as well as the drive to leave a legacy. We each have the drive to be part of The Evolution 2.0, the latest human evolution to modernity, a part of the crucial element in the cultural evolution that a select few are driving forward.

I've worked with industrial designers from Sweden, design experts in Los Angeles, alternative energy chairs in Winnipeg, impact investors in Switzerland, and the list of connections continues with one common characteristic. They are all linked to proliferation of an idea, an idea from a sixteen-year-old with ambition. If that seems crazy, it's because this expedient, iterative, and low-cost innovation has never been available to a young person at this level of ease in the history of humanity. We live in a day and age where an idea is effervescently priceless, and by this I mean its value is open to such possibility. I believe that any idea now has the potential to flourish (albeit some through major periods of iteration). Any idea has supporters waiting to be found, experts that you can receive advice from, media ready to cover the story, and masses to inspire. It is just a matter of finding the right fit or shifting your idea with each new piece of advice and being open to new ideas from others.

I began my efforts to change the world by determining an issue that was hugely problematic, with a large market opportunity that I had a lot of passion for. Solving the sustainable transportation issue became my focus. The power of the Internet and Moore's law allowed the combination of the imagination of a sixteen-year-old with new technology (thin wafer electric motors) and a group of advisers spanning industrial design, mechanical engineering, venture capital, user interface design among experts of other fields with names I had not heard of (growth hacking, looking at you!).

This is the power of a modern society. When one decides to define oneself by the possibilities of the current age, one is unlimited. When one decides to solve an ambiguous and ambitious problem, one is at the core of the innovative spirit. When one decides to dedicate himself without fear of failure, one is embracing the destruction of antiquated societal norms. And when one decides to lift the constraints of societal pressure and become independent in the truest and broadest sense, one becomes a visionary.

Cam Perron

STEPPING INTO THE BIG LEAGUES

Cam Perron's interest in the historical, but poorly documented, Negro baseball league began at the age of twelve when he began collecting autographs of retired baseball players. It quickly grew into a full-time passion, and Cam has since befriended hundreds of former players, creating baseball cards for them, reuniting long-lost friends and teammates, and organizing yearly reunions. He is helping former players get the recognition they deserved decades ago. Cam's computer skills have allowed him to track down close to a hundred former players and his research has helped a handful of former players receive yearly pensions from Major League Baseball. Cam has been working toward his business degree at Tulane University and has been featured in The Huffington Post *and HBO's* Real Sports with Bryant Gumbel *among other major media outlets.*

I have always been a baseball fan. I played it as a toddler, swinging for the fences from beside a T-ball stand; watched it, sharing stories and seventh-inning stretches with my family at the ballpark; and kept up with the history of the game, for there was so much to learn about

"America's favorite pastime" from players that took the field way before I was born.

Four years ago I stumbled across a much forgotten part of baseball history. As many older generations can relate to, one of my favorite things to do as a child was buy a sealed pack of Topps baseball cards, quickly rip open the flimsy card coating, and check to see if I was fortunate enough to receive rare baseball cards that were stashed away in lucky Topps packs. As I routinely opened another pack of cards, I found one from the Negro League, a league for black athletes that paralleled the major leagues from 1920 until the early 1960s, before black athletes were allowed to play in the major leagues alongside their white counterparts. This was new to me, and as a student of the game, I made it my goal to look into things further. When I realized that much of the league's history remained undocumented and/or nearly impossible to find online, I made it my mission to revive the league's history, and most importantly, connect with the people who contributed to this forgotten time period.

Before getting to the good stuff, I had to brush up on my history. I read books, talked with historians, and skimmed whatever scattered articles I could find about the Negro League. Unfortunately, not much about this part of "America's pastime" was easy to find, so I had to dig deeper.

I wrote to many former Negro League players, and soon I was in touch with dozens of them. Dozens soon turned into hundreds. Continually, I heard stories of meager salaries, poor living situations, and racial bigotry. This certainly wasn't the type of baseball I grew up loving, watching, and playing.

While the players spoke of this treatment and pastimes with regret, it was the lack of evidence they had ever played ball that disappointed them the most. There were few Negro League baseball cards in Topps packs and limited newspaper articles available on the Internet (as I realized at the beginning of my own journey to uncover the history of this mysterious piece of baseball history). Because of their color, the press showed little interest in them and their on-the-field accomplishments. Even though, at times, their teams would sell more tickets than the Major League clubs because their games were more exciting and skillful, these players were continually disregarded and even ridiculed. Upon the close of their baseball careers, the players would fade away, leaving their careers and teammates behind in order to escape the hatred, prejudice, and shame they felt as part of the parallel baseball league.

I was emotionally devastated by these players' stories, their memories of wanting to innocently play ball without the discrimination they faced before the Civil Rights era, and especially their current situations in life. I learned that most of them never received their well-deserved pensions from Major League Baseball, leaving them financially unstable, and few of them had any contact whatsoever with their old teammates, coaches, or fans, which made coping with their living situations even more challenging.

Now things were personal. Not only did I want to uncover the league's history, but I wanted to get as many players as possible the recognition they deserved. I used my business knowledge to help them sell signed baseball cards and photos so they could better support themselves and their families. I organized paid speaking engagements for many players, and all were eager to share their untold stories of hardship, camaraderie, and, most importantly, playing baseball. Perhaps most importantly, I worked with Major League Baseball and secured pensions for several former players.

The effects of my work became apparent in June 2010. I had been invited by the Center for Negro League Baseball Research to help with a reunion in Birmingham. On the second night, I attended a Negro League reception at the Alabama Sports Hall of Fame. During this event, I was surprised with an award for Most Outstanding Researcher, and for helping Negro League player Paul Jones receive his long-awaited pension. More than one hundred people were present, including the mayor of Birmingham, and their beaming faces told me everything that they wanted to say well before they ever voiced kind words of gratitude toward me.

That was sophomore year in high school, and within the past four years my passion for the Negro League and working with its living legends has only increased. I have now helped organize a total of four reunions with dozens of newly located players attending each year and engaging in a week of events and festivities. For years now, the Negro League has been a part of my daily life. I speak to former players weekly and talk to them as if they are my friends; actually they are my friends and some of them have become the best teachers of the game, and of life, that one could ask for. I've now personally tracked down close to one hundred former Negro League ball players through years of research and thousands of phone calls. For some reason this has taken over my life, and as an eighteen-year-old white kid from outside of Boston, I have become a household name for hundreds of elderly black athletes. Perhaps this feeling of change and impact is why I've always been a fan of baseball.

Tallia Storm

#DISCOVERYOURSTORM

Tallia Storm *is a fifteen-year-old Scottish R&B/soul singer best known for being discovered by and opening a concert for music legend Sir Elton John. With a deep, soulful signature reminiscent of the Motown Era, or perhaps Amy Winehouse, Tallia Storm and her signature "Big Hair" have been featured at events across the world, from London Fashion Week to Eva Longoria's Global Gift Gala and TEDxTeen. In Scotland, she has quickly become a local sensation, fashion icon, and notable writer. She is a regular contributor to* The Huffington Post, *and has a large social media following of fans craving her strong soulful melodies with R&B and jazz twinges. She is currently working on her debut album, and already has a song that was included in the soundtrack to the Scottish animated feature film* Sir Billi, *starring Sean Connery.*

Walking around backstage, I calm myself down. Once the lights turn on, it's time to prove myself: 20,000 eyes will be looking at me, judging me. The nerves come in spurts, and just as they're beginning to peak, Elton John walks by and gives me an encouraging nod. I walk onstage, grab the mic, and begin.

It's fair to say I have been singing all my life. My father plays jazz piano, so I grew up being surrounded by the incredible signatures of Dinah Washington, Sarah Vaughan, Ella Fitzgerald, and Billie Holiday. I didn't know why I fell in love with jazz; it just happened. The atmosphere in our home was magnetic. Music really is for the soul; comforting us, making us laugh, and sometimes even making us cry. But in our home, it was almost like a magical signal, for when we heard the keys on the piano play, we'd know "Dad's home!" and off the evening would go.

Both of my parents work, so the second part of their day was about being surrounded by music. Mum would cook dinner, Dad would play the piano, and of late, my younger brother Zac has taken a penchant for the drums (my dad said the best way to start is with the bongos!). What a joy for us all . . .

Living in the countryside of Scotland as one of four children with working parents did provide some challenges, in that our schedules were too hectic for singing lessons. My dad was also afraid that singing lessons would change my style . . . some call it my signature. At the time I remember thinking he just didn't want to be bothered, but later it transpired that *not* getting me singing lessons was the best thing he ever did for me.

Singing became all I thought about. My friends would go to swim club, hockey camp, netball, etc., and I would go home into my "cave" (my bedroom and sanctuary) and sing.

My father introduced me to the Berkeley School of Music and we bought some CDs over the Internet for warm-up routines and scale work. Soon it became part of my being. I would sit at school literally longing to be home in my cave experimenting, singing along to Sarah or Ella.

Being a songwriter, my dad was working on a project one day, which needed a session singer (as his usual lady was sick that given day). In a mild panic, he called me downstairs and asked me to sing in the demo. He literally just wanted someone to sing in the song so that other people involved in the project, such as himself, could get the feeling for it. He has a small recording studio in the house (previously our living room, which was hijacked for music). It was the first time I was ever in front of a proper microphone and I was eleven years old. Before I knew where we were, I had sung the track and he called my mum. His face looked disappointed, almost strange. I was gutted. "Oh, no," I thought. "He's calling Mum in; it must be bad!" But alas they were in shock. Yep, it appeared I could really sing.

My dad let a few pals hear me, and each of them said we really ought to pursue a career in music. So we did. We started off by doing charity events, local shows, shopping malls, wherever we could get a gig. We set up a website and so it began. It was adrenaline-fueling for sure. I remember doing a toy shop gig in this big shopping mall on a high stage. Suddenly I saw kids from my school and got a bit nervous, so from that day on I decided not to focus on the front row of an audience just in case it put me off again.

Before I knew it, my local radio station had gotten in touch with us and I started to do some local radio road shows. That's when things really started to get exciting. But my parents remained cool, almost harsh, reiterating how hard this industry was and how the goal of a lifetime career was much more fulfilling and sustainable than an overnight sideshow that so many kids had become accustomed to seeing, because of shows like *X Factor* and *American Idol*. In a sense, their honesty and approach only made me want it more. Singing would be what defined me for sure—this much I knew.

The game changer came on New Year's 2012 when my grandfather took us to Hawaii for his eightieth birthday. It was the trip of a lifetime for the family and it was beyond exciting! However, a day before we were due to fly home, my grandfather took sick and we had to change our flights, hotels; it was a nightmare. My mum booked us into another hotel as our hotel was full. We packed up and moved for one night.

At the new hotel, my dad saw Sir Elton John, his partner, David Furnish, and their adorable baby in the lift! Yikes, the legend himself was under the same roof as me!? Are you kidding me!? I began loitering in the hotel lobby, in the vain hope of bumping into the man himself. It was, in a sense, almost stalking. Eventually I had to give in. No luck. But the next morning we were at breakfast and I spotted David Furnish sitting a few tables away. This was my moment. Here I was, in Hawaii, thousands of miles from home and, in a tiny village whose population was a mere 1,800 people, I was a few footsteps from David Furnish. He could be my key!

David Furnish turned out to be the most charming person ever. He asked me all about what kinds of music I liked and what my style was, and assured me he would pass my demo to Sir Elton! I had written a letter, too, and stuck it in the envelope. *Phew*—that was it! I had taken my chance and the rest was in the hands of the God!

We left Hawaii and started flying home via San Francisco with an overnight stop. The next morning at the airport, as we were going through security, my cell phone rang. Imagine the scene; four kids, bags, belts, and shoes off, and two extremely stressed parents meandering through the crowd. I answered the phone, bemused at the foreign number. I will never forget what I heard next. "Hello, is that Tallia? It's Elton here!" My jaw dropped as my mum screamed to put the phone off going through the conveyor belt. Then fate stepped in and my battery died! *Arrrrrrrrrhhhhhhhhhhhhhh!*

My clever sister Tessie stepped into the chaos and swapped the SIM cards once we got through security, and thankfully he called back!

We had the most amazing conversation. He told me he had played my demo at his sound check in the Honolulu football stadium and his backup singers couldn't believe I was just thirteen. He said I had one of the most exciting soul signatures he had heard in years and I simply had to do something with it. He was even more impressed when he discovered that my dad had written all my tracks, and had arranged and produced them. And when I told him that my mum wrote the lyrics, he said, "You guys are like the Waltons of the music business!" I hadn't a clue what he was referring to, but my folks were in hysterics.

And so it began. He invited me to open his sold-out Scottish football stadium concert in the summer of 2012. Seventeen thousand people strong and in my hometown. It was totally surreal. I had six months to prepare and so I did—heavily.

I recall being on the stage at the sound check. I felt as though I belonged there. I wasn't afraid, a little nervous for sure but not afraid. I had rehearsed for this every minute of every day and this was it!

The experience was out of this world. People clapping and dancing to my songs and my voice? Wild! Afterward, I went backstage to meet the legend himself. There I was, entering his massive room, and the first person I spotted on the couch was Susan Boyle!

We were ushered into a private back room and there was Elton watching the football game on a TV. Behind him stood a table with literally hundreds of pairs of sunglasses. But you know what? He was the most natural, down-to-earth guy ever. He asked me how it felt, almost as if he knew that I was exploding with excitement inside. He for sure knew how the stage felt and here he was chatting with me. He gave me a big cuddle and I gave him a little present. What else do you give the man who has everything other than a custom necklace in the shape of his legendary glasses—it had "Tallia 4 Elton" on it! He loved it. Before you knew it, he shouted for my folks to come up and my mum just started to cry (I knew she wouldn't be able to hold it in—she was already crying at the sound check). There we were. Was this actually real? Sir Elton John had literally changed my life and this was the moment that we just wanted to pause and soak up—just for a little while.

I was dubbed "Tiny Chancer" by the UK press and the "girl with the big hair" was across all our newspapers, magazines, and television. It was crazy and totally surreal as I went back to school the following week as if nothing had changed, but it had!

One year on and that moment was the catalyst for so much more. I knew on June 10, 2012, that the stage was where I wanted to be. It would be my career and I would give it everything I had.

So what's the message here? Discover your inner storm and make it happen. Regrets are wasted energy. If you try something and it doesn't work, try something else.

When my parents gave me the middle name of Storm, I knew it had to be for a reason. The world better get ready for the storm as it is gathering pace now and coming to a country near you soon!

Taylor Amarel

WITH PRIDE AND HUMILITY

Taylor Amarel's *ventures started when he was just six years old. At the age of six, Taylor built an electronics circuit to automatically turn his reading light on when it was dark. At age eight, he decided to build a custom computer by himself. At age ten, he learned to program computers and created his own games. At age eleven, he started his own business repairing and building custom computers. At age fourteen, he joined a FIRST robotics team and became the lead software programmer. For two consecutive years he led the Uberbots team to win the Rockwell Automation and Innovation Award. At age fifteen, he earned a summer internship designing low-cost 3D imaging software for a major inner-city hospital. At age seventeen, he started his own business and submitted numerous patent applications for leading-edge technology. At age eighteen, he secured a job as head of IT for an energy consulting firm and now holds eight patents and works on his startup Modelyst alongside several other stealth projects.*

Three years ago, I earned the opportunity of a lifetime, an opportunity to change the world, help humanity, and use my technical expertise to truly save lives by building a superior medical imaging device.

Because of my work as the lead programmer for the Uberbots, Avon High School's robotics team, I worked closely with Dr. Joseph McIsaac, the chief of anesthesiology at Hartford Hospital, who was also a senior mentor in my school's robotics program. Within my first year as the lead programmer, the Uberbots earned the prestigious Rockwell Excellence in Programming Award as well as the Chairman's Award and the Delphi Excellence in Engineering Award. Dr. McIsaac was impressed with my motivation, professionalism, and technical expertise, so Dr. McIsaac and the Hartford Hospital offered me, at age fifteen, an internship I could not refuse.

Due to my mother's chronic illness, I knew firsthand the need for people to have access to high-quality medical care. This internship was an opportunity to give millions of people access to high-quality medical care by creating a low-cost 3D portable ultrasound system that could be used by people around the world, improving an existing medical procedure while increasing the availability of medical imaging to those who previously could not afford it. My focus was not to pad my resume, but to actually do something that helped people like my mother. While some of my peers solely focused on their studies, house parties, getting to the beach, and leisure activities, I chose a different path. I immediately saw a path toward making my mark on this world.

Portable 3D ultrasound machines have become critically important because of the need to augment the implementation of regional nerve blockade anesthesia. Formerly, when determining the position of the brachial plexus (a network of nerve fibers) for anesthetic injection, a clinician would have to visualize the brachial plexus by operating a 2D ultrasound machine and rebuild the 3D anatomical structure in her mind. Unfortunately, it is difficult to reconstruct the 3D configuration of this nerve in the mind. As a result, 3D ultrasound machines were created, but cost millions of dollars, limiting their use to people who could afford such technology. My goal for this project was to overcome these obstacles and ease the clinician's job by developing a low-cost 3D ultrasound system from existing 2D ultrasound machines.

Many people said it could not be done. Conventional wisdom would question the use of high school students to develop such an innovation. However, such a strategy was not without previous success. Dr. McIsaac had an almost impeccable track record of bringing in tech-savvy and determined high school students for his many projects. He had done so for the preceding four years, all producing incredible successes. However, some people still had doubts.

In hindsight, these doubts did not even cross my mind. Yet, it was not because I was naïve. It was because I *knew something* and was able to execute in a way most people did not.

I knew that determination, coupled with intelligence, would trump experience and institutional degrees alone. In fact, the fallacy that one must always be "trained to complete a task" can actually be dangerous in today's society, where protocols, standards, and methodologies become outdated within months. Throughout history, some of the greatest minds have changed the world through self-taught practices without institutional learning and degrees, like Einstein, Steve Jobs, and Bill Gates. In a similar way, everything I knew about programming that led the Uberbots robotics team to win awards was acquired through my own self-directed learning. No one taught me how to program. I learned and excelled at programming because I had a deep curiosity and desire to learn. Although I did not possess an engineering degree or a medical degree, I knew I could harness my ability to learn to successfully design and build a low-cost ultrasound machine. I also knew I could network with other knowledgeable individuals to build relationships that would support the growth of the project. I was determined to succeed.

This insight was the necessary foundation for meeting the assigned goal . . . to make a low-cost 3D ultrasound machine. I was solely responsible for researching and developing an appropriate mechatronic system capable of augmenting current 2D ultrasound machines to produce a 3D image. I took tremendous pride in those responsibilities. This was an opportunity to prove to myself that I was capable of successfully working in the engineering field while seriously helping others with critical medical needs. I designed the system to utilize mathematics to calculate the location and orientation of the 2D ultrasound probe and used two-dimensional ultrasound images to reconstruct 3D imaging in real time. Utilizing nothing more than a portable laptop, two web cameras, an inexpensive ultrasound probe, and an intense desire to learn and build, I finished the project using less than $200.

After successfully completing the project, the sense of achievement was enormous. With it came humility and a deep thankfulness for the gifts (time, money, and connections) that enabled this achievement. My task had been to design a system for improved medical care using cutting-edge math, science, and engineering skills coupled with an understanding of the financial realities that met clinician and patient needs. I had done it! Through this experience, my belief that engineers play an important role in society by designing solutions to complex problems in order to make the world a better place had been reaffirmed. Chronically ill people like my own mother could receive high-quality medical treatment despite their financial status.

Micaela Chapa

HOW I LOST 165 POUNDS AND SAVED MY OWN LIFE

Micaela Chapa is a nineteen-year-old young woman in Northern California who has lost 165 pounds in one year with the help of the Board of Adolescent Gastric Health and Weight Clinic at Lucile Packard Children's Hospital at Stanford University. She is planning on pursuing school and water polo next semester, where she wants to study marine biology. She is passionate about all things pertaining to the ocean. Her hobbies include painting, writing, and spending time outdoors.

Growing up, I resented going to the doctors. I awaited the inevitable lectures about my unhealthy weight. I felt like it was entirely my fault. Truth is, I had been overweight my entire life, from baby checkups to being morbidly obese at ten and eventually tipping the scales at 330 pounds as a sophomore in high school. But in circumstances like mine, it's genetic and it is nobody's fault. I grew up trying every diet in the books, starting as far back as I can remember.

In an effort to combat my weight, I had always been an active and energetic child. Playing soccer, trying gymnastics, figure skating, hula, tap dancing . . . I did it all. Eventually I found my true passion in water polo at the beginning of high school.

For me, the water became the great equalizer. I fell madly in love with the sport and all that pertains to it. I loved that my size wasn't an excluding factor. I could swim just as fast as the other girls and play just as hard. My size proved to be an advantage when used as a factor of intimidation, but I was okay with that. Getting positive attention for my size was definitely new, and it felt great.

But even during those times submerged in water, I knew I only had two paths in life. On the first path, I would stay where I was, severely overweight and living a relatively short and unhealthy lifestyle. On the second path, I would dedicate myself and everything I had to getting healthy and being able to live a long and happy life (with water polo by my side, of course).

Coming to this realization, I decided that I wanted to change my life for the better, no matter how long it took or how difficult the road would be. My mom and I began looking into my options. After a lot of research, I worked with the Board of Adolescent Gastric Health and Weight Clinic at Stanford, where I decided to opt for a surgery called the vertical sleeve gastrectomy to aide me in my weight loss.

It was about a yearlong process from my first consultation with Stanford to my surgery date, and the time in-between was filled with many trials and tribulations just to be able to qualify. I had to jump through so many hoops, but my mom and I were determined to make it happen. I was getting tested for things I didn't even know existed. They looked at my heart, lungs, and body to see how my weight would affect me in the long run. I knew that losing weight would be difficult, but I had never met a challenge I didn't feel I could face.

When I was a junior in high school, a few schools showed interest in having me play water polo for them at a collegiate level, which only motivated me further to succeed. I was determined to make my dreams come true, to be healthy, happy, and able to play the sport I loved in college. I knew and understood that getting this surgery would require me to take a hiatus from water polo in order to recover, but I had no idea for how long.

By the time Stanford was ready to present my case to my insurance company, I had found out that I was prediabetic and had sleep apnea, hypertension, and high blood pressure. I was also attending physical therapy for my knees, ankles, and lower back due to the stress my body had undergone because I had been severely overweight my entire life. One day, I got a call from my mom in class and she was in tears. My insurance had approved of the surgery and I had a surgery date. I instantly broke down in tears. I told my teacher the news and she just hugged me while I cried tears of joy.

Almost immediately, I was required to go on an all-liquid diet, which was hands down the most difficult thing required of me pre-surgery. But I was determined. I was disciplined and strict, allowing myself no wiggle room whatsoever. Even though my family and those around me were going out to eat or hosting holiday barbecues, I was in a completely different frame of mind. There was no such thing as cheating. I had no urge to undo all the hard work I had done by going out to get a burger with my friends. I realized that our society puts an emotional value on food and that all the occasional gatherings were centered around food, whether we meant them to be or not. Saying no to all my favorite foods was easy when I realized that I knew what it tasted like and that it would always taste that way. I wasn't missing out on anything, since I've tasted it all before. When I thought about what I would gain from losing weight, discipline came easy. I lost 50 pounds on the liquid diet alone, followed by another 115 post surgery.

It quickly became clear that, since the surgery removed three-fourths of my stomach, I wouldn't be able to consume enough calories to play water polo at the level I once did. At least not yet. I moved off to college five months post-op where I tried to push myself to go the distance, but I soon realized that it would only hurt my body to push myself far beyond its limits. I now needed to eat every three hours just to consume enough calories to stay functional until my stomach slowly expanded again, and by the time I was done with practice I was already at a deficit. I had a hard time with blacking out upon standing or even just periodically throughout the day. It was then that I decided that it was in my best interest to redshirt my first year of college. That way I could still be on the team and keep my four years of collegiate eligibility, but also allow my body time to recover while I slowly worked to get myself back to the level of competition I was used to. Having to sit out of the pool during practice and watching my team do all the drills I loved (and hated) so much was difficult and it made me sad not being able to play, but I knew it was for the best both for my body and for the team.

Getting the surgery was *not* an "easy way out" or a "quick fix." Rather, it was a tool to help jump-start weight loss that could be maintained with strict diet and frequent exercise. I became a gym rat, doing weight training whenever I could in an effort to tone and tighten what was being lost. I will always have to maintain my new lifestyle of healthy eating habits and exercise, but five months, 165 pounds, and countless pant sizes later, I've never been happier.

Take away from my experience that nothing is impossible. Anything and everything is attainable given the right mindset. If you're struggling with weight or battling any other demons (be they physical or psychological), just know that you are far stronger than you ever imagined you could be.

When you want something badly enough, you'll find that the only thing holding you back from achieving your goal is the fear of failure. You'll also find that if you never fail, you will never succeed. It doesn't matter how many tries it takes or how many times you fail. What truly matters is how many times you pick yourself up, dust yourself off, and put everything you have into another try. Don't wait to be proud of yourself until you've reached your goal, either; have pride in every step you take. Don't give up on a dream because of the time it would take to accomplish it; the time will pass no matter what.

The most reliable way to predict the future is to create it yourself. The only person that can decide your fate is you.

Pulkit Jaiswal

BEING FIRED FROM YOUR
OWN COMPANY

Pulkit Jaiswal is a twenty-year-old entrepreneur who loves solving real-world, nontrivial problems. Since the age of sixteen, he has built some of the most advanced image-processing technology present in search-and-rescue quadcopters. At Stanford, Pulkit worked on implementing a device that can help diagnose diseases in real time. He's currently leading a team that hopes to bag the prestigious Qualcomm Tricorder XPrize in the years to come. At the age of nineteen, he built the Internet's first swap station called Swapidy and steered it to massive profits before getting fired from his own company. He has moved on to build his second major company called Gliif. This recently funded startup hopes to bridge the gap between digital and print world by using a patented 2D tag in order to replace QR codes.

I spent the greater part of my life in the tiny island country of Singapore. Singapore is a semi-utopian society and, although everything seemed to be perfect in terms of law and order, I never felt great being a part of the richest country (per capita) in the world. I realized that the utopian nature of the society actually hindered entrepreneurial spirit. I grew up watching inspirational pieces like *Pirates of Silicon Valley* and always had the urge to do something in Silicon Valley. I was fifteen when I made a conscious decision to move out of my parents' apartment and be independent. I wanted to start a business, not because I wanted to start a business. It was simply so that I could make ends meet.

I am a big flying hobbyist. In my parents' garage, I successfully built autonomous quadcopters from cheap remote-controlled copters that I had purchased off eBay. I took my friend's GoPro camera and used it with one of the microcontrollers so that the in-flight imagery could be recorded and streamed. I also used Google Maps to allow flying hobbyists to define waypoints on the map, all autonomously without any need for a controller. At this time, autonomous flying was unheard of in the Asian flying community. I sold about fifty of these kits for $2,000 each and made a massive profit. I was pretty much the happiest kid on the planet, having made more than enough money to last me until I came out of high school. To my amazement, I landed a contract with Singapore's Defense Science Organization, and this marked the beginning of the most creative phase of my life. I wrote some of the most elegant code and built systems that help countries like the United States defend itself from its enemies. I found out what I loved to do early in life.

Fast-forward four years. After moving to Silicon Valley and having a brief stint studying at Stanford, I joined a company that had already failed twice. It was an e-commerce concept and I wanted to make it work just for the love of making things work. At one point, we were averaging about $2,000 per day in pure profits. Just when I thought we could be the next big thing in this space, I was fired from the company I helped build, right before my shares in the company would become vested and I would acquire my hard-earned ownership stake in the startup. Getting fired from your very own company is like being hit by a bus just because you didn't look both ways before crossing the road. I was broken. Looking back, I have come to the conclusion that this is actually the best thing that ever happened to me. I have the freedom to go back and do what I really do best, disrupt and solve real, nontrivial problems. If I was not making trouble, I wasn't doing something great. I rejoined my previous startup, mLab, which is on its way to replacing the medical diagnostic industry by making real-time viral diagnoses possible. I'm also serving as the chief technology officer at Gliif, which is on its way to eradicate QR codes and provide people and businesses alike with rich analytics. Gliif recently received its first round of investment a week after I joined the company, marking a great turnaround for me.

Having been through both failures and betrayal, I've learned many lessons the hard way. The single biggest business lesson I've learned is that pursuing an idea that is not truly meaningful to you is a colossal waste of time. Second, cofounding a company is almost like getting married to a person. You shouldn't just get along in the working space; you also need to be great buddies with your cofounder(s) outside of work. Never let a layer of abstraction build up between your partner(s) and yourself. Third, the lowest-hanging fruit is also the most bitter. Pursuing an idea in a field already saturated by hundreds of competitors because it is extremely lucrative is not a good way to do business. Oftentimes, things don't work out since the level of competition is so high. Fourth, don't just run after acquiring users. You also need to think a lot about generating profit. Especially in Silicon Valley, the poor performance of startups in terms of revenue generation has led to a scarcity of investment. It's almost a "must" now to be profitable before raising significant funds. Fifth, avoid getting a disease called product myopia. This is a condition that occurs when the founders of a company focus too much on the product and not on the bigger picture. They tend to forget their overall goals and end up delaying their product validation phase. Believe in building an MVP (minimum viable product) and proving your product first in the marketplace. Then, and only then, think of making it look pretty.

I could have never imagined that I would be able to join a new startup and raise $250,000 just one week after getting fired from my own company. I made it happen because I persisted. Life is all about turnarounds, and the future is such an indeterminable, but exciting, thing. As parting advice, I'd work to surround yourself with people much smarter than you (but don't tell them that they're smarter if you can help it). The objective at our age is not to earn massive amounts of money as quickly as possible. It is to earn meaningful connections. Money will follow, and if you have the right connections and work ethic, the money you make at this point will be much greater than the cash you could have made without that network. When you think you are the smartest person in the room, it's time to leave the room.

Carpe diem.

Paige McKenzie

ADORKABLE

Paige McKenzie *is the teen star of the YouTube channel hit* The Haunting of Sunshine Girl. *What began as a simple "girl and her haunted house" story has grown to a multi-webisode network with stories of zombies, ghosts, Sasquatch, and lots of Sunshine! Full of positivity, humor, and plenty of scares,* The Haunting of Sunshine Girl *has allowed Paige to spread her unique brand of adorkableness to other teens (and many adults) all over the world! At the age of sixteen, Paige (along with her mother, actress Mercedes Rose, and producing partner, Nick Hagen) cofounded the production company Coat Tale Productions.* The Haunting of Sunshine Girl *was optioned by The Weinstein Company for development into a book series with a film (or two) to follow! Paige is celiac, vertically challenged, and quotes movies as easily as breathing.*

If you base your societal standards around what you see in the media, I'm probably one of the oddest people you'll ever meet. I don't drink or party, and I don't chase boys. In fact, I prefer chasing ghosts! I'm the kind of person who would choose to stay home, as opposed to hanging out at the mall (although I will admit I love to shop . . . I am a girl, after all!).

When I was much younger, I enjoyed many opportunities to act in film and television, as well as in commercials in my hometown of Portland, Oregon. But once I turned about fourteen, those opportunities pretty much dried up. Most productions use eighteen-year-old (or older) actors to play teens since they can work longer hours and don't have to go through schooling while on set. So, when I was sixteen, I got tired of waiting and made my own acting opportunity! Along with my mom and a director friend, we created the YouTube series *The Haunting of Sunshine Girl*. Now, almost three years later, my show is very popular and has grown to become more of a network, including other series and storylines.

I enjoy what I do. I love working with my mom and I love being a part of what I consider to be cutting-edge entertainment. I also love the fact that I have been able to learn so much throughout my journey, both about myself and about making a dream come true. I love to share what I have learned with anyone who has the ambition and discipline to turn their dreams and goals into reality. Of course, my dream was to have a great, fulfilling career in show biz, but the following advice applies to whatever dream you might have!

You can say I'm positive, upbeat, and happy-go-lucky, and I would agree (although I prefer the term "adorkable"). You can say I've been successful with what I've done in my life so far and you would be right. But the truth is that I'm just a teenage girl who not only had dreams and goals, but did what was necessary to make them a reality. And while I may not be the stereotypical "sexy and ditsy" teenager you often see in the media and popular culture today, I'm proud to say that I am who I am and, because of that, have been able to positively influence several people. I'm adorkable and proud of it!

My first point of advice is to be someone that others can look up to. It's very important that those who have a strong influence on young people live an admirable lifestyle that encourages individuality, creativity, and all of the positive aspects of human potential. The work I do requires me to be in the public eye nearly every day. The one thing that has surprised me through everything I've done is the fact that many of my fans see me as relatable and as a role model. Thousands of fan messages have proven to me that a lot of teenagers look up to me. That's why I'm comfortable with who I am. I not only accept, but enthusiastically embrace, the responsibilities of being a role model.

Another huge piece of advice that helped me was this: Don't wait. If you wait for the "right time" to follow your dream, you will never find it. Now is the right time. Anyone can sit around and plan to rule the world someday or dream about conquering galaxies, but none of it matters until you take that first step toward making your dreams a reality. Dreams are simply the motivation to get up and do what we want to do. No one ever got anywhere by just "dreaming" about becoming successful.

It is crucial to always be true to your brand. Even before you have a "brand," you have a brand and an identity people see as you. I always knew I was just a cute girl who quoted movies too often and liked to stay home and sew, so I make sure that my "adorkableness" is always present in everything I do. It's important to find that thing that makes you who you are and embrace it! Because if you aren't being yourself in everything you do, who are you being?

Know your audience. You have to have an understanding of the type of person that will be interested in what you have to offer and adjust what you do accordingly. For me, I know that a majority of my audience is young people and I'm okay with that. That being said, you shouldn't automatically assume that no one outside of that group will be interested. Something else I've learned is that you have to trust your gut. Don't worry yourself to death over the little details that tend to get you down. Just go with what you feel! Chances are, if you've made it this far in life, your gut instinct probably hasn't killed you yet, so forget about being afraid of failure and go with what you believe. Worrying just causes you to come up with excuses for not fulfilling your dreams and goals.

Living by these simple guidelines has gotten me to where I am today, and I couldn't be happier. Each day brings something new and I can't wait to see where my adventures take me next. But most importantly, I hope that my story can be an inspiration to anyone who wants to fulfill a dream. As human beings, we have great potential. It's just a matter of channeling that potential into positive energy that we can use to do amazing things!

Mariah Spears

WHEN YOU BECOME STAGNANT, YOU DIE

Mariah Spears *is a twenty-year-old dancer who, in 2013, was a finalist on Fox's hit TV show* So You Think You Can Dance. *Before making the show's "Top 20" dancers, she had a lot of experience dancing, as she began dancing at the age of two. Her signature dance style is krumping, yet she is also trained in ballet, jazz, contemporary, tap, and salsa. She currently attends Chapman University, teaches dance as a choreographer, and would like to pursue biomedical engineering.*

Scared. Afraid. Alone. This equals my first experience in a dance class. Heart stuttering, I went into my first dance class, leaving my mom crying in the window. Once we started bouncing around to "The Little Mermaid" song I happened to be obsessed with at the time, however, I instantaneously fell in love with the art of dancing. Of course, at that time, my dancing consisted of bouncing around and waving at my mother's serene face, which became a permanent fixture in the window to the dance room. As my love for dance grew and matured, I began taking more than just the bounce-and-wave classes, and started taking ballet, jazz, and more technical classes.

My first ballet class turned out to be just as intimidating as the first class I ever took. These older girls, in pink tights and black leotards, seemed extremely talented (in my five-year-old eyes). I tried the hardest I could have ever imagined in this first class, but I just kept messing up. I had the wrong body type. I was already too large, too short, and too pigeon-toed to be a ballet dancer. Even at five years old, I realized that I was not very good at this style of dance, and yet I never gave up. At the end of the class, the teacher came up to my mother and told her I should quit now because I would never ever be successful in the dance world—the teacher insisted I try soccer instead.

Well, lucky for me, my mother just laughed in the teacher's face and kept me in dance because I loved it and that was all that mattered. Let me just make it clear; when I was little, I was the worst dancer around. I was uncoordinated and untalented, but I worked and worked every night for at least an hour (if not more), and that work eventually paid off. I got better with time and eventually started actually winning dance competitions instead of just receiving a participatory medal. I improved over time, and not because I drank some magic potion that made me a better dancer all of a sudden, but because I kept pushing myself and never became stagnant. *Never* become stagnant; that is absolutely the worst thing a person can do. By becoming stagnant, you become okay with anything less than your best. What I have learned is that the key to success is not being *the* best; it is about pushing yourself to be the best *you* can be. You will always wake up a better version of yourself the next day if you do that.

After years of hard work, I was featured on Fox's hit show *So You Think You Can Dance* as a member of their top-twenty finalists at the age of nineteen. To me, this was a chance to show the world that you should never take no for an answer. This experience was more than I could have ever asked for. While I was on the show, I did not realize how much of an impact I was making on people, but as I made appearances and met people on the street, I constantly heard stories of people who had stopped dancing because they convinced themselves they could not do it. After seeing me become successful they had renewed hope and began dancing again.

I have experienced many moments where I doubted my chances of having a career in dance. I was going to go to school for engineering instead of dance. Now I realize that if you love something enough, and the passion you feel for it is insurmountable, that the love you have for that activity or goal will carry you where you need to go because people will see the care you have for your craft. Whether it be dance or accounting, people will see your enthusiasm and want to work with you and for you because they know you will respect them as you do your craft.

I could go on and on about my experience on the show, and how incredible it was, and how much I learned, but in any business, in any profession, it only comes down to a few things. One, do you enjoy it? Why do anything you do not thoroughly enjoy? It is a waste of time. In the end, you may have wealth of money, but your happiness will be sparse. Two, have you worked hard and avoided stagnation? If people see that you work hard and are kind, they will want to work with you. If they like you, they will tell someone else and then that person will hire you or help you. Three, connections are key! If you make a bad impression on one person, that eventually proliferates to ten people, or maybe even more. Your reputation is valuable; guard it with your life!

So do what you love and remember why you do it, because no one will ever be able to take that from you. In the end, happiness is the key to success.

Tyné Angela Freeman

THE KEYS TO SUCCESS IN MUSIC AND LIFE

Between playing the Paraguayan harp, teaching herself Japanese, and attending Dartmouth College, nineteen-year-old Tyné Angela Freeman *is a dedicated singer/songwriter. Tyné released a charity album in support of the National Center for Missing & Exploited Children in 2013 featuring seven original compositions. (It is currently available on iTunes.) She hosted a benefit concert in South Carolina to release the record, which* High School Musical *star Monique Coleman was able to attend. Tyné is also a two-time attendee of GRAMMY Camp, a selective music industry summer camp hosted by the Grammy Foundation. In the fall of 2012, she was invited to record at the studio of multiplatinum producer Rodney Jerkins (frequented by the likes of Justin Bieber, Beyoncé, and Corinne Bailey Rae), and she was chosen in 2013 as a National Finalist in the renowned YoungArts competition (10,000 applicants, 150 finalists). Additionally, Tyné has been featured by several major publications, including* Seventeen *magazine and* The Business Journals.*

INTRO

If you're a music nerd like me, you know that the *key* of a composition is of great importance. It determines which scales and notes will be found throughout the entire piece. It also aids in determining the overall mood.

Even if you're not a music expert, maybe you've driven a car, or lived in a house before. If so, you just might possess a small, but infinitely important, metal apparatus that allows you access to those things.

If neither applies (which is okay!), maybe you enjoy spending time at your computer. I think it's amazing that the keyboard of the MacBook at which I presently type can create and direct so much beyond its fourteen-inch diameter.

Whichever examples relate to you, the *keys* (and there are many) are at your fingertips. The past year of my life has been a journey of ambition, discovery, and possibility. I see each as a different type of key, each instrumental in accessing my ultimate purpose. I'm currently wrapping up a gap year and preparing to begin my freshman year at Dartmouth in the fall. A little more than a year ago, I was recovering from rejection from my then dream school. I still remember the disappointment I felt in that moment of rejection. It was difficult then to imagine that over the next year I would be receiving grants for my startup, recording at the studio of a multiplatinum producer, and being featured by *Seventeen* magazine.

I'm so grateful for every experience and opportunity. Though I'm only just getting started, I've learned a lot, and hope I can inspire you on some level.

AMBITION

It is essential to establish a vision—similar to determining the key of a musical piece you are about to play. You must know who you are and what you will one day achieve. Then, believe in it! Make up in your mind that you'll learn from failures and obstacles. Decide that you will be motivated and strengthened by criticisms, rather than pulled down.

Deliberately exit your comfort zone, make sacrifices, and take risks for the sake of your vision.

I can remember hesitantly trying to explain the unorthodox concept of my Internet startup to friends. I also remember being one of the select few in my class interested in an Ivy League school. I was determined to attend Brown University. Even after being wait-listed, I recall holding tight, doing everything in my power to sway the ultimate decision. Despite my best efforts, I didn't end up being accepted. Then, I remember having to tell teachers, friends, and family that I had decided to take a gap year instead of attending college in the fall.

Honestly, it was uncomfortable at times. The path I took was uncommon in my community, so it caught many people's attention. I began to feel like I had to be accepted to Brown in order to prove that my high ambitions weren't in vain. People had a lot of questions, and I didn't always feel like I had the right answers. I knew rejection was a strong possibility, though I hoped otherwise. When Brown didn't come through, I was deeply upset; I had aimed high and fallen short. In my disappointment, I focused on my music. As the year came to a close, I ended up being selected to perform an original composition at my graduation ceremony. I was also chosen to attend GRAMMY Camp, a selective music industry camp held in Los Angeles. Both of these experiences helped me develop immensely as an artist, and further solidified my passion for the craft. I also entered my music-focused startup in a nationwide social entrepreneurship competition, and was chosen as a finalist. I traveled to Washington, DC, to pitch my concept, and was awarded two seed grants for the venture.

Despite being denied acceptance to the school I worked hard for, I knew my potential. I knew what I was passionate about and what my vision was. That gave me the courage to continue trying and putting my all into each new endeavor. My college efforts may have been premature, but I had to realize that a rejection is simply a redirection (and later I would end up attending Dartmouth, which isn't a terrible school, either!). I couldn't let it define me or convince me that I was inadequate. I had to recognize that it was a matter of timing, and continue moving forward with confidence.

DISCOVERY

Physical keys (which I'm constantly misplacing) unlock physical doors. But the most important keys in life must unlock and ignite the potential within you.

I only applied to one school in South Carolina, where I've grown up, and definitely didn't expect to spend another year in my suburban hometown. Even after deciding to take a gap year, I was interested in traveling abroad or doing an internship in New York City or Los Angeles. While I am positive that these experiences would have been life-changing, I'm so grateful to have spent the year in South Carolina. I ended up applying for an internship at a local music academy and receiving the position.

Passions and gifts are within. I realized that I had to make the most of whatever geographic location I found myself in. I've kept working toward my vision, and some amazing opportunities have presented themselves. It's important, though at times difficult, to have a vision, but it's also important to keep an open mind. Sometimes the plans we lay out fall apart in our hands. We just have to accept that every experience is shaping us and leading us onward. That's something I've grappled with on many occasions. In fact, I'm doing so at this very moment. It's an ongoing and gradual growth. I'm still learning to see events that happen along the way as check-in points, leading to the ultimate destination.

Throughout this year off, I've also developed vastly as an individual. My experiences have prompted me to dig deeper and begin gaining a better understanding of myself and the world around me. I've been able to strengthen indispensable relationships and form completely unexpected ones. I became part of the Thiel Foundation's Under 20 community after attending their summit in New York, and the community has been incredible. Recently, I attended their summit in San Francisco, at which I was invited to perform a musical selection. This year, I also participated in a national competition called YoungArts. There were about 10,000 applicants, and I was one of 150 finalists flown to Miami, Florida. They orchestrated an amazing creative experience called YoungArts Week, during which we performed, had master classes, and further explored our crafts. Through each program, I've met wonderful people who share my passions, and have been vastly inspired.

During the winter, I was blessed with the experience of recording and releasing my first charity album. I created it in support of the National Center for Missing & Exploited Children after being moved by the story of a fifteen-year-old girl in my community who went missing last August. The record features seven original compositions and is currently available on iTunes. I hosted a benefit concert to release the album, which *High School Musical* star Monique Coleman was able to attend. I met Monique a few months prior to the concert after winning a competition to sing the theme song for an international makeup company. I spent time in Los Angeles recording at the renowned Rodney Jerkins Studios, frequented by the likes of Justin Bieber, Corinne Bailey Rae, and Beyoncé.

This year has shown me that life keeps on moving and in a positive direction if you allow it to. Not getting into Brown momentarily felt like the end of the world. I quickly realized that it wasn't, as other opportunities presented themselves. I was instead prompted to continue moving forward. I've traveled around the country alone for the first time, spent time learning about the random plethora of subjects that interest me, been struck with new ideas, and tried out crazy notions like playing the Paraguayan harp. Ultimately, my gap-year experience has helped me develop a deeper passion for life itself. It has helped me appreciate what I've been surrounded by, and possessed, all along.

POSSIBILITY

There is a world of possibility right at our fingertips. This holds true whether I'm hunched over my keyboard typing up a business plan draft, or improvising on the piano keys onstage. My piano and computer keyboards consist of seventy-eight and sixty-six keys respectively (yes, I counted them). Neither can be bound by their physical limits; their possibilities are literally endless.

I'm constantly reminded of how blessed I am in having the liberty to pursue my passions, to develop, and to believe in a vision. Even being invited to contribute to this project was an honor and has been an eye-opening experience. Furthermore, I'm so grateful for the people who have been next to me along the way, the passengers who have made this journey all the more enjoyable and spontaneous.

Whenever I look back, I marvel at how vastly the present differs from what I expected. But I think the beauty of life often lies in its unpredictability. This past year has truly taught me to begin embracing the unexpected. As my beginning comes to an end, and I move toward this next stage, I'm grateful and anticipatory. There's truly no algorithm, no surefire plan. Failure is recurring and unavoidable. I still have letdowns, and I still make wrong turns all the time. But as I move forward, I can often feel pieces falling into place.

The key to moving forward lies at your fingertips even at this moment, as you flip these pages and read on.

OUTRO

I know this past year has only been an iota of all I will experience. Life is a continuous song, an ongoing chorus. I have to put my mind in the right position in order to progress. In that vein, you must be conscious of your disposition and understand the importance of having a vision. Let yourself be propelled by passion and inspired by the infinite possibilities. The power of all we hold within is vast. Consciously take time to improve and discover yourself. Strengthen your mind, realize the power of your attitude, and recall that mistakes are just alternate routes.

Within the key is potential, and the key is in your hands. Use it to determine the essence of who you are and what your purpose is. Use it to ignite your ambitions, to unlock your potential. Use it to drive you onward and remind you that even seemingly incorrect notes ultimately play into the song.

Then, turn up the music and enjoy the ride.

Lou Wegner

HOW HUNDREDS OF KIDS HAVE SAVED THOUSANDS OF ANIMALS

Lou Wegner is an accomplished teen actor, having been in Nickelodeon's The Thundermans, *Clint Eastwood's* Trouble with the Curve, *ABC's* Modern Family, *and many other well-known films and TV productions. Though this is truly admirable for a person so young, his greatest achievement by far is his work with abandoned and endangered animals. At fourteen, he started Kids Against Animal Cruelty, "KAAC," and it has grown from a single voice to more than 50,000 members. There are fifteen chapters across the nation, which are solely run by teens. Members are active in animal issues including banning pet store puppy mill sales, eliminating the use of gas chambers at shelters, saving wild mustangs, and preserving America's western frontier. Lou and his nonprofit organization are also lobbying to educate his generation on responsible pet ownership. "KAAC" is one of the country's fastest-growing animal rights groups, thanks to many notable supporters.*

I have always been surrounded by animals. My mom, Diana MacNeill Wegner, is a huge animal advocate, and she was only eight years old when she wrote a letter to President Richard Nixon protesting the use of horsemeat (wild mustangs) in dog food. I grew up in a home filled with rescued dogs and surrounded by photographs of my mom and dad with tigers, whales, endangered sea turtles.

At the age of three, my parents enrolled me in Jack Hanna's summer zoo camp in Columbus, Ohio. I had firsthand experience learning about the larger world we operate in and the animals that struggle to survive alongside us humans (like certain species of rhinos, elephants, tigers, and many others that are slowly becoming extinct). Conservation, preservation, environmental concerns, recycling, responsibility, and accountability were new concerns for me. I didn't understand until much later that those eight summers at camp would impact my life immensely, and that kindness was a key component in understanding how we treat each other, animals, and the planet.

After eight years spending summers at the zoo, my parents exposed me to a different world. I spent two summers at the Ohio Wildlife Center's rehabilitation youth camp. I was deeply saddened by the number of wildlife maimed, poisoned, shot, and killed for amusement. Raccoons, opossums, deer, coyote, hawks, owls, skunks, groundhogs, snakes; we cared for them all. They had worth, feelings, and deserved to be protected, and were treated as equal to humans. I will never forget my first encounter with a coyote named Hope. She could never be released back into the wild because she had become too used to humans. She didn't fear us, and that endangered her. I became attached to Hope. She loved people and just wanted to play. Humans destroyed many like her, but human kindness also saved her life.

I left Ohio for California at the age of fourteen to become an actor in Hollywood. Little did I know that move would impact my life in a direction that was totally unexpected.

Kaileigh Brielle, the director of my first film, *Be Good to Eddie Lee,* noticed that I had included animal rescue on my resume. I had little experience as an actor and added my love for animals to enhance my chances for a job. It worked. I earned the role of Jim Bud on the spot. She found it remarkable that a fourteen-year-old kid would be concerned with animal rescue and asked if I had volunteered at any of the local Los Angeles animal shelters. I had not. I found an adoption event at the Baldwin Park Animal Shelter and volunteered. Walking through those glass doors changed my life forever.

I remember the first thing that hit me when I arrived at the shelter . . . the number of people lined out the door with their pets. I walked slowly past trying not to stare but I couldn't escape the disturbing question of why they were there.

The shelter director, Mr. Lance Hunter, gave me a personal tour. It was tough. I wasn't expecting crying and barking dogs. I wasn't expecting euthanasia . . . animal death row. There were cats, bunnies, reptiles, and a horse. Mr. Hunter explained that the shelter was full and that the people lined up at the door were turning in their animals. Either they didn't want them or couldn't care for them any longer. Animals coming in the front door meant that animals in the back unfortunately had to go (this did not include the large number of strays that were picked up by animal control). The shelter was full. I froze. Animals "had to go" . . . my heart sank.

Animals are abandoned/surrendered for many reasons: barks, chews, too expensive, cries, old, not playful, too playful, animal is pregnant, animal is surrendered with babies, home is in foreclosure, moving to a new home, owner has passed away, veterinary bills are too expensive, etc. City and county shelters nationwide are beyond capacity. Animal control has the difficult task of picking up strays, taking in unwanted pets, caring for those pets, and then euthanizing them when the shelter runs out of room; a tough, thankless, and emotional job.

Millions of pets across the United States die yearly. Millions . . .

I left the shelter knowing that I had to do something to reach out to our generation. Through education and the sharing of information we could help make a brighter future for these shelter animals and reduce animal cruelty. It was very clear to me: Animals are not disposable and are deserving of respect.

I gathered some friends and took to the streets with signs, "Adopt from Your Local Shelter, Save a Life, Be Pet Responsible, Spay/Neuter." I continued to volunteer at the Baldwin Park Shelter, thankful to be mentored by Lance Hunter, Baldwin Park staff, and volunteers—Robin Harmon, Stephanie Levy, and Elaine Seamans. A friend suggested we go a step further and expand our cause using social media.

Kids Against Animal Cruelty was born on Facebook in the summer of 2010. We numbered a couple of good friends and parents: Shira Rich,

Nicole Cummins, Justin Cygnor, Lori Rich, my mom and dad. Our mission statement reads, "We are Animal Rights Knights fighting for the rights of all animals," and our logo became a shield with two swords. Our quest: save as many lives as possible, find forever homes, and help end animal cruelty.

The Kids Against Animal Cruelty Facebook page exploded and branched into sixteen U.S. state chapters run by kids/teens. Our first international chapters opened in Belgium, Greece, and Nepal in early 2014. KAAC grew to more than 22,000 members with 50,000 more in partner and coalition support worldwide.

KAAC kids and teens volunteer at adoption events and use social media to network animals on death row in shelters across the country. We share information about pet responsibility and bring attention to animal cruelty and endangered animals around the globe. We work closely with animal shelters, county and city animal control, rescues, shelter volunteers, and fosters to help find safe and permanent homes.

People always ask me what KAAC stands for, and I always go back to Hope, the coyote, and the kindness of the people that cared for her and saved her life. Kindness to people, animals, and our planet is what we are all about.

Olivia Bouler

SAVING THE GULF

ONE DRAWING AT A TIME

An avid birder at a young age, **Olivia Bouler** *wept when she heard about the 2010 oil spill in the Gulf of Mexico. Knowing birds were going to suffer, Olivia wrote to the Audubon Society about her fund-raising idea: to give bird drawings to people who donated to wildlife recovery efforts, setting a goal of 500 originals. The response was incredible, raising more than $200,000 for organizations helping wildlife in the Gulf region and having more than 31,000 people sign up for her Facebook page: Olivia's Birds. Her story has appeared on many media outlets including CNN,* The Today Show, CBS Evening News with Katie Couric, Larry King Live, People *magazine, and Disney's Friends for Change. Olivia has received many honors and accolades for her work, including being named an "Audubon Artist Inspiring Conservation" and a "White House Champion of Change," meeting President Obama. In 2011, Olivia wrote and illustrated* Olivia's Birds: Saving the Gulf, *which is in its second printing. Now a sophomore in high school, she is currently writing and illustrating a graphic novel and enjoys speaking to fellow young people around the country about birds and saving their habitat. And, of course, she still enjoys bird watching any chance she gets.*

I grew up loving birds and appreciating the works of French-American painter John James Audubon and author Rachel Carson. Audubon's paintings showed the beauty of birds, while Carson's book *Silent Spring* caused the use of DDT (a chemical known to kill many birds, namely the almost-extinct bald eagle) to cease. They both proved to me, at a young age, that one person and their unique talent can truly make a difference.

In April 2010, I watched TV as images and videos flashed of people trying to save hundreds of birds covered in oil, as a news reporter went over the facts. The explosion of an oil rig killed eleven people and hundreds of animals, and dumped 4.9 million barrels of oil into the Gulf of Mexico. The BP Oil Spill would become known as one of the worst environmental disasters in human history.

With the inspiration of my two favorite artistic environmentalists, I started a project called "Olivia's Birds: Saving the Gulf" on May 3, 2010. The idea was simple: For each person who donated to an environmental organization like the Audubon Society, I would send them an original drawing of a bird. It was my way of saying "thank you" to these people for helping preserve the beauty of birds in the world.

I used social media to promote my cause and, after giving away my first 500 drawings, AOL caught wind of what I was doing. They rallied with me to help plan a fund-raiser to send out my prints to their users who would donate to the cause. Shortly after, I teamed up with the Disney's "Friends for Change" campaign where they spread the message of animal habitat preservation to thousands of young kids to highlight the importance of our environment and habitat.

I never would have thought that we would raise more than $200,000 for Gulf recovery efforts, but we passed that mark about a year ago. The money was used to establish a volunteer center in Moss Point, Mississippi, for people who came to clean the birds from the oil spill.

It's hard to believe that this small idea created this much of an impact, but really all it takes is a passion, a simple concept, and a talent that you're willing to share, to make the world a better place.

Vanessa Restrepo Schild

A SEVENTEEN-YEAR-OLD SCIENTIST

At seventeen, **Vanessa Restrepo Schild** *envisioned a world where excess water from floods could be sucked out of the afflicted areas and recycled to provide water energy benefiting communities all around the world. With an undying ambition, she headed to the Internet and ultimately invented a new line of biotechnology. One day before the final presentation, she had corrected and perfected her technology and was ready to present it. Both local and national TV channels arrived waiting to hear her story. After being covered both locally and nationally in Colombia, she was invited to attend the National Science Fair, and sit in the Iberoamerican Meeting of Digital Cities to talk about her project. After that, she published her first patent and entered the Biotechnology Group at the University of Antioquia with Dr. Lucia Atehortúa (a nationally renowned scientist), who would serve as her mentor. She was selected as winner of "Young Women Talent in Science and Technology," named a "Student World Leader" in The Start-Up of You Fellowship, appointed by the Biotechnology Roundtable Oxford as a delegate of Colombia, and invited to be the Kairos Society President of Colombia. She is a 30 Under 30 award recipient in Colombia.*

When I was in elementary school (or "primary school" as we call it in Colombia) and high school, I dreaded every second of class time after the first school bell rang in the morning until the final ring at 3 p.m. Sitting still in a chair all day staring at a teacher who molded the class schedule around the pace of an "average" student wasn't getting me anywhere. What was the good of simply memorizing concepts if we weren't allowed to get up and apply them anywhere? And what was "average" in a classroom anyway?

Yet, because I was still young (and there are laws in place that require young people to be in school), I decided to mix my classroom education with my own personal education outside the classroom. I began dabbling in psychology, English, art, and soon found my love of science. I started using it as a tool to learn about and solve local problems in my community.

I grew up in Antioquia, Colombia. Forever engraved in my brain are the myriad memories of me as a little girl walking across the street with my mom reminding me to cover my face so I wouldn't inhale car smoke. I was living in a country not known for being environmentally friendly, and definitely not known for technological innovation (Colombia's GDP is hovering around $387 billion, less than the valuation of Apple). But from a young age, I remember always questioning why these cars were harming our environment and why our air pollution was so noticeably bad. I wanted to change that . . . with science.

Hours of books and online resources led me to a quote by T. S. Eliot: "We shall not cease from exploration, and the end of all our exploring will be to arrive where we started and know the place for the first time." So I vowed to keep learning and exploring science as a tool and solution to worldly problems, both outside and inside the classroom.

In tenth grade, I was lucky enough to be placed in a science class with a teacher who changed my life by taking an interest in my own personal journey. She quickly caught on to my passion for scientific discovery and exploration. As I began realizing teachers have a life and wealth of knowledge outside the class curriculum, she began brainstorming with me after class about projects I was pursuing outside of the classroom. She began introducing me to specific scientific magazines that she knew would pique my interest. And she encouraged me to attend events in my local community to learn more about the developments of new technologies within different fields of science.

At each of those events, I increasingly learned the importance of personality. I wasn't afraid to introduce myself to the speakers and other attendees, which lead to open doors and a multitude of opportunities. At one event, I met a science fair talent hunter who championed my entrance into the "science fair scene" (I hadn't even known there was a scene around science fairs) and ultimately led me to get my first patent published in the Colombian Superintendency of Industry and Trade. With that experience under my belt, I applied to university with a new goal: meet Lucia Atehortúa.

Lucia Atehortúa was, in my eyes, the most important researcher in biotechnology at my university. She also happened to be the director of the Biotechnology Research Group in the University Research Center and the Biotechnology Lab on campus. She was also very well connected in the community. On the first day of classes, I started knocking on her door and, after many tries, quickly realized I needed to find another way to catch her. She seemed to travel regularly to give talks about her work. She was also frequently at the Research Center to hold/attend important industry-changing conferences. I went to the university's science department and asked if they needed any help cleaning equipment (flasks and such), as I figured being around the space would only increase my chances of meeting her or people close to her. Yet, I was told they had more experienced students (juniors and seniors) who were already filling those jobs.

Determined, I made friends with the students cleaning the flasks, professors who worked with her, people from the research administration, and everybody I could possibly think of. I explained the project I was working on and my goal of speaking to Professor Atehortúa. Finally one day it paid off when a friend of mine who worked in the lab came running to my class to tell me that Professor Atehortúa was in the lab that day. I excused myself from class and ran as quickly as I could to the lab to meet her. My friend introduced the two of us. Professor Atehortúa paused and looked at me before saying that she had read an article about me winning a science fair a while back and that she had wanted to meet me.

For the next couple of hours we had an in-depth conversation about our dreams in the field of science, the endless possibilities if science continued to advance (or advanced at a faster rate), and a dream of her own. As we discussed one of the projects she was working on, my brain started churning and I blurted out, "I can do it!" But she looked back at me, gave a friendly laugh, and said that not even any of her doctorate students had dared to try. Regardless, I asked for her e-mail address and made a note to send her an e-mail that night.

A couple weeks later we met up for a second time, but this time I brought a proposal for how I might go about executing the beginning stages of her idea. She spent the first ten minutes of the meet-up reading over my proposal and tearing it apart. She outlined all the reasons why my proposal wouldn't work, why the technology wasn't ready for it yet, and gave me some insightful questions to think about in terms of how to develop the technology to get there.

One month later (and after many revisions of the proposal), I was directing a research project in the University Research Center—the youngest ever to do so—and had achieved my goal of meeting Lucia Atehortúa, who became my mentor. Over the past couple of years, I've gone on to be a government representative for women in science in Colombia, contributed to a variety of social changes through advising public budgets, started my own company, and conducted research at the University of Oxford in synthetic biology and 3D printing new types of biomimetic materials.

Reid Hoffman once said, "The fastest way to change yourself is to hang out with people who are already the way you want to be." As I strive to use science and technology to fuel my interests and improve my country, I live by these words, forcing myself to always surround myself with people smarter than I am and a learning environment that allows me to test out my hypotheses rather than sitting still all day.

Leora Friedman

WRITING THE LYRICS TO A LITTLE GIRL'S DREAM

*At the age of fifteen, **Leora Friedman** and her sister started a service project in their hometown called Music is Medicine. The two spent a summer performing at a local children's hospital and writing songs of inspiration for the patients. After the program's initial success, Leora grew so passionate about the cause that she was determined to continue it in order to impact more patients. In 2009, she received a $3,000 Key Change Grant from DoSomething.org and the GRAMMY Foundation. Now a senior at Princeton, Leora and a team of college students have grown Music is Medicine into a national organization that harnesses the power of music to make a difference in the lives of seriously ill children. So far, Music is Medicine has worked with Emmy-nominated singer/songwriter Drew Seeley and YouTube sensation Savannah Outen, and has been promoted by* Forbes, The Huffington Post, *and, more recently,* Glamour *magazine,* MTV, *and* Glee's *Darren Criss, among other media.*

"Hi! My name is Leora, and I am the CEO of a nonprofit organization called Music is Medicine." I stare wide-eyed at the person in front of me with a big, silly grin on my face. "Our mission is to harness the power of music to make a difference in the lives of seriously ill children." That's my typical introduction. It's the way I briefly capture who I am—my professional identity that in the past two years has come to permeate and consume much of my personal identity as well. That's the way I convey who I am to the new people who enter my life. However, those few explicit but impersonal words hardly scratch the surface of what Music is Medicine does, what it means to me, and how it has affected my life.

My organization embodies my passions, values, and personality. It is me, and I am it. According to *Merriam-Webster's,* a nonprofit describes an entity that is "not conducted or maintained for the purpose of making a profit." But in my experience of growing and running a seedling nonprofit organization and aspiring to transform it into an impact powerhouse, I find this definition incredibly lacking. A nonprofit isn't defined by what it does *not* do, but by what it *does* do. It is a systematic effort to help others and improve lives exponentially. When I discovered that leadership, business strategy, and innovation could be applied through the art of changing lives, my entire worldview shifted. The world became a far more beautiful, riveting place, and I finally believed in myself and in my capacity to make a difference. But, interestingly, this professionally motivated personal revelation was not a product of winning an award or grant. It was simply a response to meeting a little girl named Brooke.

"Go on and try to tear me down." I softly sang the lyrics to "Skyscraper," Demi Lovato's inspirational tune. "I will be rising from the ground. Like a skyscraper, like a skyscraper." The differences that separated Brooke and me melted away as I sang—she, a teenage girl with cancer; I, a teenage girl with a guitar. I looked up; her mother's eyes glossed with tears and Brooke's smile lit the room. In that moment, for once in my life, everything felt okay. The refreshing spirit of a strong, graceful thirteen-year-old girl with a gentle heart and fortitude of steel had dissolved my weariness from juggling academic pursuits and the management of Music is Medicine. She was an angel and a soldier. After meeting Brooke and her mother for the first time, I knew three things: I knew they were special, I knew Music is Medicine was destined to help them, and I knew I'd never be the same.

I met Brooke through Music is Medicine's Donate a Song project, a program that leverages the talent and fame of artists to inspire, fundraise, and increase awareness for pediatric patients. Donate a Song is a wing of Music is Medicine, a service-project-turned-nonprofit born when I was in high school. At fifteen, I went from singing Taylor Swift songs in the shower to performing them in children's centers and even writing my own lyrics for seriously ill children with my older sister. After transforming my own music into a tool for social change, it became my goal to do the same for musicians around the world. All artists deserve to use their music to influence girls and boys like Brooke, and all girls and boys like Brooke deserve to be inspired by artists. It's really a win-win situation.

Music has always been a huge part of my life, so when the program magically started to transpire only months after I drafted a strategic plan for Donate a Song, I was beyond thrilled. Johns Hopkins embraced the idea and connected us with Brooke. Brooke was apparently a huge fan of *Another Cinderella Story*'s Drew Seeley, who ultimately wrote an incredible song for her called "Fly." Brooke is also featured in the song's music video, which aims to tell the story of Brooke and Drew's Music is Medicine experience. "How do you smile when you don't want to? How do you laugh when it's easy to cry?" Drew sings in the chorus.

When I first heard "Fly," tears filled my eyes. They were both sad and happy tears. I was sad for Brooke's unfair struggle, but happy for her strength that Drew so lucidly expressed in the song he wrote for her. Here was a song that people across the globe would be able to listen to and be empowered by. Brooke would now not only be able to influence me and her closest friends and family members, but she, through her strength, would be able to touch the lives of people everywhere.

In August 2012, Brooke lost her battle to cancer. When I learned the news, the music stopped. I cried again, but this time the tears only streamed from sadness. Often I try to extract positivity from everything, but this time I simply couldn't. For a little while, I mentally distanced myself from Donate a Song and from Music is Medicine. My goals became blurred by the tragedy and heartbreak of an incurable disease. Sadly, I recognized what I'd always known—music cannot fix everything.

Fortunately, though, I quickly realized the need to move forward. The pediatric oncology team at Johns Hopkins told me that "Fly" was

Brooke's legacy; it helped fulfill her and her mother's dream of using her story to contribute to the ongoing and frustrating, but immensely important, fight against pediatric cancer. The program also deeply impacted the artist, Drew Seeley, who now serves on our Board of Directors and is as dedicated as ever to advancing our cause. Musicians from around the world e-mail me daily wanting to get involved in our work, and I'm now more motivated than ever to grow Music is Medicine in order to share more stories of strength, raise more awareness, and continue finding fresh ways music can be used to help these patients.

"I'm so glad I met you," Brooke said to me the first day she met me. I looked at her curiously, but mainly gratefully. Because in that moment, I knew that I would be forever glad to have met her, too.

Karan Kashyap

MIKEY'S RUN

A MISSION TO AID BOSTON
MARATHON BOMBING AMPUTEES

*Karan Kashyap is a freshman at MIT who cofounded the nonprofit
organization Mikey's Run after the Boston Marathon bombing in 2013.
In order to help new amputees who had been victims of the terrorist
attack, Karan and two classmates set the goal of raising $1 million. Since
April 2013, they have raised more than $220,000, including $100,000
from Oprah Winfrey, who spoke of the organization in her 2013 commencement speech at Harvard University. Over the last year, Mikey's Run
has been featured on* The Today Show, CNBC, CNN, PerezHilton.com, New
York Daily News, *ABC, and other national and local news outlets and
publications.*

On April 15, 2013, terrorists created chaos during the Boston Marathon by planting pressure cooker bombs in several locations along
the marathon course. Three people were killed and dozens more were
injured, including several people who lost limbs from the blast or
from resulting amputations. I had been there on April 14, just twenty-
four hours before the bombing; in fact I was walking the very same
path where the terrorists placed those bombs. My name is Karan

Kashyap, and I'm eighteen years old. I am the cofounder of Mikey's Run, a charitable organization that raises money to assist victims of the Boston Marathon bombing. This is my story.

Exactly four months before the devastating act of terror, I was in my living room celebrating my Early Action admission to the Massachusetts Institute of Technology. December 15, 2013 at 12:15 p.m. is when my dream came true: I got into my dream school! The acceptance letter was followed by an invitation to Campus Preview Weekend, which would take place from April 11–14. I could hardly wait to set foot on campus for the first time.

A few months later I arrived on campus. Preview Weekend was full of activities and excitement. It was a time for admitted students to mingle and explore, and I saved some time to attend academic expos such as a computer science open house. It was here at MIT that I met Corey Walsh and Harris Stolzenberg, who would become my Mikey's Run cofounders. Yet, at the time, we were completely oblivious to what fate had in store for us.

On the night of April 14, I left Boston and headed back to my home in Dallas, ready to resume classes the following day at the Texas Academy of Math and Science. Just hours later, on Monday morning, I heard what had happened. I was shocked, but at the same time I felt fortunate that my family and I were safe. The MIT Class of 2017 Facebook group went crazy with posts. People were linking others to news stories, providing their own opinions, and suggesting some course of action for us to make a difference. Harris Stolzenberg had a unique story. His younger brother Mikey was a quadruple amputee. In 2008 Mikey lost his arms and legs due to a bacterial infection, but bounced back, amazingly continuing to play lacrosse and football. He had already fought through many of the struggles that Boston Marathon victims would soon have to face. Mikey could inspire others in a very unique way, and he became the inspiration for Mikey's Run (as you can tell by the name).

Corey and I helped Harris refine his vision. Together, we designed a website in two days using a template and reached out to other nonprofits for guidance. For instance, we decided to partner with The Scott Rigsby Foundation, another charity working to raise money for amputees. The original goal was to raise some money to help people affected by the bombings. The three of us come August would be MIT students and Boston residents, so we thought it would be nice to do something for our future community. Raise a few thousand dollars? How about fifty grand? Let's shoot for double that! After discussing this, we finally agreed to aim for a million dollars. It was a hefty goal but one that would challenge us. Even if we couldn't reach it, we'd have a target to work toward.

Within the first week we raised $20,000 and were featured on CNN, *The Huffington Post,* ABC, and other news media. Our main strategy at the beginning was simply to utilize social media. The following week, we received a check for $26,000 from a philanthropist. We were then featured on CNBC and received a $15,000 boost in donations thanks to airtime. Our donation total climbed to almost six figures within the first six weeks, and then Oprah happened. Oprah Winfrey, who heard about our cause, mentioned Mikey's Run in her Harvard Class of 2013 commencement speech. She followed this up with a donation of $100,000! Oprah said she was very proud of our hard work, and word of her donation brought us even more media attention and donations. The viral news caused by Oprah's donation led to more television and news appearances, including the featuring of Mikey's Run on *The Today Show* in August 2013.

Now, we're at well more than $200,000, only a fifth of the way to our goal of a million. But this is only the beginning. Although I'm just an incoming college student, I learned that by simply finding a meaningful cause and wholeheartedly pursuing success, anyone has the ability to make a difference in this world!

Siouxsie Downs

PARTING, HEARTFELT ADVICE TO FUTURE DOERS

Siouxsie Downs *is a nineteen-year-old CEO, college dropout, and roller derby player. She is currently working on STEM education accelerator programs for her company, IQ Co-Op (iqco-op.org), hosting a radio talk show, developing landmine detection hardware, and creating advanced atomic energy systems. Atomic energy has been her passion for the longest time and she is collaborating with Conrad Farnsworth on a company to usher in a new era of clean nuclear technology.*

Well, here we are. This is the end of *2 Billion Under 20,* and you have heard stories and advice from dozens of amazing people. Here is just one more that is less of a story and more of the lessons from my successes so far.

I am a business owner. I founded IQ Co-Op in May 2013 and started down this crazy path of becoming an entrepreneur and juggling literally twelve different projects at once while working, going to school, and still trying to make ends meet. I also received a contract from the government for my demining hardware used by the military. I am writing a book, *HackerSpace Rising.* I am in charge of marketing for a band

and record company. I've cold-e-mailed my fair share of CEOs and nuclear engineers just hoping to get them to agree to a conference call. It is the same song and dance that many others experience. I love it though. I had to create my own path to presumed success. Short of illegal activities, there really is no wrong way to do it. You "fake it 'til you make it" in a lot of ways. If you have passion, drive, and a few skills in your toolbox (that I have outlined below), you can do just about anything you want.

I may not know you personally, but if you are reading this, I know how you feel. Earnestly, I care for your future, and for every chance you have to improve the future of this world. There aren't enough people that like what they do, so I dearly hope you do not live your life in vain. You are following your dreams. It is a combination of abject fear of the unknown intertwined with the elation of small victories. This is the advice that I can give you, and I hope it helps you to go boldly where few have dared to venture.

Find something to be passionate about. I love thorium. I love molten salt reactors. I can honestly say that energy production and humanitarian engineering work is my main passion in life. I have been told to shut up since 2009 because of my slight neurosis regarding the switch from uranium PWRs to MSRs. I have designed plans, crunched numbers, cold-called CEOs and scientists, and am seriously contemplating getting a periodic table tattoo with TH and U in green glow-in-the-dark ink (I am sadly not joking about this). Be *that* kid. The obsessed one that knows anything and everything about a given subject. Live your passion, and use it to make life better for yourself and those around you. If you live for art, create an exhibit. If you write, come out with a book. Never let other people's self-imposed limitations stop you from doing anything. Living a life that excites you every day and adds value to your life or others is uncommon. *That* is real success.

Know what is wasting your time and let go. It may be a project, a hobby, or a person. If it does not help you achieve your dreams, let it go. Your obligations are what you choose them to be. Choose wisely. I started a nonprofit when I was sixteen. I fought against its obvious failure for about two years before letting it go. If you lock yourself within imposed obligations, you will be guilt-ridden and ineffective with the rest of your time. Eventually you will find yourself procrastinating by planning your time so carefully that you never actually start or complete anything. This is especially true if you have two or three side projects that you are trying to put off. Always planning and never doing is both toxic and contagious. If you don't have an interest in continuing with something, then don't. Time is a precious currency in this life, so don't waste it. You can never regain it.

Accept rejection and failure. If you are too wrapped up in being scared to fail, you will always be too terrified to try. Failure depends on your expectations and ability to learn. "Earn your '*nos*.'" Every time you fail, you learn what not to do, which teaches you how to modify your plans. If you never try to get past a roadblock because you are likely to fail, then you are setting your own limits for success and productivity. Think of when you were young. If you never learned to give up, what would you accomplish? Make this your goal: Relearn how to persevere. You won't die. There is relatively little risk associated with most of our attempts at success. And yes, there may be some monetary risks or sacrifices of time, but this is the beauty of being twenty and younger; we have so few true responsibilities! No families, little debt, no real concerns other than maybe car payments, rent, and student loans. If there is one time in our lives we can bounce back from failure better than any other, that time is now. Talk to people older than you. If you are an older person, embody a youthful mindset and couple it with your experiences and resources to date. You'll be unstoppable! Many will say that fear of failure held them back a lot in their life, and that it is the one thing they truly regret.

Know how to speak and write! If you want to be taken seriously, and take away only one thing from my thoughts, memorize this. Make it your mantra. If you cannot convey your thoughts coherently to others, you will be of little use. Or even worse, you will be thought of as an immature teen when trying to make a serious proposal because you let "text speak" slip in to your white paper or e-mail. Oops.

Master the art of networking. Know who is who in the industry or craft you are interested in, and contact them! I cold-e-mailed a tech CEO that appeared on the media network I worked for and was offered a job to work with nuclear engineers (I was seventeen). Keep track of your connections. I carry a notebook with me that I use to jot things down in every day, and there are several pages of contact information with notes about how I met each person. Who do your connections know? Facebook is a great tool. It's called "social networking" for a reason. Utilize that. Use this to find mentors, friends, schedule coffee meetings, and connect with other people that can help you achieve your goals.

See how *everything* is connected. Most of my success is attributed to simply being able to see how things are related. Who knows who? What group was at the last two events you attended? What programs do you have a shot at finding like-minded people in? What other things are they working on? Opportunities arise from seeing hidden connections and taking risks. A tip to practice this: Start mind mapping everything, from news articles and life goals to who knows who. Mind maps are a lot like those brainstorming activities you did when you were in elementary school. They have one central idea, and that connects to other associations. Those leads to others. And each association is unique. Look up "InfoRapid" to see this done with information from Wikipedia articles (this is also super useful for research). Try this with everything from contacts to life goals. You will never see the world the same way again.

Learn how to learn. Seriously guys, we are smart, but we are far from all knowing. It is far more useful to know what you don't know and how to obtain the knowledge that you need to complete a task. Unfortunately, this is one of those things that is harder to teach someone to do. Start off by learning something new every day and utilizing that knowledge. Take an online class, for *fun*. Crash a college class that interests you. Host meet-ups and intellectual conversations. Join a community. If you become excited to learn new things, you will become a lifelong learner. Curiosity is king in learning. To paraphrase Mark Twain: "Never let your schooling interfere with your education." Cling fiercely to that spark of curiosity.

Thrive through independence. I am sure that nobody really wants to read this, but if you are a sub-twenty-year-old who has goals, ambition, dedication, drive, or any sort of "doer" spirit, please, do not expect to have much in common with most people our own age (yet). If you can only trust one person in this world, it is yourself. Unfortunately, in addition to that, you are the easiest person for you to deceive. Be honest with yourself and know what is in your head. Only you are in charge of your life. This includes your bank account. This is often overlooked, but vitally important. If you do not learn to take control of your finances, you will never make it out of the proverbial parents' basement, literally and/or metaphorically. There are a million and one ways to do this; use Excel, get an app, or just pay attention to where your money is going. Personally, I find that using a good budgeting app is a godsend. Or create your own; you are a smart cookie. Just be mindful of all transactions you make. If you find yourself with a cup of Starbucks in hand every morning, you would be amazed to find out that your coffee fix costs you about $110 a month pretax. Know what makes money and what is an unreasonable expense, and you will be better prepared for whatever comes your way.

Be humble. Be happy. Honestly, a lot of us "high achievers" could do with a good dose of humility. Whoever comes in contact with you in the future will greatly appreciate humble confidence over self-conscious arrogance. Being told you are special all your life rarely sets you up for a smooth transition into the "real world." Everyone is special. Accept that. Enjoy other people's differences and unique interests. Do what you love and love what you do. I know that this is easier said than done, but simply find ways to be content in your life. Life isn't a zero-sum game! Just because some other kid in Silicon Valley made a cool app doesn't mean that your needlework skills or saxophone talents are any less valuable. Appreciate their abilities and develop yours. Embrace your own life and your own independence. Don't hold yourself up to anybody else's standards but your own.

Anybody can accomplish great things if they put in enough work to achieve their goals. It is all about how much you push yourself and forge your own path. Nobody is going to force you to succeed or fail. Nothing will determine that fate but what you do with the cards you have been dealt. You are fully capable of making any opportunity for yourself. You know yourself better than anyone else, so live a self-determined life. We are on this earth only once. What will you do with the chance you have to change the universe? Please, if nothing else, just give a bit more thought to that crazy venture idea you had last summer, or rejoining that garage band you loved playing in since eighth grade. We don't have to "grow up." Youth is a state of mind and a way of life. Youthful spirit in life will help you reach impossible heights because you won't know where the "adults" would have told you to stop. You will stay hungry, stay foolish, stay forever young, and keep working on chasing your dreams to the ends of the earth.

So cheers to the 2 Billion Under 20 who will change the world, and the other five billion who are rooting us on. We've got a lot of work to do.

ACKNOWLEDGMENTS

No one who achieves success does so without acknowledging the help of
others. The wise and confident acknowledge this help with gratitude.
—ALFRED NORTH WHITEHEAD

There are so many people we'd each like to thank that it is quite
overwhelming to conclude our gratitude in just a few pages. Even after
sorting through hundreds of unique, value-providing stories that some
of the world's most ambitious, thoughtful, and talented young people
started sharing with us just a couple short years ago, selecting seventy-
five anecdotes to piece together for this generational message to
you, and editing every story at least a half dozen times collectively,
acknowledging everyone who has helped us individually over the years
with our respective careers, as well as throughout our partnership
beginning 2 Billion Under 20, is not easy.

In order for us to share our thanks both individually and collectively, we will break our collective voice for a couple paragraphs so
it is easy to tell which one of us is sending our appreciation to select
people in our lives, and then return to the "we" voice when showing
gratitude for all the people who helped us during this project.

ACKNOWLEDGMENTS FROM STACEY

It goes without saying that I owe the biggest thank you to my mom and dad. You taught me what it means to learn, love, and live and gave me (and still give me) every opportunity in the world to do so. Thank you for making the best parent team possible: Mom for packing my lunches every day, making sure I was safe crossing the street to school, and for taking me to sports practice and music lessons. Those are some of the things that influenced who I am today. Dad for getting on a plane every week to fund it all and for always being there to hike with me when I needed it most. Thank you to both of you for your commitment to working so hard to give Scott and me the best education money can buy and for your commitment to teach me the valuable lessons you've learned along the way. Thank you for teaching me that hope is not a strategy and that only thoughtful action gets results. I can only hope to give my future kids the kind of life you gave me, but know that you inspire me every day to work toward that.

To Scott for being the best brother, friend, and business partner a girl could ask for. Thank you for building Lego homes for my Barbies, encouraging me to go to Xavier, and working together with me to create our shared idea for the future. I can't wait to continue building with you and see all that we are able to accomplish and do in the future.

To Patrick for being there through thick and thin throughout some of the biggest transition periods of my life. And even though it was hard at the time, thank you for making me leave Palo Alto.

To my best friends, who always believed and were inspirations the entire way. Words can't even describe how grateful I am for all of you and your friendship and help throughout the years: Andrew (Andy) Aude, Casey Blake, Jake Schulte, Julianna Garreffa, Kaylee Buchholtz, Michael Costigan, Nick Arnett, Paul Henry, Patrick Stoddart, Surekha Naidoo, and many more.

To Richard Branson, Alex Welch, and Jerry Murdock for taking a chance on my brother and me when we were so young. You truly gave us an opportunity of a lifetime that, while we can never truly repay, we will be forever grateful and do our best to pay forward. This book is, I hope, one micro-example of that. To Michael Fertik, Taz (John) Hammond, and Rich Cisek for teaching me that there is an infinite world of knowledge and lessons out there and that I haven't even begun to start to know a fraction of it. Thank you for encouraging my continuing curiosity and supporting me inside and outside of Reputation.com.

To my GRAMMY Camp family, especially Kristen Madsen, Michael Garcia, Steve Baltin, Priscilla Hernandez, and Julia Friedman, for showing me at a young age that anything is possible if I put my mind to it and that no one and nothing in this world is unreachable. You all continue to inspire me each and every day with your ideas, dedication, work ethic, and kindness.

To Jared for birthing the idea of 2 Billion Under 20 and for your willingness to share your vision for it with myself and the world. We've definitely learned a lot throughout the entire 2 Billion Under 20 process, but there is no one I would rather have learned it with. We make a great complementary team. I'm looking forward to building out the future of 2 Billion Under 20 with you and witnessing all that you accomplish beyond it!

ACKNOWLEDGMENTS FROM JARED

First and foremost, I'd like to thank my wonderful family. Starting from the top, Grandpa Ronny and Grandma Sue-Marie, I'm sending my love all the way to Napa! A key conversation with Gramps early on helped guide our decision to reach out to as diverse a group as possible beyond the techies and entrepreneurs Stacey and I had originally pegged, which has definitely added to the power of this book. To Grandpa Phil and Grandma Maddy, I love you both so dearly. Given that I've shared many triumphs, updates, and challenges with you over the course of this book's creation, I would hardly be surprised if you had my elevator pitch down to a science by now!

To Uncle Howie, one of the best role models I could ask for in a family member, thanks for always "getting it." It's good to know you're there for me no matter where you are. To Aaron, I asked you to contribute to this book for a reason. You have, oh so quietly, motivated, inspired, and astounded me over the years. Watching you grow and being your brother are things I don't outwardly express thanks for enough, but do know you mean the world to me and that you are destined for great things, on and off the pitch.

To my cousins: Lindsay, Julia, Spencer, Hallie, Michael, Lauren, Danielle, and Alex; I hope my friends who have contributed to this book have inspired you and will continue to inspire you as you all grow older and take on the world. As for others in my family . . . Michael and Ellen, Marc and Elena, Aunt Erica, Craig and Nicole, Brian and Amy, Lauren and Johnny, Anne, Rachel, Jesse, Grandma Barbara, Joy and Mike, Angella ("Mama Ang"), Noah and Tomer (who are close enough to be my younger brothers), and everyone else in my vast extended family, thank you for all the love you share with me, time we are blessed to spend together, and guidance along this path. I hope I've made you all proud.

To Dad, thanks for instilling in me a special type of kindness to others that is increasingly difficult to find in this world. Know that the same gentleness you helped raise me with can be found in the way I help lead and be of service to the 2 Billion Under 20.

And to Mom, I don't know where to begin. Through highs and lows, you are there for me, and this book (alongside anything else I'm fortunate enough to create and accomplish in this lifetime) is not possible without your early sacrifices, undying love and support, and thought-provoking comments in many of our weekly conversations. I love you.

To those who took a chance on me early on. David Hassell, I'll always be grateful for the chance you took on me when I was sixteen. Your constant mentorship, exampled both personally and professionally, and care to point out my various mistakes and offer new paths of thought has shaped my life more than almost any other individual in the last four years. Aaron Burcell, thanks to you as well for allowing me to help in the creation of Learnist early on. You're another individual who validated my "intrepidity" early on and challenged me to be better. Keith Ferrazzi, our time working and learning together has been relatively short to date, but you've taught me a world of lessons, most perhaps unconsciously, for which I will always be grateful. Thank you, and keep up the hustle in decoding human behavior.

To other individuals who have actively or passively mentored me along the way, shared important insights pertinent to this book's success, and/or my personal development: Sophie Vlessing, Brian Smith,

Dr. Geoffrey Miller, Eben Pagan, Joe Polish, Gry Sinding, Hiten Shah, Charlie Hoehn, Neil Strauss, Nick Terzo, Shep Hyken, Seth Rogin, John Lee Dumas, Greg S. Reid, Shane Metcalf, Justin "JB" Bauman, Brent Crews, and many others I've been humbled to pull expertise, mentorship, and guidance from over the years, thanks for the world-class education you've given me that few schools, if any, could ever provide.

And Stacey, thank you for your partnership and friendship on the journey of bringing this book to the world and, more importantly, introducing the much bigger, much bolder 2 Billion Under 20 mission with me. I couldn't have asked for a better coeditor, cofounder, and co-ass-kicker. You've taught me plenty (and I'm sure, will continue to do so), compensated amazingly well for my weaknesses, and challenged me personally to "step up my game" on this project. I know you have my back when most needed, and I hope you know I truly have yours as well. I'm excited to lead this movement with you well beyond this book's release, and eager to continue building the incredible friendship we've worked for over the last couple years. Thanks for all you do.

ACKNOWLEDGMENTS FROM US

We'd like to thank Blake Masters for contributing a masterful foreword and putting his unique stamp on this project. Blake is one of the most thoughtful people we've come across, and it is an honor to share this book with him. As does *Zero to One,* his bestselling book with Peter Thiel, our book preaches new, innovative thinking for an upcoming generation of entrepreneurs, doers, and thinkers, so Blake's input in *2 Billion Under 20* provides the perfect prelude to our contributors' stories.

Thanks to all of our contributors! Your generosity in sharing very personal anecdotes, triumphs, challenges, missions, solutions for societal challenges, inspirations, and more has made this book as profound and insightful as we'd hoped. We greatly appreciate all the time each and every one of you put into writing, rewriting, and editing your contributions to *2 Billion Under 20,* as well as all the resources, ideas, connections, support, and excitement you've shared with one another and the two of us as we've brought this book from idea to published product and important generational message. The community we've developed with all of you and the hundreds of other highly talented, impressive, and thoughtful Millennials we've come in contact with over the last few years constantly inspires us and motivates us day in and day out to find more meaningful ways to inspire the 2 Billion Under 20 to find and act on their passions in life, and then work together to solve the world's most pressing problems. And this is only just the beginning.

It's important to shout-out some of the various communities, groups, and individuals that have supported us since Day One. A big, heartfelt thank you to the Thiel Foundation. Without your Summits and the inspiring speakers you invite on a regular basis to speak to your attendees, this book would not exist. Without your online community, we would not have found each other as coeditors, let alone the first few dozen contributors to this book. Keep up the insanely important work you all do on a daily basis. We appreciate it greatly, as do the thousands of young people whose lives have benefitted and who have found their "tribe" because of your work. Thank you to Coca-Cola, GLAAD, Lamp Post Group, Craig Bonn, Ron Zuckerman, TEDxYouth, and other groups or individuals that supported us with very early press coverage, backing, and stages to spread our message.

Cheers to Erin Tyler and Pamela VanVolkenburgh for some great additions and work on this project.

Also, thank you to our various promotional partners who helped to spread 2 Billion Under 20 far and wide to as many people as possible over the last few months. Although we had to write this acknowledgments section in advance of finalizing marketing plans for the book's launch, we greatly appreciate all the efforts of organizations, conferences, companies, and individuals who stood by our side in delivering this book to you. Understand how important a role all of you play in activating and uniting a new wave of young people who are ready to tackle the world's biggest hurdles.

To everyone who has heard about 2 Billion Under 20 over the last few years when it was still a well-kept secret from the world, and championed our book, community, and brand's mission to their friends, families, and others, we thank you.

Thank you to our agent, Chelsea Lindman, and the entire team at St. Martin's Press for your hard work on this project.

And finally, thank you, dedicated reader. By reading this book, you have now accepted the challenge of "spreading the virus" and getting more young people to do amazing things with their lives. If you're a younger reader, we anxiously await your decision to join the 2 Billion Under 20 and lock arms with all of us as we create a better future. If you're part of the "Other 5 Billion," we hope you now have a better understanding of the Millennial and Gen-Z generations, and we also eagerly await partnerships with you, the mentors, leaders, and organizational heads who will benefit from an ever-enlightened younger generation and work to inspire them further alongside us. We hope you've all been touched in some way by the stories shared in this book and are more excited than ever about our future.

ABOUT THE EDITORS

STACEY FERREIRA

Stacey is the twenty-two-year-old cofounder of 2 Billion Under 20 and CEO of AdMoar, an online marketplace that matches brands with YouTube Influencers for product placement opportunities on their channels.

Previously, Stacey was the cofounder of MySocialCloud, an online password storage and management solution, that was acquired by Reputation.com in 2013. In addition to AdMoar and 2 Billion Under 20, Stacey travels across the world to speak about marketing and entrepreneurship. She has been a U.S. State Department "Expert Speaker on Entrepreneurship" and spoken in places like Russia, India, Greece, and many more to spread the lessons she's learned from building MySocialCloud and now AdMoar with her brother Scott.

She has been noted by MSN as one of "19 Ridiculously Successful College Dropouts Who Prove You Don't Need a College Degree" next to Mark Zuckerberg (Facebook), Evan Williams (Twitter), and Zack Sims (Code-Academy). She was named as one of the "50 Startup Founders You Need to Follow on Twitter" on *Forbes,* and was named by *Business Insider* of one of few "Successful College Dropouts" next to Aaron Levie (Box) David Karp (Tumblr), and Daniel Ek (Spotify). She was also selected from more than ten thousand girls to be the "Pretty Amazing" role model and cover girl for *Seventeen* magazine in 2013.

In her spare time, she enjoys talking to other entrepreneurs, promoting women in STEM, reading, and going on spontaneous adventures. She can be reached at stacey@2billionunder20.com or on any social media platform imaginable.

JARED KLEINERT

Jared is the nineteen-year-old cofounder of 2 Billion Under 20. He is also the Chief Test Subject of The Gap Year Experiment, where he helps readers and peers take control of their own education, an in-demand speaker around the world, and a marketing specialist for legendary authors, entrepreneurs, and brands like #1 NYT Bestselling Author Keith Ferrazzi, the founder of UGG Australia, March of Dimes, Samsung, and others.

Jared's spoken to audiences of 20 to 1000+ around the world, from TEDx stages to corporate boardrooms, about Millennial empowerment, youth entrepreneurship, community-building, and more. He's shared the stage with various thought leaders including Peter Diamandis, Kevin Harrington, Les Brown, Charlie Hoehn, and even Pitbull.

He previously was an early team member at enterprise software start-up 15Five, as well as edtech start-up Learnist, and successfully started (and spectacularly failed) two start-ups of his own at fifteen and sixteen years old. At seventeen, he was named the "Definition of Social Entrepreneur" on *Forbes,* and has since also appeared in *Fast Company, TechCrunch, Business Insider, The Huffington Post,* and other media outlets.

Jared spends most of his time studying, interacting with, and befriending the world's smartest and most talented young people, and figuring out how to unite them in solving the world's most pressing problems after having learned professional relationship-building under David Hassell, named "The Most Connected Man You Don't

Know in Silicon Valley" by *Forbes,* and Keith Ferrazzi, the world's #1 expert on the subject. He can be reached at jared@2billionunder20 .com, or wherever the next plane flight takes him.

To connect with the inspiring young people we've featured in this book, visit www.2BillionUnder20.com and join our growing online and offline communities!

If you'd like to join our online and offline communities and work alongside us to inspire an entire generation to find their passions, work wholeheartedly toward making a difference in their chosen fields of endeavor, and unite in solving the world's most pressing problems, check out www.2BillionUnder20.com where we have set up resources, a vibrant network, and important content for you.

Want to interact with our community and invite the *2 Billion Under 20* to your school, conference, or company HQ so we can share more stories and information about Millennials with your audience? Fill out a quick form we've put together at www.2BillionUnder20.com/Tour and we will see you soon!

Have a group of ambitious young people at your school, company, or city whose stories you'd like to share in your own edition of *2 Billion Under 20*? We're interested in sharing our entire editorial process, from e-mail templates to style guides and marketing plan, with a highly select group of organizations who wish to unite their talented young people, showcase their stories as we have with our original contributor group, and ultimately create their own self-published, special edition of *2 Billion Under 20*! If you're interested in learning more, and to see if you qualify, e-mail us at stacey@2billionunder20.com and jared @2billionunder20.com.

If you're the founder, CEO, or high-level executive of a company looking to break into the Millennial marketplace or better capitalize on your brand's positioning currently, reach out and see what we can do for you as Millennials become 50 percent of the global workforce by 2020, 75 percent of the global workforce by 2030, and eclipse consumer spending of Baby Boomers by 2018 (when Millennials are estimated to spend almost $3.4 trillion!). We can be reached at stacey @2billionunder20.com and jared@2billionunder20.com.

And if you are ready to make a difference, but are still stuck, just let us know. We can be reached at stacey@2billionunder20.com and jared@2billionunder20.com. We will be happy to hear from you.

I hope, in some small way, this book gives you the inspiration and tool kit you need to go out and take action.